Transformations on the Highveld: The Tswana & Southern Sotho

William F. Lye &
Colin Murray

Transformations on the Highveld:
The Tswana & Southern Sotho

Barnes & Noble Books

Totowa, New Jersey

Editor: M E West

Grateful acknowledgements are due to the Mauerberger Foundation for generous financial assistance in the publication of this volume.

First published in the USA 1980 by Barnes & Noble Books, 81 Adams Drive, Totowa, New Jersey, 07512

ISBN 0-389-20112-X

Cover photograph: In the highlands of Lesotho
(R Levetan)

Printed and bound in South Africa

Contents

Preface

William Lye:

'I wish to acknowledge the long line of scholars whose research has influenced mine and whose ideas permeate this brief synthesis. Though they cannot be identified by name, they will surely recognize their part. Professors Leonard Thompson and Hilda Kuper cannot go unnamed, however, because of their particular guidance to me. Documentary resources have been generously provided by the South African Museum and the McGregor Museum and by the Government Archives of every province of South Africa and of Lesotho and the Public Records Office in Britain. Rhodes University, the Witwatersrand University and the Universities of Cape Town, Natal and the Orange Free State; missionary repositories of the PEMS in Lesotho, the Wesleyan Methodist Missionary Society in South Africa and London, and the London Missionary Society, have all also been most generous in the use of their papers.

'Provost R. Gaurth Hansen and Vice President Bartell C. Jensen of Utah State University have provided travel support as has the Mauerberger Foundation of South Africa. The excellent typing of my manuscript was done by Remona Atkinson. The hospitality of Martin West, Christopher Saunders and the Philips made pleasurable the final phase of revision in Cape Town. Lastly, I must recognize the tolerance and support of my wife Velda.'

Colin Murray:

'I am indebted to a number of people for practical assistance and informal discussion: David Cooper, Piers Cross, John and Judy Gay, Bob Hitchcock, Carol Kerven, Andrew Spiegel, John Taylor, Helga Vierich; to John and Jean Comaroff for permission to use unpublished material from their respective Ph.D. theses; to students at the London School of Economics who have helped to explore some of the ideas in this book; and, above all, to the villagers of Ha Motšoane in northern Lesotho for their friendship and hospitality and for making fieldwork, in 1972-4 and again briefly in 1978, such a rewarding experience.'

Both authors would like to thank Martin West, general editor of this volume, for his valuable assistance and his work in co-ordinating their contributions.

Further Reading

At the request of the publisher, notes and references have been omitted from the body of the text. The reading lists for each chapter, which can be found at the back of the book, are intended to provide a guide for the reader who wishes to read more widely around the subjects discussed here, but they are not lists of works referred to by the authors; these would be far more numerous.

1

The Tswana and Southern Sotho People

COLIN MURRAY

The Problem of Definition

The human population of Southern Africa is very diverse. Yet there are important senses in which it must be studied as a whole. Monica Wilson and Leonard Thompson, editors of the *Oxford History of Southern Africa* (1969, 1971), stressed as its dominant theme the 'interaction between peoples of diverse origins, languages, technologies and social systems, meeting on South African soil'. Such interaction is the raw material of the historian and of the sociologist. How can we make sense of it?

This chapter is an attempt to answer two questions. Who are the people under study in this book, one of a series on People of Southern Africa? And how can we study them? The two questions are closely related because the meaning of a classification, whether it is based on racial or ethnic or other criteria, derives from the way in which it is used in practice. How we identify the population with which we are concerned depends on the sorts of problems we are interested in. The boundaries of language, culture, economy and nation–state do not coincide. For this reason, it is by no means self-evident that the most significant boundaries within the population of the sub-continent are ethnic boundaries. The reader should therefore bear in mind two further questions that recur, explicitly or implicitly, throughout the text. Firstly, what are the boundaries that enable us to distinguish the Tswana and the Southern Sotho peoples, collectively referred to as Sotho–Tswana, from other peoples who inhabit Southern Africa and who are the subjects of other volumes in the series? Secondly, are there other boundaries of over-riding significance?

Language and the Question of Numbers

The basis of the classification implied in the title of this book is linguistic. The languages spoken by the Sotho–Tswana are all closely related. They belong to a distinct Sotho group within the south-eastern zone of Bantu languages, which also includes the Nguni, Venda and Tsonga groups. The Sotho group is conventionally divided into three main language clusters: Northern Sotho, spoken in the northern and eastern Transvaal; Tswana or Setswana, spoken in the northern Cape, the western Transvaal and Botswana; and Southern Sotho or Sesotho, spoken in the Orange Free State and

Early morning in a Lesotho village, against the backdrop of the Maluti range.

A Tswana wedding. The groom's relatives leave to return to their village.

Below left: Tswana homesteads near Taung in Bophutha Tswana. Right: Houses in the King's village, Matsieng, in Lesotho.

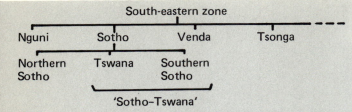

fig. 1   The Sotho–Tswana as defined in this book
speak dialects of the Tswana and Southern Sotho
language clusters, which belong to the Sotho
group of the South-eastern zone of Bantu
languages.

Lesotho. The Sotho–Tswana as defined in this book, however, comprise speakers of the Tswana and Southern Sotho languages only (fig. 1).

The Tswana language cluster contains numerous distinguishable dialects (fig. 2). These are local, tribal or clan dialects which contribute to a common written form of the Tswana language. A classification of the kind shown in the diagram is neither absolute nor necessarily comprehensive. Indeed, the linguists themselves do not agree about it. It is simply an approximate identification of linguistic affinities. It represents one kind of evidence with which we can seek to make sense of complex historical relationships. The historical contingencies of the classification can be shown by two examples, one of inclusion, the other of exclusion. Some groups of Transvaal Ndebele origin (Nguni, not Sotho) so completely adopted the language and culture of the Tswana that they were classified by the experienced ethnologist N J van Warmelo within a category of Eastern Tswana peoples. On the other hand, the language of the Kgalagadi, who live on the western fringes of the Tswana area (and from whom the name of the Kalahari desert was derived), is considered sufficiently distinct from mainstream Tswana not to be placed in the above classification of the Tswana language cluster. Yet Kgalagadi culture is very similar to Tswana culture. Largely on the basis of evidence of 'archaic' elements in their language, the Kgalagadi are thought to be descendants of the first wave of immigrants of Sotho–Tswana stock into Southern Africa.

The Southern Sotho cluster, by contrast, contains little dialectal variation, although C M Doke's inclusion of the Lozi language is controversial (fig. 3). Lozi is spoken in Barotseland in western Zambia, nearly a thousand miles north of Lesotho and the Orange Free State where Southern Sotho is spoken. Their linguistic affinity derives from the northward migration of Fokeng and other Sotho clans led by

A Note on Orthography

There are two orthographies of Southern Sotho in use today: one in Lesotho, based on the written form developed originally by the French missionaries of the Paris Evangelical Mission Society (P E M S); the other in South Africa, following a conference in 1959 which sought to standardise conventions for the rendering of Sotho languages from the oral into the written mode. Thus, for example, the term for bridewealth is written *bohali* in Lesotho and *bohadi* in South Africa, *lifaqane* becomes *difaqane*, and *Moshoeshoe* becomes *Moshweshwe*, although the pronunciation is the same in both areas. However, the Basotho of Lesotho are deeply proud of their language and literary tradition, and understandably resent external pressure to rationalise their orthography. South African oral and written forms of the language are directly associated with Bantu Education, a system abhorred by the Basotho, and attempts to standardise them therefore raise issues of acute political sensitivity. The issue does not have the same political implications in Botswana.

The policy in this volume will be to use the standard 'South African' orthography throughout, since it is a better guide to pronunciation, with the exception of proper names and formal titles, where we shall defer to local usage.

the warrior chief Sebetwane in the years 1822–4, which is described below. Sebetwane set up the Kololo kingdom of Barotseland in the upper reaches of the Zambezi. It lasted for only one generation but this was enough to establish the language of the conquerors. Lozi is still basically recognisable as Southern Sotho but it is heavily influenced by elements of Central Bantu languages.

The relative uniformity of Southern Sotho is attributable to the incorporation of various Sotho clans under one political authority, the chief Moshoeshoe I, in the second quarter of the nineteenth century. These clans formed the Basotho nation, whose territorial base was the western foothills of the Maluti range of the Drakensberg and the lowlands of the Caledon valley. Today the Basotho of Moshoeshoe, as they describe themselves, are distributed between the independent kingdom of Lesotho, the tiny barren 'homeland' of Basotho QwaQwa, on the northern edge of Lesotho, and the 'white' farming areas and industrial centres of the Orange Free State and the southern Transvaal. They have developed a vigorous literary tradition. Works by Basotho writers include histories, collected proverbs and praise-

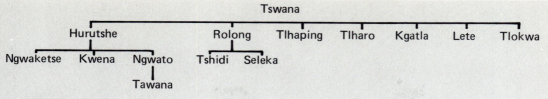

fig. 2   The relationships between the various
Tswana dialects are a matter of linguistic con-
tention. This classification is taken from C M
Doke's authoritative handbook on The Southern
Bantu Languages.

fig. 3   The Southern Sotho language cluster.

A meeting on horseback in Lesotho. Horses were
introduced in the nineteenth century, and are a
common means of transport, particularly in the
mountains. The characteristic blankets worn here
show some of the variety of designs.

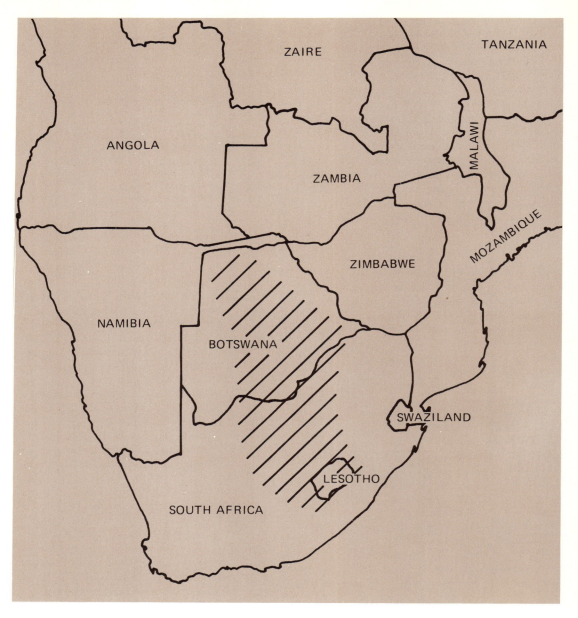

fig. 4 The shading indicates the approximate area of Southern Africa in which the Sotho-Tswana represent the majority of the population. About three-quarters of the South African Sotho-Tswana were resident in the 'white' areas of South Africa in 1970. One quarter were resident in various 'homelands'.

poems and original fiction, as well as religious works and school texts. The fortnightly newspaper *Leselinyana la Lesotho* (A Little Light from Lesotho)

has been published in Sesotho for more than a hundred years.

A glance at the map (fig. 4) shows that the Southern Sotho and Tswana peoples are distributed between three different nation–states: the Kingdom of Lesotho, the Republic of Botswana and the Republic of South Africa. Although there are minorities of Nguni origin in Lesotho, they were all incorporated politically into the Basotho nation. They all speak Sesotho today. The indigenous population of Botswana contains significant numbers of non-Tswana, most of whom acknowledge the authority of Tswana chiefs. These include the Kgalagadi, in the south and west; the Sarwa (Bushmen), some of whom still live by hunting and gathering, in various parts of the country; the Kalaka (or Kalanga, of Shona origin) in the north-east; and the Herero, Yei and Mbukush in the north-west, around the Okavango delta. Botswana government policy seeks to eliminate 'tribalism' and to foster a sense of national identity, so that ethnic identities were not recorded in the Botswana census of 1971. It is not known therefore what proportion of the country's population these minorities represent today. Having been politically incorporated, however, people of non-Tswana origin speak Setswana in addition to their own language. Significant differences relate not so much to foreign (i.e. non-Tswana) origin but to political status within the great Tswana tribes to which they belong, such as the Ngwato, the Tawana, Kgatla, Kwena and Ngwaketse. It is as well to distinguish, nevertheless, two senses of Tswana identity in Botswana. One sense is membership of a community of Tswana origin; the other sense is citizenship of Botswana.

Official South African sources provide breakdowns of the African population of South Africa by reference to ethnic identity or home language. This breakdown is functionally related to the government's policy of separate development in the sense that the number of languages officially classified corresponds with the number of African 'homelands' identified as independent or potentially independent 'national' entities. For this reason the linguistic classification implies clear-cut boundaries where there is, on the ground, a continuum of gradual variation. As Van Warmelo has pointed out, in reference to the linguistic categories used for South African census purposes, 'these are not languages but clusters of dialects, some so marginal that they are classifiable as intermediary between clusters'. A further difficulty is that many Africans, particularly in the polyglot black townships of the Rand, speak more than one home language.

Subject to these problems, it is possible to derive from census results from the three countries an approximate figure for the total number of the inhabitants of Southern Africa who may be classified as Sotho–Tswana in the sense defined in this book. There were more than five and a half million Tswana and Southern Sotho in 1976 (fig. 5). Two further qualifications must be made, however, relating to the distribution of this population. The first point is that the *de jure* populations of Botswana and Lesotho include absent migrants who are regarded as

COUNTRY	CATEGORY	ESTIMATED NUMBER (MILLIONS)(1976)
Botswana	*De jure* citizens	0,712
Lesotho	*De jure* citizens	1,214
South Africa	Tswana	2,103
	Southern Sotho (Seshoeshoe)	1,698
	'Sotho-Tswana'	5,727 TOTAL

fig. 5 The Sotho-Tswana population in 1976, based on census results and projections from Botswana, Lesotho and South Africa. The figures given are no more than approximate estimates, in view of the uncertainties and sources of error discussed in the text.

citizens. Perhaps 160 000 temporary migrants from Lesotho are employed in South Africa at any one time. Estimated absentees from Botswana in 1976 were 46 000, most of whom were likewise employed in South Africa. Further, there are unknown but substantial numbers of people born in Lesotho and Botswana who have been away for so long that they have effectively been absorbed as permanent residents of South Africa. Many of them are recorded in the South African census, but as 'foreign Africans' rather than as members of particular ethnic groups. This category also includes temporary migrants from Lesotho and Botswana. Therefore the number of Tswana and Southern Sotho who are physically present in South Africa is rather greater than the figures in the table reveal.

The second point is that the populations identified in the table as Tswana and Southern Sotho (or Seshoeshoe), who comprise about 20 per cent of the indigenous African population of South Africa, do not 'fit' their respective 'homelands' of Bophutha-Tswana and Basotho QwaQwa. Two sets of figures are necessary to understand this lack of 'fit'. One set relates to the physical distribution of a particular ethnic population between its 'homeland' and the 'white' areas of South Africa. The other set relates to the physical presence in many 'homelands' of ethnic minorities who 'belong' in terms of official policy to other 'homelands'. These figures and their implications are discussed in chapter 6, with reference to the transformation of political communities.

Is There a Common Culture?

A Tswana theologian, Gabriel Setiloane, has written, 'No study of a culture is adequate which

Camels of the Botswana police at Hukuntsi, in the sandy scrub of the Kalahari desert.

fails to catch the inwardness of that culture. Previous accounts of Sotho–Tswana society have failed precisely in this way.' Here is a challenge to the outsider who seeks to study Sotho–Tswana culture or society. Understanding of its 'inwardness', Setiloane implies, can only be derived from Sotho–Tswana experience itself. His book, *The Image of God among the Sotho–Tswana*, is a statement of faith in the uniqueness of that experience. It is an attempt to define the essence of Tswana belief, as distinct from the orthodox Christian theology of western Europe. Setiloane argues that, despite the radical changes which have taken place through contact with the West, 'the Sotho–Tswana are, in their inwardness, still stubbornly Sotho–Tswana'.

This book takes up the challenge. What is the Sotho–Tswana experience of life? What are the boundaries of Sotho–Tswana culture and society? How can an outsider grasp its 'inwardness'? And is this elusive quality accessible only to the theologian and not to the sociologist? These are questions which directly concern us. Setiloane is a Methodist minister whose family comes from Kroonstad in the Orange Free State. He has lived and worked in South Africa, England, Switzerland and Botswana. Does he himself remain 'stubbornly Sotho–Tswana'? He wrote his book in English, a language whose forms of expression have been forged from

an experience and historical consciousness altogether different from those of his own people. His rendering of Sotho–Tswana thought into English is an implicit denial that its subtleties are inaccessible to outsiders.

There is a contradiction here. On the one hand Setiloane insists on the unique 'inwardness' of his own culture. On the other hand he demonstrates that one culture can be translated, albeit approximately, into the terms of another. The simplest way of resolving the contradiction is to question the integrity of the Sotho–Tswana experience of life. It may seem presumptuous for an outsider to do this. But the works of other Sotho–Tswana writers demonstrate the difficulty of defining the essence of that experience.

For example, in his novel *Blanket Boy's Moon* (1953), A M Mopeli-Paulus describes the anguish of a man from Lesotho who passes through the degradations of life in Johannesburg, the City of Gold, and who returns home only to be trapped as an accomplice in the ritual murder of his friend. He seeks spiritual resolution first through dagga (cannabis) and then, in self-imposed exile in Moçambique, through conversion to Islam. He finally achieves it through the hangman's rope in Maseru. His life is a parable of the conflicting pressures of a larger world than is encompassed by his native mountains and valleys. In *Down Second Avenue* (1959) Ezekiel Mphahlele vividly portrays slum life in the township outside Pretoria in which he grew up, in a way that evokes the experience of thousands of urban Africans in all parts of South Africa. He is a novelist and critic who lived in Nigeria for many years. Is his inner life 'essentially' that of a Pedi from the broken hill country of the northern Transvaal? Again, Naboth Mokgatle in *The Autobiography of an Unknown South African* (1971) traces his family origins to the diverse Tswana tribes whose haphazard conjunctions on the highveld are attributable to the early nineteenth-century upheaval known as the *Difaqane*. He is at pains to identify his ancestors because he is in some sense a 'continuation' of them. Are they the well-springs of his consciousness? At the end of the book, Mokgatle's answer is unequivocal. His oppression as a black South African is the crucible of the 'sickness' from which he must recover in lonely exile. Finally, Stimela Jingoes in his autobiography *A Chief is a Chief by the People* (1975) combines an account of his activities with the Industrial and Commercial Workers' Union in South Africa, which was founded by a man from Malawi, Clements Kadalie, with a strong element of nostalgia

'Landscape from Bechuanaland' from Drei Jahre in Süd-Afrika *by Gustav Fritsch (1868).*

for the tradition of chieftainship in Lesotho and for the comfortable certainties of a rural life that no longer survives. Yet his own ancestry is Swazi.

These accounts of their own lives make it very clear that the experiences of Sotho–Tswana individuals cannot be reduced to their lowest common denominator, defined as *the* Sotho–Tswana experience. By the same logic, because culture has to do with learning, a universal human ability, anyone who represents *a* culture as an integral package, the private property of a given population, is guilty of reifying the concept of culture. That is, of treating it as a tangible object instead of as an aspect of the human condition. It follows that the 'inwardness' of Sotho–Tswana culture on which Setiloane insists is an illusion. Consider the parallel difficulty of defining western civilisation. Does it refer to the Christian injunction to love your neighbour? The internal combustion engine? The music of Mozart? All these are evidence of remarkable human achievement. But they are the cultural heritage of mankind as a whole. They are not biologically transmitted.

The fallacy of attempting to define the essence of a particular culture derives from a false assumption— that the boundaries of the culture coincide with

those of a given human population. The fallacy is a popular one. Even anthropologists, professional students of culture, are guilty of reifying the concept in this way. Let us briefly examine how they do so.

Practitioners of *volkekunde*, the study of cultures, in the Afrikaans universities seldom disguise their ideological subservience to the politics of racial segregation and, latterly, of separate 'national' development. A number of prominent academics, originally trained in the German ethnological tradition, devoted their careers in South Africa to making these ideas philosophically respectable. The best known was W W M Eiselen, who was a close friend of Hendrik Verwoerd, Prime Minister of South Africa from 1958 to 1966. Eiselen was influential in formulating the policy of separate development; and government propaganda reflects this influence directly. The *South Africa Official Yearbook*, for example, is permeated by a laborious effort to identify particular cultures with particular 'national' populations.

The tendency to reify the concept of culture is also found in the liberal British tradition among anthropologists who regard the 'translation of culture' as the central problem of their discipline. That values and morals are relative to social context is a professional assumption that anthropologists take for granted. But this relativity can be construed in various ways. In a weak sense it need imply no more than rejection of an earlier view, no longer intellectually respectable, that some cultures are inferior to others. But it is also used in a stronger sense to justify a view of culture as a distinctive 'world view', an integrated symbolic system of meaning whose 'code' it is the anthropologist's special task to decipher. In circumstances such as those of South Africa, such a view of culture can carry direct political implications: firstly, that particular cultures are uniquely appropriate to particular populations; and secondly, that cultures are less eclectic and less mutable than in fact they are. An assertion of the unique integrity of particular cultures thus not only reifies the concept of culture, it can also be used to legitimise the political philosophy of separate development.

The anthropologist Max Gluckman recognised this danger of unwitting complicity with official ideology when he wrote, shortly before he died in 1975: 'I as a South African and as a professional anthropologist am seriously disturbed by recent work in anthropology which, because of the developing interest in symbolism within cultures, confuses the problems of differences and similarities in cultures with the problems of differences and

Young Tswana children.

similarities among human beings'. In other words, Gluckman detected a subtle intellectual convergence between historically disparate traditions: on the one hand, the liberal recognition that a culture is uniquely meaningful to its human exponents; on the other hand, the ideological rationalisation of *apartheid*, based on the idea that Xhosa culture is uniquely meaningful to a population classified as citizens of the Transkei, that Tswana culture is uniquely meaningful to a population classified as citizens of BophuthaTswana, and so on. Why should anthropologists appear to endorse such propositions when most black people concerned emphatically reject them?

The lesson from all this is two-fold. Firstly, the concept of culture should never be used in a sense that implies a finite and exclusive aggregate of things learned by a given human population. Secondly, a culture cannot be studied in an historical vacuum. Whether it takes the form of an appeal to Sotho–Tswana 'inwardness' or to the need to defend 'western civilisation', an assertion of cultural integrity serves intellectual or political interests of one kind or another. Whether these are progressive or reactionary cannot be determined from first principles but only from analysis of particular historical conditions. It follows from this that Sotho–Tswana culture cannot be abstracted from history as an object of study in itself.

Failure to recognise this can have some odd consequences. In 1976 an American freelance journalist, Eugene Linden, wrote a book called *The Alms Race*. Its purpose was to investigate the American impulse to give aid to the Third World, in the light of its consequences for the recipients. Linden chose the barren and impoverished mountain kingdom of Lesotho as an obvious example of a 'basket case'. He was critical of development initiatives in Lesotho since independence in 1966, largely on the grounds that they undermined the integrity of Sesotho culture. They exposed Basotho, he pointed out, to the corrupting influence of western materialism. His anxiety was quite misplaced. In the first place, he misconceived Sesotho culture as an integral package that cannot accommodate alien influences without itself being undermined. In the second place, his anxiety was at least one hundred years too late. The Basotho have been incorporated in a larger political and economic system since the mid-nineteenth century. Throughout this period they have been directly exposed to 'western materialism'. The persistence or otherwise of

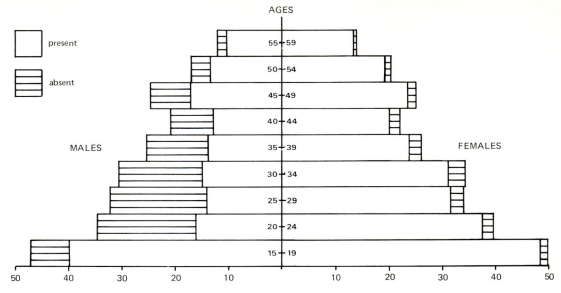

AGES

MALES   FEMALES

present
absent

55–59
50–54
45–49
40–44
35–39
30–34
25–29
20–24
15–19

50 40 30 20 10   10 20 30 40 50

fig. 6   The distribution of the population of Lesotho in 1966, by sex, residential status and age cohorts 15–59. Census results revealed a masculinity ratio of only 49 resident males per 100 resident females in the age range 20–39. Such a low ratio is typical of the labour reserves. It has profound sociological consequences, which are examined in chapter 7.

Sesotho custom must therefore be related to the changes that have taken place in the lives of Basotho as a result of their incorporation. This argument will be illustrated in detail with reference to various aspects of custom amongst the Sotho–Tswana.

What, then, do we mean by Sotho–Tswana culture? It is an abstraction which is significant in the following respects. Firstly, the languages spoken by the Tswana and the Southern Sotho peoples are closely related, in a way that I have outlined. Secondly, although there are many variations of detail, it is possible to identify an approximately common tradition, a cluster of moral rules and social arrangements which are recognisable to most contemporary speakers of those languages as 'the manners and customs of our grandfathers'. Thirdly, the term Sotho–Tswana is often used to define people's identity, either by insiders who claim it or by outsiders who impose it. Such uses, as will be seen, are by no means mutually consistent. These are the senses in which the phrase Sotho–Tswana culture is used in this book. It implies no mystifying 'essence' of Sotho–Tswana humanity, for their humanity they have in common, by definition, with mankind as a whole.

The Transformation of Society

Does the phrase Sotho–Tswana society have any meaning? The Sotho–Tswana today are distributed across several international boundaries. They are at present subject to the administration of six governments: those of Lesotho, Botswana and South Africa; of the newly 'independent' Transkei and BophuthaTswana; and of QwaQwa, the Southern Sotho 'homeland'. They are peasant cultivators, commercial livestock farmers, urban commuters. They are Christians and traditionalists, they are down-to-earth country people and sophisticated townspeople. Many of them spend their working lives as migrants who oscillate between their rural homes and employment in the 'white' urban areas of South Africa, in the mining, manufacturing, construction and service industries. Many of them are unemployed, and their families have the greatest difficulties in making ends meet. Differences of this kind are found within the population of Southern Africa as a whole. Therefore there is no bounded set of social relationships today that we can usefully identify as Sotho–Tswana society. Many years ago Isaac Schapera, the anthropologist who is best known for his exhaustive historical and anthropological studies of the Tswana, insisted that chief and district administrator, missionary and medicineman, trader and teacher, migrant miner and peasant, all had to be studied as participants in a single social system, that of Southern Africa as a whole. We share this view. It poses the problem of what perspective is appropriate for seeking to understand the experience of the Sotho–Tswana, defined as a minority population within Southern Africa.

Let us briefly outline two possible approaches. Neither is adequate in itself. One approach would be to reconstruct, from oral tradition and written sources, a social system which no longer exists but which may be considered approximately representative of the Sotho–Tswana tradition. The unit of analysis would be a tribe or a chiefdom, an independent polity having its own territorial base, a hierarchy of hereditary offices, and a relatively self-sustaining economy based on livestock and crop cultivation, with some trade and craft specialisation such as iron-working. We would discover high rates of polygyny—men marrying several wives—among the ruling families; preferences for marrying women defined as cousins in kinship terms; rituals of kinship for propitiating the ancestors and marking births, marriages and deaths; communal rituals for initiating the youth, for invoking the rain and for ensuring protection from malevolent powers; and elaborate social arrangements for ensuring the transmission of property, office and tradition from generation to generation.

An alternative approach would be to develop a perspective within which to understand the lives of Africans who live in the rural areas of Southern Africa. We would describe and analyse conditions which are not peculiar to the Sotho–Tswana peoples but which are typical of the labour reserves from which migrant workers are drawn to meet the needs of South African industry. These labour reserves are the black 'homelands' within South Africa itself, including the Transkei and BophuthaTswana; the independent kingdoms of Lesotho and Swaziland, and the Republic of Botswana. Southern Moçambique and Malawi may also be included as historically important suppliers of labour to the mining industry. Collectively these areas comprise what may be called the rural periphery of Southern Africa, by contrast with the industrial core where migrants are employed—the mines of the Witwatersrand, the Orange Free State and Natal—and the heartlands of secondary industry: the major conurbations of the Pretoria-Johannesburg-Vereeniging complex, Durban, Port Elizabeth and Cape Town. The terms rural periphery and industrial core are analytically convenient because they enable us to transcend the boundaries of nation–states when seeking to understand the regional economy of Southern Africa. The flow of migrants across these international boundaries on a large scale makes it impossible to understand the economy of any one of these countries in isolation.

Because of South African influx control and pass laws, migrant workers' families remain behind in the rural areas, where many live in overcrowded squalor and where they seek to scrape a partial livelihood from exhausted and over-grazed soils. Our analysis would focus on the relationships between migrants and their dependent families, and on the consequences for the elderly, the young, the sick and the unemployed of general dependence on the earnings of absentees. We would find a gross imbalance between the sexes in the rural populations—women far outnumber men, especially amongst young and middle-aged adults (fig. 6). Family life is ravaged by the separation of spouses and the absence of fathers. There is a crisis of security in old age. The energies of the vast majority of people are devoted to sheer survival under difficult conditions. We would also find evidence of increasing differentiation between rural households—most people are poor, but some are very much poorer than others.

The challenge in presenting an account of the Sotho–Tswana today is to integrate these two approaches. They would appear to have little in common. No traditional chiefdoms survive as independent political entities, with the partial exception of Lesotho. It is impossible to conceptualise a Sotho–Tswana economic system today, for the Sotho–Tswana participate, variously but inevitably, in the regional economic system of Southern Africa as a whole. But custom seldom merely dies. Some aspects of it are undermined with the passage of time. Other aspects of it are invigorated. Social relationships do not merely wither away—they are transformed. The Sotho–Tswana still engage in disputes within the framework of customary law, and rationalise their behaviour with reference to the morality of their grandfathers. They have also acquired new values—with education, with Christianity and the habits of an urban consumer life-style. New forms of religious behaviour have partly replaced the old forms, but the new idiom is often inspired by the old idiom. Many of the younger generation in Lesotho still go to initiation schools. Other Sotho–Tswana despise these schools as relics from the past.

The object of our study is therefore the transformations that have taken place in political, economic, kinship and ritual relations. Much of Sotho–Tswana custom persists. In this sense people remain, in Setiloane's phrase, 'stubbornly Sotho–

Tswana'. But it is misleading to represent the persistence of custom as cultural bedrock impervious to superficial change. The changes in people's lives are themselves fundamental. Rituals for the ancestors persist, even amongst members of Christian congregations. Many Sotho–Tswana, both rural and urban, continue to perform their customary obligations in this respect, and fear the mystical consequences, in the form of illness or misfortune inflicted by the ancestors, of failure to do so. The dead, in other words, are still regarded as moral arbiters of relations among the living. Yet the pattern of relations among the living—between elders and juniors, between men and women—has undergone significant change. This suggests that the relationship between ritual practice and everyday life is a very complex one. Likewise, the institution of bridewealth persists among many of the Sotho–Tswana peoples. As will be seen, however, it is not the same institution in the late twentieth century as it was in the middle of the nineteenth century. Accordingly the problem which recurs in the later chapters is how to analyse the relationship of Sotho–Tswana custom to the changing lives of the Sotho–Tswana themselves. We are particularly concerned with those who retain their roots in rural communities. But before we proceed it is necessary to know something of the origins and history of the people in question.

Sol Plaatje: A Breaker of Boundaries

The life of Solomon Plaatje (1876–1932) well illustrates the diversity of Sotho–Tswana experience. A full member of the Rolong tribe (a branch of the Tswana), he took part in the defence of Mafeking during the Anglo–Boer War, and recorded his experiences in a diary which has only recently been found and published. He was a co-founder, in 1912, of the African National Congress. His book *Native Life in South Africa* (1916) is a moving account of the human misery arising out of the Land Act of 1913, and a scathing attack on its political sponsors. As a journalist he wrote throughout his working life about the grievances of blacks in South Africa. He also wrote a novel, *Mhudi*, which celebrates the importance of tribal custom and the relevance of an African historical perspective. He travelled widely in Southern Africa. He visited Britain, the United States and the Belgian Congo. He spoke many languages, and drew his inspiration from many sources, not least of which was Shakespeare.

'While reading *Cymbeline*, I met the girl who afterwards became my wife. I was not then as well acquainted with her language—the Xosa—as I am now; and although she had a better grip of mine—the Sechuana—I was doubtful whether I could make her understand my innermost feelings in it, so in coming to an understanding we both used the language of educated people—the language which Shakespeare wrote—which happened to be the only official language in our country at the time. Some of the daily epistles were rather lengthy, for I usually started with the bare intention of expressing the affections of my heart but generally finished up by completely unburdening my soul. For command of language and giving expression to abstract ideas, the success of my efforts was second only to that of my wife's, and it is easy to divine that Shakespeare's poems fed our thoughts.

'It may be depended upon that we both read *Romeo and Juliet*. My people resented the idea of my marrying a girl who spoke a language which, like the Hottentot language, had clicks in it; while her people likewise abominated the idea of giving their daughter in marriage to a fellow who spoke a language so imperfect as to be without any clicks. But the civilised laws of Cape Colony saved us from a double tragedy in a cemetery, and our erstwhile objecting relatives have lived to award their benediction to the growth of our Chuana-M'Bo family which is bilingual both in the vernaculars and in European languages.'

The language which Shakespeare wrote was indeed accessible only to a small educated élite, in South Africa at the time Plaatje was writing. But Plaatje himself was largely self-educated. His reminiscences reveal the extent to which it is possible for individuals to transcend boundaries of tribe, language and modes of thought. At the same time they show clearly how such boundaries are used to define, for example, the limits of marital eligibility. The theme is a familiar one: 'Would you let your daughter marry a . . .?'

2

Early History and Upheaval

WILLIAM F LYE

According to their legends, the Sotho and Tswana peoples originated from the 'Cave of Lowe', or from a bed of reeds at Ntswana-tsatsi ('Where the sun rises'). To confirm their commitment to that understanding many mothers announce the birth of their child by placing a reed across their door. Theories of the origins of this interesting people abound, but detailed proof escapes confirmation because of the lack of a literary heritage. Nonetheless some basic facts lend understanding and this chapter will start by offering a survey of what is known and believed by scholars today.

The Setting

The Sotho people traditionally occupied the bulk of the high interior plateau country of South Africa, roughly framed by the Kalahari Desert on the west, the Drakensberg Mountains on the east, the Limpopo River on the north, and towards the Orange River on the south-east and south-west. The dominant physical characteristic of the area is relatively flat land, isolated from the coastal plain by an escarpment which surrounds it on three sides. This plateau tilts slightly so that its highest edge converges with the Drakensberg Mountains on the east. As it extends north and west, it drops gradually in altitude. Numerous small flat-topped hills break the monotony of the plain, especially near the eastern mountains. The eastern and southern mountains afford an isolation to the plateau which is accentuated by the thirsty Karoo and desert on the west. In the north and north-east the plateau drops off to the Limpopo River, where the altitude averages less than 660 metres, but then a dense tropical vegetation hosts diseases for man and cattle and deters travel.

The plateau is drained by the Orange-Vaal River system with its numerous tributaries. This system is little use for transportation, however, because of the irregularity of the flow and its direction towards the Karoo.

The climate of the area depends on wind patterns which bring rains from the Indian Ocean during the summer. The abrupt rise over the Drakensberg forces the winds to disgorge the bulk of their waters on the coastal side before they enter the plateau. What they retain beyond that point they precipitate in progressively smaller amounts as they travel westward, until they exhaust themselves on the desert. For the plateau as a whole, half of the area can

The generic name, Sotho, which is widely adopted today, is accepted by all but a few of the Western Tswana clans and derives from their own language. 'BaSotho' translates from their language as 'Black People'. The origin of the name, like that of the people, is shrouded in antiquity, and invites speculation about who coined it and why. Despite the fact that a few clans do not apply it to themselves and it lacks a general historical application, it serves adequately the need for a designation for similar cultures.

In the early contact period, Europeans generally spoke of the group as Tswana, probably because the line of their entry from the southwest led them first to that sub-group. 'Sotho', however, has the virtue of deriving from their own language, of being widely accepted by the people to whom it refers, and possessing no pejorative implication. It serves as well as any alternative, because of its currency, its brevity, and its lack of ambiguity. It will therefore, be used in the historical chapters to refer to the whole language group, as distinct from the sub-sections under consideration: the Southern Sotho, Tswana, or any of the individual chiefly names when they are identified specifically.

expect drought one year in every three.

Over the long history of occupation we have no record to verify that rainfall has reduced, but even within the short period of recorded history we have convincing proof of the gradual desiccation and denudation of the land. Overgrazing by cattle, sheep and goats, destruction by the natural fauna, burning of the natural grasses, increasing densities of human population and cultivation have all reduced the natural ground cover and led to severe erosion.

Ground water is an important contributor to the usefulness of the plateau. It underlies the surface over a wide area, in a limestone reservoir. Fountains, or springs, tap this reservoir, making limited areas especially productive. Where rain is scarce, fountains become the predominant foci for habitation.

The natural vegetation of the plateau is grass; hence, the term 'highveld' applies to that portion above the bush and tree line, at an altitude of roughly 660 metres. Because of the altitude, even the portions of the plateau which approach the tropics enjoy bracing winters and cool summer evenings, which limit the spread of brush and the attendant tsetse fly menace. Where the altitude declines, in a large arc roughly following the bend of the Limpopo, bush-

veld takes over and restricts the encroachment of cattle-keeping people.

The Occupation of the Land

This land appears to have supported human occupants for a very long time. Remains of ancient humanoid Australopithecines date the earliest known occupation to perhaps 1,8 million years ago. Hunter–gatherer modes of life introduced at that time dominated until very recent times as far as the scanty archaeological remains confirm. Although the physical type of the occupants varied, most recently the modern San, or Bushmen, predominated with cultures which are still well known in the western extension of the plateau.

Perhaps 3 000 years ago, the hunter–gatherers began to be pushed aside from the choice lands to make room for pastoral cultures of genetically similar types, perhaps kin to those now referred to as Khoi. Whether they migrated into the area or whether they evolved from existing people as a result of acculturation with external contacts is unknown. What is known is that the domestication of cattle and sheep became a way of life in the area approximately 3 000 years ago.

More complex cultures followed during the period from about 1 700 to 1 400 years ago. The newer life-style added the use of implements manufactured from iron and other metal-smithing, the production of pottery ware, and the domestication of grain crops. Again, who the first iron-using farmers were is a mystery. Thus far only a limited number of sites have been discovered to indicate the extent of spread of the new life-styles; however, more sites have recently been added. Perhaps the most spectacular find was made by a young boy named K L von Bezing. In 1956–7, when only 10 years old, he uncovered a few pottery sherds. Later, when he became more aware of their worth, he led archaeologists to the site near Lydenburg. They uncovered a fine array of pottery, bone, ivory, copper, shell and stone objects. The most interesting items, however, were two large and five smaller terracotta heads. The radiocarbon datings from this site suggest their manufacture during the fifth century A.D. Other recent finds in the Transvaal date to the third or fourth century A.D.

Only inferential links justify identifying these finds with living populations. Nonetheless, it can be asserted that the coincidence of agriculture, permanent dwellings, pottery and metal crafting, and cattle and sheep domestication, describe the historical culture of contemporary Bantu-speaking peoples in the area. Perhaps the early arrivals were the ancestors of modern Bantu-speaking peoples, including the Sotho. As more archaeology is completed in the region, a more adequate indication of dating and distribution may be made known. These mute finds cannot now be linked with existing populations without some literary or at least oral traditions of the living people. Thus far these have not been claimed.

A reasonable case can be made for the belief that the more complex cultures migrated into the area from the north, presuming the chronological sequence of the appearance of iron technology southward throughout the continent of Africa. That does not necessarily presuppose that the entire population migrated, nor that all the elements of the more complex society migrated intact. A more plausible postulate suggests that the pre-existing populations hosted immigrants of greater or lesser numbers in sequence, and adopted the more advantageous aspects of their culture. Certainly, observable variations in the physical types, manner of speech and customs of modern Africans seem to indicate a variety of degrees of fusion of distinct elements over a lengthy period of time. It points to a complex pattern of populating, migrating and acculturating in the southern veld over an extended period.

The Emergence of the Sotho People

What archaeology cannot reveal, the living people provide in their traditions. Despite the lack of proven links between the mute ancient remains and the contemporary inhabitants, certain indicators suggest that link. Virtually all contemporary Bantu-speaking societies share a material culture analogous to that of the buried ruins, at least until their modification through contact with others; they also maintain a tradition of migration from the north.

Those scholars who are most familiar with the language of the Bantu-speaking peoples and who have studied African village life first hand over long periods tend to propose more conservative interpretations regarding Bantu origins, while those whose study depends upon translations and collections of the traditions made by the former tend to be more speculative. The reader needs to be aware that the data is fragmentary and that speculations are not proven fact.

The remembered traditions of the Sotho generally confirm the widely accepted belief that they, too, migrated from the north, and dispossessed or absorbed the earlier San inhabitants of the plateau. A tentative theory based on those traditions suggests a rather explicit sequence for the arrival of various

Sotho lineages. The earliest to arrive were probably the Kgalagadi in the west, and the Fokeng in the east. Isaac Schapera used the Kgalagadi's own lists of kings to propose that they had arrived in the thirteenth or fourteenth centuries, but recent archaeological evidence seems to suggest an earlier date. Perhaps the known tendency among pre-literate societies to elide or telescope their rulers' genealogies explains the discrepancy. The intermixture of these pioneers with earlier occupants is clearly attested by their physical traits, their dialectic peculiarities and, especially for the Kgalagadi, in their mode of living. Succeeding invaders apparently drove the Kgalagadi to the borders of the desert, where they had to adopt the hunter–gatherer life of the San.

The Hoja were also early pioneers. They too became displaced and were forced either west to the desert or eastward across the Vaal River. Like the Kgalagadi, those who remained became absorbed in a client relationship with their more powerful successors.

The next entrants, the Tlhaping and Rolong, occupied most of the grazing land between the Vaal River and the desert. Their immediate relationship with their predecessors is vague, but they probably absorbed some of them, at least temporarily.

The most important influx of Sotho speakers followed next, bringing the direct ancestors of the dominant Southern Sotho and Tswana lineages. They may have entered as a single community, but they soon broke up into the Hurutshe, the senior lineage, and the Kwena, who later subdivided further into the Ngwato, Ngwaketse, Tawana, Kgatla, Pedi, Hlakwana, Tlokwa, Sia, Phuthing and others. Some writers connect the Hoja and Rolong to this dominant genealogy also, though they generally concede the relatively earlier arrival of those two.

Virtually all of these ancient Sotho lineages subsequently split further into several chiefdoms of varying autonomy, and dispersed locally until they had inherited the land from the Caledon River valley on the south-east to the borders of the desert. Not all of the Sotho were necessarily descended from these lineages, though most of the Tswana and Southern Sotho chiefly families appear to have been. Nor had they completely occupied the land. Dispersed among them and scattered along their southern flank were independent communities of San and Khoi. Immigrant Nguni and other Bantu-speaking people shared with them the eastern part of their lands. In addition, all the Sotho communities absorbed aliens within their own ranks. However, in general each Sotho community preserved the key elements of speech and customs by which it identified itself (see figs. 7 and 8).

By the end of the eighteenth century their occupation of the plateau had reached its greatest extent. They had by then expanded vigorously. The Southern Sotho occupied the land south and east of the Vaal River to a line as far south as Thaba Nchu and Thaba Bosiu, possibly further. Hoja villages claimed the western extremity of the area. The Taung, who were either a branch or a close affiliate of them, occupied lands south of the Vaal to Thaba Nchu. The Kwena clans settled mainly along the

Tswana huts. An illustration by Charles Davidson Bell, surveyor and artist, who accompanied Dr Andrew Smith on his expedition, from Andrew Smith's Journal of his Expedition into the Interior of South Africa, 1834–1836, *edited by William F Lye.*

Caledon valley north of Thaba Bosiu, and had already divided into several distinct chiefdoms. The ancient Fokeng villages lay interspersed between the Kwena and extended south beyond Thaba Bosiu, where they mixed with early Nguni and San settlers. At least one Fokeng chiefdom, the Patsa, occupied land north of the Caledon near the Vaal. North of the Caledon to the east, along the Wilge and the Elands Rivers, dwelt the Sia, the Tlokwa and the Phuthing, all closely related chiefdoms descended from the Kgatla, a Tswana chiefdom.

The Tswana chiefdoms dwelt north and west of the Vaal, and claimed a larger territory than did the Southern Sotho. The lands farthest west served the Kgalagadi, who sought to avoid the dominance of stronger chiefs by settling the sparse desert. Next, on the Kuruman River, lived the Tlharo. The Tlhaping and their allies occupied the land around

Dithakong and Kuruman.

The Hurutshe settlement, Kaditshwene, was one of the largest towns in Southern Africa. The Kgatla resided on the banks of the Crocodile River, the Ngwaketse dwelt near the present site of Kanye. The Ngwato dwelt furthest north at the Shoshong Hills. The Kwena dispersed north and east of the Ngwaketse. Each Tswana village possessed cattle posts as well as their towns, and many had spawned autonomous sub-chiefdoms, already separated from their main towns.

Though common origins linked these two great divisions of the Sotho family, geographical separation and the passage of time had already begun to create cleavages between them. These distinctions would only become greater as a result of the turmoil of the *Difaqane*, the wars which broke out early in the nineteenth century, and with the arrival of European missionaries and immigrants thereafter.

The Difaqane: Breakdown of Traditional Order

As the Sotho expanded southward over the plateau for many generations, their main opponents were San. These Bush people occupied all the land as their extensive hunting preserves, possessing no permanent villages. The more intensive agri-pastoral life of the Sotho made their encroachment on the hunters' lands relatively easy.

The process by which the Sotho expanded occurred as an outcome of their political succession. When a chiefdom grew beyond the carrying capacity of its territory, or beyond the administrative convenience of one chief, contending heirs would fight over their father's patrimony. The victor would inherit the homeland; the vanquished would take his following away to find land where he could rule autonomously. The vulnerable lands of the San made the process easy.

Eventually, as the Tswana reached southward in the west, they encountered a different type of people: Kora pastoralists, Khoi people, who, though they did not occupy permanent villages, had the support of cattle, and possessed more formidable weapons. These Kora had themselves migrated into the area from the south, crossing the Orange River to escape the encroachment of Europeans at the Cape of Good Hope.

By the mid-eighteenth century signs of change appeared. The Rolong, under Tau, established themselves on the Harts River, and sought to con-

1. Tswana
Early Migrants:
  Kgalagadi
  Hoja
  Tlhaping
Rolong Lineage:
  Tshidi Rolong
  Seleka Rolong
  Rapulana Rolong
  Ratlou Rolong
Hurutshe Lineage:
  Kwena
  Ngwato
  Ngwaketse
  Tawana
  Kgatla
  Tlharo

2. Southern Sotho
Early Immigrants:
  Fokeng
  Patsa (Kololo)
  Hoja
  Taung
Kgatla Lineage:
  Phuthing
  Sia
  Tlokwa

3. Other Bantu-Speaking People
Northen Sotho (Kgatla Lineage):
  Pedi
Southern Nguni:
  Xhosa
Northern Nguni:
  Hlubi
  Ngwane of Matiwane
  Kumalo of Mzilikazi (Ndebele)
  Zulu
Highveld Nguni (N. Nguni origin):
  Lesotho Group
  'Transvaal Ndebele'
Shona (Zimbabwe)
Herero and Ovambo (Namibia)

4. Non-Bantu-Speaking People
San (Bushmen)
Khoi
  Kora
  Griqua

fig. 7 *The ethnic relationships of the Tswana and Southern Sotho and their neighbours.*

28

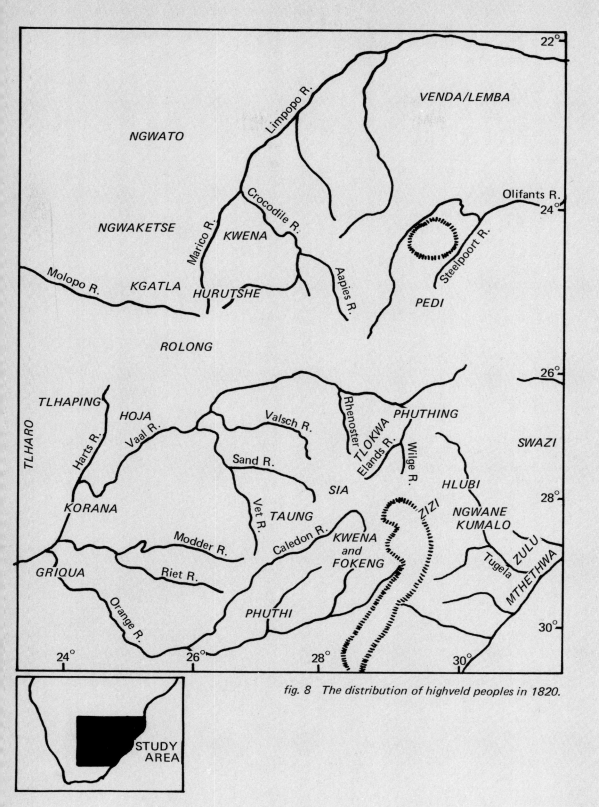

VENDA/LEMBA

NGWATO

Limpopo R.

Crocodile R.

NGWAKETSE

Marico R.

KWENA

Olifants R.
24°

Steelpoort R.

Aapies R.

PEDI

Molopo R.

KGATLA

HURUTSHE

ROLONG

26°

TLHAPING

HOJA

Valsch R.

Rhenoster R.

PHUTHING

SWAZI

TLHARO

Harts R.

Vaal R.

Sand R.

TLOKWA

Elands R.

Wilge R.

HLUBI

KORANA

Vet R.

SIA

TAUNG

ZIZI

NGWANE
KUMALO

28°

Modder R.

Caledon R.

KWENA
and
FOKENG

ZULU

GRIQUA

Riet R.

Tugela

MTHETHWA

Orange R.

PHUTHI

30°

24°

26°

28°

30°

fig. 8   The distribution of highveld peoples in 1820.

STUDY
AREA

22°

29

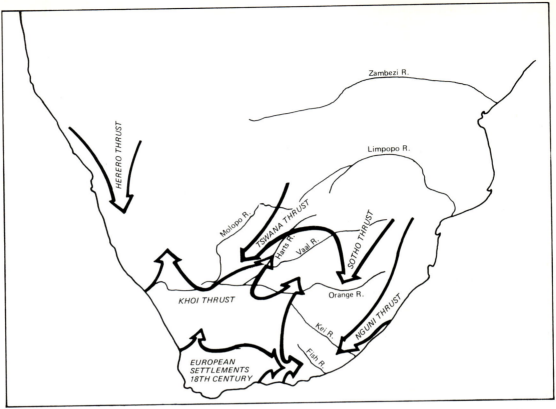

fig. 9 Southern African confrontation zones in the eighteenth century.

solidate their power by subjugating their Tswana neighbours, the Tlhaping and Tlharo, who preceded them in the region (fig. 9).

The Tlhaping, however, had by that time already allied with the Kora through a series of marriages between their senior chiefs and Kora wives over three generations. When the Rolong incursion became intolerable, the Tlhaping called upon their Kora friends, who broke the Rolong hegemony by killing Tau. This engagement blunted the Rolong advance. They retreated to their old country and segmented under the four heirs into autonomous units in the more traditional pattern. ThenKora and their Khoi kin continued to oppose Sotho expansion for the rest of the traditional era.

Though the Kora alliance with the Tlhaping ended the Rolong experiment with consolidation, pressures on the land led the Ngwaketse to experiment in a similar manner at the end of the century. The Southern Sotho never produced effective amalgams before 1800, but Mohlomi, the almost legendary chief of the Monaheng Kwena, sought to

generate cooperation. He died without creating any permanent political institutions, and the wars of the *Difaqane* swept away all but his memory.

On the coastal plains of the east, however, the Nguni experienced even greater pressures on their confined lands. They carried out more consistent efforts to consolidate. By the end of the eighteenth century, the Nguni, too, had occupied the lands available to them. They had spread as far south as the Fish River, and were grazing or hunting beyond. They probably thrust forward more rapidly than did the Sotho because their land was more fruitful, and because they were confined between the sea and the Drakensberg. At the Fish the Southern Nguni became blocked by another reverse migration of the Khoi, who fled in that direction from the Cape.

As the frontier passed beyond the Northern Nguni clans, they had ever reducing opportunities to segment and move to unoccupied land. This new internal pressure led the proliferating clans to seek alternative solutions. Early offshoots found their way out of the area on to the plateau, where they competed with the Sotho, and were called Matebele (Ndebele) by their Sotho neighbours.

More than the actual shortage of land, the loss of

autonomous space on which to build a chiefdom may have been the catalyst for revolution. Escape was not desired by all the Nguni chiefs, for some enjoyed the fruitful plain and, perhaps, desired to dominate the budding trade with Europeans who had settled at Delagoa Bay.

Whatever the causes, as the opportunity for segmentation diminished, chiefs began to substitute aggregation in its place; that is, they moved to incorporate weak neighbours to enhance their strength in competition against their foes. Those chiefs who competed for mastery over the area adopted military structures for their chiefdoms in place of their traditional age grade systems. These changes appear to have evolved over time, one chief adopting the innovations of his neighbour and adding something new to gain the advantage. Eventually Shaka, king of the Zulu, coalesced all the people of the north coast into a great conquest state. Those who resisted either succumbed to the assegai or fled away. The refugees who escaped, thoroughly conversant with the new fighting strategies, burst upon their unsuspecting neighbours to precipitate a holocaust in every direction. Such was the *Difaqane*, as the Sotho victims named the wars, 'the Scattering'.

These wars reached the Southern Sotho about 1822. Three of the Nguni chiefs who fled from the Zulu crossed the Drakensberg with their adherents and their salvaged possessions, seeking security far from the turmoil. Instead, they took that turmoil with them. Virtually every Sotho community from the Drakensberg to the Kalahari fell prey to the plundering bands loosed by the wars.

The first major refugee from Shaka's fury was the great Hlubi chiefdom, possibly the largest among the Northern Nguni. The senior chief fell to the invaders and the chiefdom split into two sections. The smaller section, headed by the heir, fled south along the edge of the Drakensberg to seek asylum amidst the Xhosa villages. The majority followed a lesser chief of the 'right-hand house', Mpangazita, up to the highveld.

Their first encounter with the Southern Sotho community was against the Mokotleng branch of the Tlokwa, who lived near the Wilge River under a regentess named MaNthatisi. Because of their strategic location near the mountain pass, the Tlokwa had long traded with the Nguni for metal goods. Their recent squabbles with a Hlubi chief gave cause for the refugees of that chiefdom to vent their frustrations on their neighbours rather than to seek asylum amongst them. Without warning the Hlubi band attacked the Tlokwa villages, driving out their

hapless victims. MaNthatisi led her followers westward while Mpangazita rested at her village, devouring her people's cattle and crops. However, with such a large following Mpangazita soon exhausted the food supply and, as his pursuers were still close, he roamed on.

He followed the route taken by MaNthatisi, sacking as she had the Kwena and Fokeng villages en route. They caught the Tlokwa at the Sand River and pushed them on again, but only after suffering heavy casualties and discovering that the Tlokwa had devoured the crops. They next followed the Caledon southward on the west bank, while MaNthatisi travelled a parallel route on the east bank. The Hlubi settled temporarily at Mabolela while the Tlokwa stopped at Peka just across the river.

Next, the Tlokwa decided that they had to destroy the Hlubi menace. The Hlubi anticipated their coming and drove them off, but at heavy cost. Then the Hlubi decided to teach the Tlokwa a lesson. They crossed the river while the Tlokwa men were absent foraging for food. MaNthatisi, seeing them appear, hastily gathered her women and children, 'armed' them with hoes, and arrayed them in fighting order. The sun's rays, gleaming off the shiny iron tools, startled the approaching Hlubi army. They broke and fled, only to encounter the returning Tlokwa warriors. The disordered Hlubi retreated to Mabolela, where they settled on the summit of a flat-topped hill, called in Sesotho a *qhobosheane* or natural fortress.

During the two years from the time they entered the highveld until they settled down, the Hlubi and their Tlokwa victims plundered the Southern Sotho communities along the Upper Caledon. In that time they had triggered off the mauraduing career of MaNthatisi, whose name became synonymous with the *Difaqane* for her Sotho victims, and for those who learned of the wars from them. Her victims, in turn, fled across the Vaal to convey the same pattern of plunder amongst the Tswana.

By 1824 the Hlubi had newly settled down only to face a renewed threat from their old Nguni depredator, Matiwane, chief of the Ngwane. The Ngwane had originally driven the Hlubi from their homeland and had settled there. Matiwane had gained the reputation of being the Nguni warrior next only to Shaka in strength, but he failed to build up state structures which could compete, and Shaka drove him away in his programme of creating a cordon of desolation around the Zulu kingdom.

The Ngwane followed the route of the Hlubi to the highveld, falling first upon another Tlokwa branch and their Sia neighbours who had remained near the passes. They apparently remained in the east for a time, and then migrated to Senyotong, a short distance north of Thaba Bosiu, where Moshoeshoe, a Kwena chief, had settled near his old Hlubi foe. Matiwane followed a similar pattern of plunder against the local Sotho communities as had Mpangazita before him.

Following an intense period of fighting between the two Nguni foes, Matiwane crossed the Caledon to settle at Mekwatleng, near the Hlubi retreat of Mabolela, where he could 'fight them every day'. In 1825 he trapped Mpangazita and killed him, concluding a five-day battle. With the death of their chief, the Hlubi broke up. Some joined their conquerors and fought as equals in the Ngwane army, others fled to Moshoeshoe, and still others fled northward to join another Nguni refugee, Mzilikazi, or eastward to rejoin their kinsmen below the Drakensberg.

After the death of Mpangazita, Matiwane became the undisputed master of the Caledon area and raided as far south as the Xhosa lands. Moshoeshoe and his Kwena followers became his tributary; MaNthatisi fled back north to Khoro-e-betlwa, to her own defensible hill. The other Southern Sotho chiefs had either fallen under the rule of one of these three chiefs or had become vagabond.

About two years after Matiwane defeated the Hlubi, Shaka's impis appeared on the highveld. Some people claimed that Moshoeshoe had lured him there and, whether that story is true or not, it is clear that something alerted the Zulu king to the presence of a rival along the Caledon. In 1827 he sent an impi captained by his brother, Dingane, who drove Matiwane south and captured many of his cattle. Even though Matiwane regrouped and attacked the Zulu army, they kept his cattle as they returned home. This event proved a severe blow to Matiwane's prestige, and Moshoeshoe's alleged part in his defeat rankled amongst the Ngwane soldiers.

Finally they induced Matiwane to invade Moshoeshoe's stronghold. Moshoeshoe repulsed them, and on their way home they faced a surprise attack by Mzilikazi, who had come from his northern outpost. His failure to defeat his own vassal, Moshoeshoe, or to avoid the increasing menace of other Nguni invaders led Matiwane to seek out a new home in the south, where his soldiers had captured much cattle. The Thembu country, where cattle abounded and crops thrived as in his homeland, promised a haven.

Matiwane trekked south with his large following of Ngwane, Hlubi and Sotho early in 1828. Travel proved difficult. Some of his people fell victim to grass fires along the Tele River, others suffered attacks by petty Sotho chiefs who had become emboldened by Matiwane's defeats, and others froze to death in the early winter frosts of the southern mountains. They finally reached the Thembu country only to discover it was not the haven they sought. Rumours of a Zulu raid had alerted the local Thembu chiefs to seek aid from the European colony. When Matiwane arrived, the combined force of Africans and colonists routed them completely.

Many of the survivors from Matiwane's armies returned to Lesotho to seek admission to Moshoeshoe's growing state. Their chief passed through that area en route to his original home, and there he was murdered by Dingane, who had succeeded Shaka, in 1828.

The third Nguni refugee provoked similar disruptions in the chiefdoms of the north. Mzilikazi had been chief of the Northern Kumalo clan until he succumbed to Shaka's domination. Then he became a regimental commander in Shaka's army, but over his own warriors. By 1823 he rebelled and fled from Zululand to the high interior with about 300 young warriors and what few family members survived the wars. He gradually fought his way across the plateau until by 1825 he had settled at the junction of the Apies and Crocodile Rivers where the Tswana branch of the Kwena had formerly thrived.

There he built the Ndebele kingdom after Shaka's model. Unlike Mpangazita and Matiwane, however, he survived for over ten years amongst the Sotho, and then moved successfully to continue his empire over the Shona people beyond the Limpopo River. Being relatively few in numbers, and in an alien land, the Kumalo found every opportunity to add to their strength. They often absorbed other refugees from Zululand, and also many of the young men of the Tswana clans which they destroyed. In doing so they adopted a unique structure in which each type of subject, Nguni, Sotho and later Shona, received a specific caste status in which intermarriage and intermixing were stringently restricted (fig. 10).

Even though the Ndebele were few in numbers, they struck terror in the minds of their neighbours. Their permanent base on the Apies enabled them to launch attacks on all sides. Their usual technique was haughtily to warn their foes of their coming, and then surround them by night. At dawn they would drum their heavy shields like thunder to startle their sleepy victims. Then they stormed the village, stabbing their short assegais into everyone in sight and firing the huts. No one survived except the

'The onset of Ndebele warriors', from Andrew Smith's Journal, 1834–1836. *The Tswana and Southern Sotho people were unprepared for the onslaught of the Nguni invaders in their lands, who were totally mobilised and trained according to entirely new methods developed in Zululand. Not only did the Sotho–Tswana lack the military tradition developed amongst the Ndebele, but also they used less formidable weapons.*

young men who could be drafted into the regiments and young maidens who could reward the valour of the fighters.

Though his tactic worked stunningly well on the Tswana tribesmen, the more distant Kora and Griqua villages in the south, with the advantage of guns and horses, staged repeated plundering raids on the cattle outposts which the 'Matebele' (the name given them by the Sotho) established beyond their villages. Even though they frequently failed, the persistence of the Kora and Griqua undermined Mizilikazi's dominance over the area, and when their raids were joined by more direct attacks by Zulu impis, Mzilikazi fled further westward to the

Marico River in 1832. Again, he subdued the local Tswana communities, including Rolong and Hurutshe. In fact, few Tswana chiefs escaped disruption except the Tlhaping, who lived further south under the tutelage of Scots missionaries.

Despite a continuation of Kora and Griqua raids and Zulu attacks, Mzilikazi ruled his large domain with remarkable success until the arrival of European trekkers. In August 1836 he encountered their first parties, and though he resisted at first, he soon fell prey to their arms. They drove him northward. Many Tswana subjects remained loyal to him and assisted him in rebuilding his state north of the Limpopo River, where it survived to the end of the century.

The removal of Mzilikazi's kingdom meant the end of direct Nguni threats for the Sotho people. The *Difaqane*, however, included more disturbances than those caused by aliens. For many the attacks were the work of their own kinsmen who had been uprooted from their lands by the Nguni invaders. MaNthatisi and her Tlokwa became the first Sotho victims of the wars, but she proved to be a capable

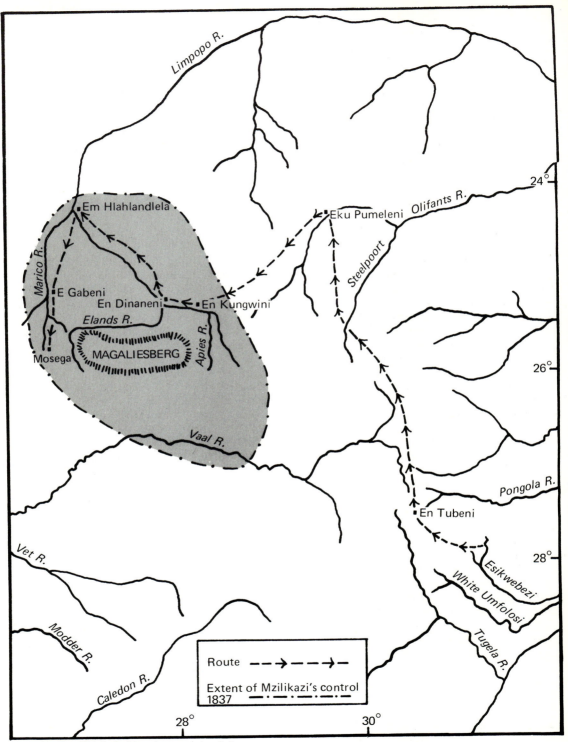

Limpopo R.

24°

Em Hlahlandlela

Eku Pumeleni   Olifants R.

Marico R.

Steelpoort

E Gabeni
En Dinaneni   En Kungwini

Elands R.

Apies R.

Mosega   MAGALIESBERG

26°

Vaal R.

Pongola R.

En Tubeni

Vet R.

28°

Esikwebezi

White Umfolosi

Modder R.

Tugela R.

Route	- - -→- - -→-
Extent of Mzilikazi's control 1837	-·-·-·-·-·-

28°   30°

fig. 10   The Ndebele kingdom south of the
Limpopo River.

leader. She ruled in the name of her young son, Sekonyela and, despite the explosion of war, refused to relinquish her power. While other chiefs fell victim to the wars, she held her people together, repeatedly fought the Nguni bands, and copied their methods as she dispossessed many of her neighbours, devouring their sustenance.

This Tlokwa heroine was a tall, slim woman of great strength. in peaceful times she bore five children. Her people loved and trusted her. Out of affection, they named her 'Mosayane', 'the little woman', a far cry from the horrible reputation accorded her by white men of her day. Europeans who met her after she had settled down and retired from the leadership of her people admired her elegant figure and her open countenance. Andrew Smith compared her favourably with Moshoeshoe. By that time, however, she had passed her control over to her son, Sekonyela.

Contrary to legend, MaNthatisi did not lead her troops in battle, though she planned their strategy and sat in court to make policy. When she was driven from her fields and herds by the Hlubi, she only temporarily sought aid from her brother, the chief of the Sia. She chose to oppose her enemy alone, and this became the archetype of the plundering chiefs of the *Difaqane*. She adopted the methods of her attackers in a succession of raids up and down the Caledon River in order to support her destitute followers. By making that decision she added to the disruption and weakened the ability of the Southern Sotho clans to resist and end the wars.

Being driven from their lands, her band, like the Hlubi before them and her victims afterwards, had to wander with complete family units with what few cattle and possessions they could keep from their plunderers. In the haste of their flight they neglected the elderly and very young, who suffered privation and frequently fell behind to become prey to the next wave of attackers, or to the victims of their own most recent raids. In these circumstances, to use the name of traditional clans to identify the wandering hordes becomes meaningless. Each band consisted of the followers of an identifiable leader and as many of his or her original subjects as survived, but also numerous adherents from whatever source they could be collected: victims of their raids, stragglers from their own plunderers. In order to survive, the wandering bands had to be numerous enough to overpower their victims and to capture the supplies they needed. But, being numerous, they had to stage ever more frequent raids to support themselves. Further, as horde after horde broke upon the country the means of support diminished.

Agriculture ceased, flocks and herds were slaughtered throughout the Southern Sotho area.

Those who did not enter a plundering horde had to sustain themselves in the ruins of their land. Crops and herds became magnets to other plundering bands. Many retreated to remote hideaways in the mountains where they reverted to hunting and gathering the wild foods as their means of subsistence. A few even adopted cannibalism as a result of their destitution. As late as 1834, Dr Andrew Smith described the plight of such people along the Upper Caledon:

'But few natives were seen during this part of our journey and if we except a small village which belonged to an uncle of the Mantatee king [Sekonyela] we cannot say that we passed anything like a regular establishment. Many small hordes were dispersed over the mountain sides, but these had neither a fixed nor regular abode, they sought their shelter in the crevices of the rocks and wandered from place to place as the game migrated. Though the country might therefore be said to be almost depopulated, such, we had sufficient evidence before us, had not always been its condition. The ruins of several large villages were passed, the environs of which were thickly strewed with human bones and even the appearances around the remains of the huts showed that numerous lives must have been sacrificed even at the very doors of the houses.'

Once the worst raids had ended MaNthatisi and Sekonyela settled at Khoro-e-betlwa, and Moshoeshoe led his refugees to Thaba Bosiu, where many victims of the wars amongst the Southern Sotho congregated under their protection.

Before the reconstruction had taken effect in the Caledon country, many dispossessed chiefs fled northward to carry the devastation to the Tswana. From the fragmentary evidence of occasional literate travellers and rumours spread by the victims to the Griqua and the frontier mission stations, we know that the entire country north of the Vaal was swept by roving bands of Southern Sotho refugees, even prior to the emergence of Mzilikazi. Some reports of devastation amongst the Tswana reached the Griqua country before the end of 1822. Perhaps these were victims of bands organised by the Phuthing and the Hlakwana clans, two of the earliest victims of the Hlubi. In December of that year the Griqua reported stories of disorder across the Vaal, and in January 1823 two Wesleyan missionaries, en route to open a station amongst the Seleka Rolong, gained the distinction of being the first Europeans to see such a rabble. Their own witness was marred by their ignorance of the language. Nonetheless, they saw

Warriors of the Difaqane, *from* Relation d'un Voyage d'Exploration *by T Arbousset and F Doumas (1842). Left, 'Marimo de Leribe'; above right, 'Le Marimo ou Cannibale Béchuana'; below right, 'Guerrier Matabele'.*

that the band was near starvation. Some people were greedily devouring the partly cooked flesh and marrow of their fellow-wanderers. The missionaries narrowly escaped, apparently because of the terror they created in the approaching warriors by their ghostly white skins and their strange covered wagon.

Thereafter, rumour filtered through to Kuruman, the frontier mission station amongst the Tlhaping, telling of the tragedy. Frightened refugees blamed the invasion on a giantess with one eye in her forehead, who loosed swarms of bees in advance of her soldiers. Her name was MaNthatisi. These rumours led most of the Tswana and their European contacts to call the *Difaqane* the 'Wars of the Mantatee'. In fact, neither she nor her people crossed the Vaal. The refugee hordes comprised Southern Sotho victims of raids by her and her Nguni foes. They carried the wars to the Tswana and, in competition with Mzilikazi, laid waste to that land as completely as MaNthatisi and the Nguni bands had ravaged Lesotho.

The destitute hordes united and separated in a confusing web of events. Most of their story was lost in the conflagration which destroyed so many chiefdoms. Fortunately, Sebetwane and Moletsane, two of the most successful leaders, lived to report their experiences to literate travellers, thus augmenting the fragmentary accounts of their victims.

Marauders amongst the Tswana appear to have first sacked a branch of the Hoja just north of the Vaal River, and then various villages of Kwena, Rolong and Hurutse. Later, they attacked the Ngwaketse, at first succeeding, and then being repulsed by the renowned Ngwaketse chief, Makaba II. After that defeat, the invaders attacked the Rolong at Khunwana. Their chief described the invaders as hungry wolves, ill-suited for war, but victorious because of their great numbers.

Invaders next appeared in the south, heading towards Dithakong, an outpost of the Tlhaping. The Tlhaping deserted that town in terror until they were stopped by their missionary, Robert Moffat, at Kuruman, who had obtained aid from the Griqua.

The best-known battle of the *Difaqane* then occurred on 26 June 1823, at Dithakong. A hundred mounted Griqua and a thousand Tlhaping foot soldiers, in the company of Moffat, approached the

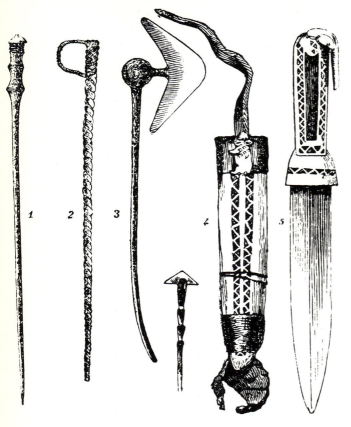

Engraving by George Baxter in Robert Moffat:
Missionary Labours and Scenes in Southern Africa *(1842)*. 'No. 1. A Bechuana needle or bod-
kin, about 6 inches long. 2. Its sheath, made of
brass wire. 3. A war axe, the handle of rhinoceros
horn, about two and a half feet long. 4. The sheath
of a knife. 5. The knife, six inches long, with a
carved ivory handle.'

horde. A group outside the town began the battle,
soon driving off the frightened Tlhaping. The Griqua fought on for two and a half hours until a second
band poured out of the town to join the fight. Moffat estimated the entire horde at between forty and
fifty thousand individuals. Though they had never
seen guns and horses, the enemy repeatedly advanced in winged formation, trying to surround the
Griquas. Only their horses enabled them to escape
after each telling volley. The Griqua pushed them
back for eight hours before the enemy finally broke
and fled. Five hundred warriors fell in the battle. The
Griqua captured a thousand head of cattle from the
horde, probably the prize of recent battles. Even after that complete rout, the marauders moved to

Nokaneng, where they destroyed the victims who
were returning from the last disaster. Then one part
of the horde fled back to Lesotho while the rest wandered north.

Moffat recognised their language as a dialect of
what he knew, and described them as indistinguish-
able from Tswana except for the grease and charcoal
they smeared on their bodies, though they carried
shields of the Nguni style and strange weapons, including a kerrie with a sickle-shaped blade with a
sharpened outer edge. Their winged fighting formation was also new to him. Although they possessed
cattle, they were starving and would stop in the
midst of battle to grab up raw meat and devour it.
He also observed cannibalism. Perhaps the horde
had only recently banded together, and the cattle belonged to the more successful division. Clearly,
many of the participants had not benefited from the
long line of victories attributed to them.

Moffat entered the battle to retrieve stragglers left
behind by the escaping warriors. From these hapless
victims he learned the identity of their leaders,
confirming that they included Nkgarahanye,
Tshane and Sebetwane, three Southern Sotho
chiefs. The first two died in the battle and their people retreated to Lesotho, while Sebetwane headed
northward. Captives verified that they knew the
people called 'Mantateezi', but that they were not
associated with them, substantiating MaNthatisi's
story that she never crossed the Vaal.

The general outline of these raids conforms to the
route ascribed to Sebetwane. His Patsa branch of
Fokeng suffered their first defeat by MaNthatisi at
their kraal along the Sand River in the middle of
1822. At the time he was only nineteen or twenty
years old, but he rapidly assumed the leadership of
his people. After seeking refuge south of the Vaal, he
appears to have fled northward around the end of the
year. During the early stages of his career he
changed the name of his people to Kololo, by which
they gained fame. Though little is known of his early career, it is known that he sometimes joined
Moletsane, his brother-in-law, chief of the Taung.

After his participation at Dithakong, he travelled
north, attacking Rolong, Hurutshe, Kgatla and
Kwena villages. After his defeat of the Kwena,
Sebetwane occupied their town, Dithubaruba. At
the end of 1824 he attacked the Ngwaketse, the only
group who had defeated him during his early
advance, and killed their chief, Makaba. The next
year he again attacked the Ngwaketse under their
new chief, Sebego. In 1826 Sebego recruited two
European traders and drove Sebetwane from
Dithubaruba. Sebetwane and his surviving army

fled to the hills. Thereafter, perhaps in 1829, Mzilikazi's impis attacked both him and the Ngwaketse. Sebetwane retreated northward attacking the Ngwato and other northern chiefdoms and settled again in 1834. From his new home he ventured a raid into the Kalahari desert, but he lost many cattle and men to drought and, perhaps, to the poisoned arrows of the Bergdama. His son died there of a poison wound. Thereafter, he moved further north beyond the Tswana, and built up a great kingdom over the Lozi people along the Upper Zambesi River.

Moletsane, Sebetwane's ally, had a reputation as a fighter even before the wars. When they began, he fled across the Vaal before he could be attacked, and concentrated his fighting against the Seleka Rolong. In a spectacular raid he drove the Seleka from their village, which had become a mission post. His warriors found gunpowder in the vacated mission house and tried to roast it. The explosion burned several warriors.

The Taung narrowly escaped a punitive expedition from the Griquas for that raid but instead the Griquas decided that Sehunelo, the Seleka chief, had destroyed the town in order to obtain the mission property. Once the commando left, the Taung completed the ruin of the Seleka, following them as they retreated up to the Molopo River. The Seleka joined other Rolong in the north and resisted the Taung in the famous 'Battle of the Chiefs', in which seventeen leading Rolong, including three of Sehunelo's brothers, and the father of Moletsane were killed.

Moletsane probably joined Sebetwane in the north during their battle with the Hurutshe, but he soon returned south to escape the threat of Mzilikazi. After repeated battles between himself and the Rolong, Moletsane sought missionaries to settle with him, but failed. He then concentrated his attacks on cattle posts of Mzilikazi. In retaliation for one of those raids, Mzilikazi pillaged his town in 1829. Moletsane escaped only to be met by a band of Griquas who took the rest of his stock. Completely broken, Moletsane followed his plunderers to Philippolis, where he obtained refuge. He joined the Griquas in one more raid against Mzilikazi in 1831, and then settled down. When the wars ended he returned to Lesotho where, in 1836, he finally obtained missionary teachers.

By 1825 the *Difaqane* had passed beyond the Southern Sotho, but it continued to plague the Tswana for another few years. The defeat of the conquest states of the Hlubi, Ngwane and Ndebele reduced the violence, but by then the Sotho and Tswana chiefdoms faced an utterly altered destiny.

Most communities had lost their lands, at least temporarily, and had to rebuild in new areas. Their new homes were often in the same general area, but some migrated for long distances. Of the latter, only Sebetwane retained sovereignty over his people. Many ruling chiefs died, and many leading chiefdoms weakened, leaving the reconstruction to new leaders or to less important chiefdoms.

The search for recruits to replace the losses of war produced the fusion of many chiefdoms into larger units, and the incorporation of large numbers of aliens within traditional chiefdoms. The *Difaqane* marked the most serious threat to survival the Tswana and Sotho had ever faced, but they would face even more troubles thereafter.

The Aftermath: Bastards and Bergenaars

Following in the wake of the *Difaqane* and the intrusion of Nguni conquest states amongst the Sotho, the recurrent troubles with the Khoi peoples revived. The Kora and their part-Khoi kinsmen, who had become entrenched permanently along the south-western flank of the Sotho, had arrested their southward advance even before the *Difaqane*. They posed an even greater threat after the wars, because they obtained weapons hitherto unknown amongst the Africans, and they dispersed in independent clans and villages, having neither unified purpose nor command; hence, they could not be treated with nor subdued by a single encounter, nor could their raids be predicted. The result was an attrition of the already weakened Sotho chiefdoms for an entire generation.

These Khoi and mixed societies can best be understood as the first frontiersmen of the expanding Cape Colony, though they remained beyond its control and were often hostile to it. As typical frontier folk, they borrowed freely the technology of the society which spawned them, but remained jealous of their independence. They stood unique in respect to their primary origin, being different from either the intruding colonial society from which they escaped, or the people into whose lands they encroached. They originated as Khoi, but had early mixed with the Europeans and slaves of the colony, and would freely mix with the Tswana peoples near whom they went to live.

Four types of these pre-trek frontier people can be distinguished, though they often cooperated. First to arrive were the Kora. They retained much of their traditional culture, having left the colony before the end of the seventeenth century. They divided into two classes: the *Bolanders*, who left the colony first, and the *Ondervelders*, who left only after having learned Dutch. Both groups divided further into numerous independent clans with their own petty chiefs, though they often joined together in the event of war. By the time of the *Difaqane* the Kora had dispersed widely along the Harts and Vaal Rivers on the southern flank of the Tswana.

The second Khoi group to settle the frontier were the Griqua, the creation of irregular unions of Khoi women and white and slave males. They first accepted the name Bastard as a title of distinction. They spoke Dutch and were well acquainted with the use of guns and horses. By the end of the eighteenth century they had congregated beyond the colony under their leaders, Adam Kok II and Berend

Griqua hunter and Griqua women, from Thomas Baines: Explorations in South-West Africa *(1864).*

Berends, who had received recognition from the colonial government. They then crossed the Orange River and claimed five springs in what had been Kora country, near the junction of the Orange and Vaal. There they accepted missionaries, and in 1813, under the influence of the Rev. John Campbell, changed their name to Griqua, a corruption of the name of their leading clan. They also named their main village Griqua Town and adopted a code of laws and a court system. The colonial governor recognised these changes, though the Griqua remained autonomous. Their government combined the patriarchal authority of their captains, the influence of the missionaries, and the intrusion of colonial authority, which, while refusing to take direct responsibility, confirmed the captains in office and authorised frontier magistrates to assist them in settling disputes. Despite the multiplicity of authority, the Griqua remained a turbulent people. They settled down only after a long period of wandering and shared the land with Kora and San inhabitants, who were even more restless than they. Like the Kora, they subsisted on pastoralism, which led to their further wandering. They also became the focus of new runaways from the colony, most of whom resisted their authority as they had the colony's.

Springing from these Griqua, a third class of people even less ready to settle down were dissident offshoots who resented the encroachment of missionary and colonial influence. The *Hartenaars* were an early form. In 1814 they fled from Griqua Town and settled along the Harts River where they subsisted by plundering Tswana, Kora, San and Griqua villages. Their rebellion ended in 1818 when the colonial frontier magistrate, Andries Stockenström, led a Griqua commando to force them back to Griqua Town. By 1822 a more dangerous rebellion propelled the majority of the Griqua from their settlements when the missionaries obtained the election of Andries Waterboer as captain of Griqua Town and the colony established an official agent there. These new rebels took the name *Bergenaars* (Mountain people) because they lurked in the hill country to the east and west of Griqualand, from whence they preyed on their neighbours.

The last category of part-Khoi frontiersmen were recent arrivals from the colony who persisted in using the name Bastards. They normally left the colony because of conflicts with the law. Having left most recently, they were well supplied with guns and ammunition and contacts among the trekboers from whom they easily obtained more. This made them invincible as foes and invaluable as leaders. Accompanying these Bastards were runaway slaves

Contemporary drawings demonstrate the unique culture of the Khoi and mixed peoples who pressed against the southern frontier of the Sotho peoples. Notice the evidences of European influence in their clothes and weapons.

Kora man riding a horse, and Bastard, from Thomas Arbousset: Voyage d'Exploration aux Montagnes Bleues *(1842).*

and renegade whites who preferred life with the half-castes to the restraints of the colonial society. All three classes of renegade fitted more naturally with the dissidents than with the settled Griquas.

The history of the Khoi frontier is largely the account of attempts to create cohesion out of these disparate elements. The failure of that effort produced instability which threatened not only their own survival, but the rehabilitation of the Tswana and Southern Sotho from the effects of the *Difaqane*.

Contacts between the Sotho and the Khoi frontier folk can be divided into three periods: the first was the settlement phase before 1820 in which both groups were establishing their villages over the highveld in comparative peace, and were also establishing a boundary between them. The second period was that of the *Difaqane* and the confusion which followed in which the renegade Griqua and Kora added to the immigrant hordes in disrupting the life of the Tswana and Southern Sotho. The last phase followed on the *Bergenaar* assault and lasted through the period of the rise of new polities amongst the Southern Sotho and the revival of communities amongst the Tswana.

The earliest contacts must have begun at the opening of the eighteenth century, when the most southerly-placed Tswana, the Tlhaping, had settled on the Nokaneng River, near the Langeberg Mountains. From this base they traded with the Kora, who occupied sites south of the Orange River into which the Nokaneng flowed. The Kora named these Tlhaping 'Briqua', Goat People.

This early contact developed into a pattern of annual trade. Tlhaping traders settled permanently near the Orange, where they intermarried freely with the Kora, while the Kora visited beyond the river at the Tlhaping towns. The Kora eagerly sought Tlhaping products. They traded cattle for such Tswana items as tobacco, ivory spoons, bracelets and earrings of copper, beads of copper and iron, barbed assegais, axes and awls of iron, and skin karosses. The Tlhaping opened long-distance trade routes to the north and east to obtain these products of African craftsmen. These early associations

appear to have been peaceful, and the distance between their settlements minimised pressure on the land. It is known, for example, that the Tlhaping royal house had married their main wives from the Kora for three generations by 1820.

Before this period ended in the *Difaqane*, two changes had marred the relationship: firstly, boundary pressure gradually increased, and secondly, Griqua immigrants crossed the Orange to complicate the association which had flourished. Regarding the first change, the senior Kora clan migrated to land along the Harts, which until then had been claimed by the Rolong under their chief, Tau, the Lion. Tau had made himself the dominant chief over the Tswana in the area, had subjugated the Tlhaping, and had begun to threaten the Kora on the Orange River. Together, the Tlhaping and the Kora retaliated against Tau in five skirmishes, which ended in his death. The Rolong then broke and retreated northwards while the Kora occupied Taung, the Rolong town. This probably occurred about 1760. Thereafter, the Kora turned on their former Tlhaping allies. The pressure increased so much that the Tlhaping fled from the Nokaneng to settle near the Kuruman, where they remained after 1790. Even at their new settlement the Tlhaping did not reach safety. Another clan of Kora, led by a renegade white colonist, Jan Bloem, sacked their new village and left them destitute.

The arrival of the Griquas beyond the Orange around the turn of the century at first led to peaceful contacts. They aided the Tlhaping against the Kora. After 1814, the *Hartenaars* used their base on the Harts River to join in the plundering of Tswana villages, with great success because of their superior arms.

The Khoi groups contacted many different Tswana and Southern Sotho chiefdoms, including the Tlhaping and Rolong, and beyond them the Hurutshe and Ngwaketse, and to the east the Hoja on the Vet River, who were the advance migrants in that sector. South and west of the Hoja lived the San who, while providing a buffer between the Khoi communities and the Southern Sotho, suffered from aggression by their neighbours on both sides.

The first phase of association created several effects: boundary lines became delineated between them, at least in the west; social intercourse led to a more complex hybridisation of the Khoi peoples; the interchange of goods had already established the superiority of Tswana crafts, and had led to the establishment of commercial production of goods in Tswana towns, and long-distance trading by the Tswana with people further north and east to supply the demands of Kora trade. On the negative side, marauding Kora and Griqua bands, though the plundering was still on a small scale, were already setting the dominant pattern for their relationship in the years to follow.

The second phase, the *Difaqane* period, lasted from approximately 1822 until 1826 or 1827. While the Sotho faced total warfare by dislocated hordes of refugees to which they were unaccustomed, the small-scale raids of Kora and Griqua bands paled in comparison. But the period coincided with the revolution of the dissident Griqua *Bergenaars* of greater numbers and superior arms than those whom the Tswana had fought earlier. Just as the Tswana became weakened through warfare, the *Bergenaars* became increasingly formidable. The Griqua dissidents swarmed off to the Langeberg mountains in the direction of Tlhaping and Tlharo chiefdoms. Those in the east camped on lands of the San along the Modder River from whence they raided northward amongst the Hoja and Taung, whose villages were widely dispersed over the land, and eastward to the Fokeng and Kwena clans along the Caledon valley.

The raiders easily captured cattle and children for illicit trade in guns and ammunition with frontier boers, whose farms reached ever closer to the Orange River. Because they rebelled from ordered society, the *Bergenaars* fought with no restraints and were urged to further excesses by Bastard recruits from the colony. The sons of Jan Bloem egged on the eastern rebels while Coenrad de Buys gave particularly strong leadership to those in the west.

As the invading *Difaqane* hordes dispersed or moved on, the *Bergenaars* intensified their raiding, partly because of the weakened state of their victims, but also because the departure of the invaders had freed the *Bergenaars* from any restraint. The colony and the missionaries also failed to strengthen the traditional captains in their efforts to subjugate the rebels.

This second phase in Khoi–Sotho relationships also produced some constructive results. The Griqua captains rescued Tswana chiefs on several occasions. The first attempt occurred in 1823, when the united captains stopped the advancing horde at Dithakong. After the battle the Griquas gathered the broken fragments of the horde and either settled them in their own lands or sent them to the colony to be apprenticed to the farmers. A second example occurred when the Griquas went to defend Sehunelo against Moletsane. Though they mistook Sehunelo's role and punished him instead, they then went on to attack the *Bergenaars* and retrieved some cattle. The

Bergenaars had recently captured the cattle from a Southern Sotho chief, Khatlani, so the Griquas restored them to him and allowed him to settle under their protection. A third example was the 'Battle of the Chiefs', in which Berend Berends's Griquas assisted the Rolong in driving back Moletsane. Again, when Moletsane finally broke against the Ndebele of Mzilikazi, the Griquas gave him haven at Philippolis until he could safely return home.

Refugees flocked from the wars into Griqua lands. Mothibi and his Tlhaping followers settled under Waterboer in 1825; Rantsane and Baramonake and their Hoja people obtained protection from Cornelius Kok; and numerous individual refugees also found shelter. The extent of this migration may be judged by the estimates of missionaries that they constituted the majority of the population in every Griqua community by 1828.

Above, Griqua men riding oxen; below, Griqua family at home. From Andrew Smith's Journal, 1834–1836.

Apparently the refugee chiefs retained command of their people under the umbrella of Griqua government, while individual refugees accepted direct control of the Griqua captains. Though many Sotho participated in mission churches and schools, when the disturbances ended both individuals and organised chiefdoms freely returned to their home country, suggesting that relatively little incorporation took place.

Perhaps the most effective role of the Griquas during this phase was as intermediaries who prepared the Sotho for the full force of white intervention in their lands. The refugees who returned home surely conveyed their knowledge of the alien culture, as

With the destruction of Sotho dominance over the highveld, the people retreated to protected areas. Those who remained exposed went to unusual extremes to defend themselves, such as building their huts on stilts to be safe from lions.

they had observed it modified by the Griquas, back to their villages. Griquas taught the Sotho the danger of horsemen with guns and conveyed to them the value of missionaries as teachers of the new technology and as protectors. In addition, the presence of the Griquas deferred the full entry of European settlers for a generation while the Sotho prepared.

The final phase of Sotho relations with the Griquas and Kora marked the rise of a black alternative to Griqua power. First to emerge was the Ndebele state north of the Vaal, followed by the conglomeration of Sotho refugees under the leadership of their own kind, such as the Southern Sotho kingdom of Moshoeshoe.

In the first case, the Kora under Jan Bloem and the Griquas under Berends united Griquas, Kora and Sotho in numerous attempts to dislodge Mzilikazi. Though they failed, the effort created a potential for cooperation. In the later case, Moshoeshoe could attribute a large measure of his success to the continuing erosion of Southern Sotho power after the *Difaqane* by the Kora and *Bergenaar* raids. Had the

Difaqane ended in peace, the Southern Sotho might have reverted to their traditional segmentary organisation, which would have rendered them more vulnerable to the intrusion of the white men. The plundering raids continued the unrest sufficiently to induce surviving remnants to unite under Moshoeshoe, and to encourage refugees to return to Lesotho to seek his protection. A similar result effected the growth of mission communities amongst the Tswana.

In each period a different set of conditions obtained, resulting in different relationships between Khoi and Sotho, and by the end of the period the Sotho had been permanently modified by those contacts.

3

Reconstruction of the Sotho States

WILLIAM F LYE

The breakdown of order amongst the Tswana and Southern Sotho during the *Difaqane* relates directly to their less advanced stage of aggregation as compared to the Northern Nguni, who had coalesced into the Zulu kingdom. The refugee hordes, spawned by the revolution amongst the Zulu, easily challenged the segmentary chiefdoms of the Sotho, arresting the political evolution of the scattered and destroyed communities. Nonetheless, almost immediately, the victims began to invent responses which ensured their eventual survival. The Southern Sotho, who suffered first, created the most successful structure, but only after extensive experimentation. The Tswana, more dispersed from the beginning and suffering the effects of war and subjugation longer, generated their own responses which prepared them for the challenges to come.

The great variety of responses of the Southern Sotho, which ended in the creation of a paramountcy over the entire area, began with panic, disruption and participation in the plunder of the countryside by their own chiefdoms. Before the wars began they recognised no central authority. Mohlomi, the senior chief of the Kwena, attempted to achieve a measure of cooperation in the early years of the century. He received deference due his genealogical primacy, and he added a reputation as a sage, rainmaker and diplomat. Wandering among the chiefdoms of the Sotho, and beyond, he achieved personal alliances through selective marriages and his diplomatic services. Though he is revered as the precursor of a united Lesotho, Mohlomi died in 1816, leaving no permanent institutions upon which the Sotho could rely in war or build upon later. The *Difaqane* found the Southern Sotho divided in their traditional segmentary chiefdoms.

The first victims of the wars, such as the Tlokwa, Sia and Phuthing, resided along the inner slopes of the Drakensberg mountains but before the end of 1822 every important chief along the Caledon suffered attacks. The dominant chiefs suffered most because they possessed the largest flocks and herds on lands which were most exposed. Less important chiefs, consigned to remote areas, survived better to become the nuclei around whom the broken peoples gathered.

The Sotho first responded negatively by flight and by forming bands modelled after those of their predators, but later sought to restore normal life. Sebetwane, chief of the Kololo, however, was a most unusual case.

Sebetwane and the Kololo

While others remained in the Caledon country, Sebetwane led his followers, including refugees from other clans, on an epic trek of about fourteen hundred kilometres to the upper Zambezi. There he built a conquest state over the Lozi and other peoples, but before reaching this, he roamed the west and north for years, contesting for land with other hordes and with the Ndebele kingdom. There he adopted the transhumant life style required by the riverain environment. Even when established, he had to keep guard against Ndebele in the south-east, Tswana in the south-west, and unpacified Lozi in the north. He incorporated the Lozi according to the dictum 'All are children of the chief'. He married Lozi women and encouraged his soldiers to do so. He freely appointed the Lozi élite as headmen and counsellors, thus creating an integrated society. His son, Sekeletu, broke with these practices, allowing the Sotho to oppress the Lozi until they rebelled and regained their country.

Though the state which Sebetwane created survived him, malaria weakened the alien rulers. The elders died out quickly, and the youths lost their vitality and determination. When Sekeletu succeeded his father, and broke with his policies, the kingdom withered and crumbled. Some Sotho remnants returned to Lesotho; others joined their scattered kinsmen amongst the Tswana clans.

Despite the shortness of Kololo rule, the impact of Sotho culture still survives along the Zambezi. The Sotho language and magical and ceremonial practices, and the bilateral descent system which blended Kololo practices with the Lozi matrilineal descent system are still practised.

Sebetwane was unique among the Sotho. He alone developed a conquest state; he alone established himself far away from his home country. Furthermore, his integrated society differed from any of the conquest states of his age. Only Mzilikazi achieved anything comparable, but his was an imposed rule, and his society was stratified rather than integrated. Nonetheless, long-term significance to the Southern Sotho and Tswana was achieved by those chiefs who rebuilt their polities in their own country.

Sekonyela and the Tlokwa

Just as the Tlokwa were the most notorious of the plundering hordes of the *Difaqane*, so they were singular in their efforts to restore order. When the wars had passed, Sekonyela led his followers to the flat-topped mountain retreat, or *qhobosheane*, called Khoro-e-betlwa. This natural fortress became the nucleus for the largest congregation of Southern Sotho for several years. The site was on the north bank of the Caledon in lands formerly held by the Monaheng, and about 160 kilometres west of the Tlokwa homeland. He also settled a second hill near enough for messages to be shouted from hill top to hill top. Andrew Smith described Khoro-e-betlwa (Merabeng) in these words:

'Here there was no choice of roads as in the instance of Thaba Bochu [Thaba Bosiu], and even the one was more rugged and broken than the road by which the latter was to be ascended. At first it was of

Sekonyela, the Tlokwa chief, son of MaNthatisi, retained his warlike reputation throughout his career as he tried to compete with Moshoeshoe for leadership over Southern Sotho people.

considerable breadth, but near the narrow ravine along which it extended on approaching the summit of the hill, it became narrow and steep.

'Prior to the occupation of this hill by the Mantatees there was a free access to its summit by this ravine, but since their selection of it for a residence the break in the perpendicular rocky wall, which, like a belt encircles the hill towards its summit, has been obliterated by art. A stone wall of great thickness and not badly built has been carried across, from precipice to precipice, so as to complete what nature had left imperfect. In this wall a small passage just sufficient to admit men and cattle has been left, and during the night is secured by a strong wicker gate which thus makes it a perfect enclosure. Immediately inside of the gate, upon the highest points of the hill from which the approach was to be commanded, piles of large stones were everywhere observed, having been collected for the purpose of being hurled upon any who might venture to attack the citadel.'

From his capital Sekonyela ruled a mixed following of Tlokwa, and other Southern Sotho, and some of the Hlubi and Ngwane survivors of the wars. His supporters numbered about 24 000 by 1833, according to the missionaries who met him. His success in attracting followers can be attributed to his military skill. His location in the heart of the land vacated by the leading Kwena chiefdom naturally attracted some of them to return. Those refugees who fled across the Vaal found the Tlokwa retreat to be the first they could return to from the north. Ratsebe, the Phuthing plunderer, was one. The promise of cattle, which a great fighter could share, attracted others.

Sekonyela's lands extended fifty kilometres to the north and east as far as the sources of the Caledon in small dispersed villages of twenty to one hundred huts. Headmen, including Mmote, his brother, ruled these villages under him. Beyond the villages, small destitute communities squatted, eking out a livelihood from wild game and plants. Sekonyela exchanged his permission for them to remain on his land for the advance warning they provided of the approach of enemies.

Despite his apparent strength, Sekonyela had inherent weaknesses. He defended his people well in battle, but he lacked judgement in peaceful situations. He desired other men's cattle. Even when no cause impelled him, he preyed on his neighbours, not always with success. His proclivity for raiding led enemies to notice him above other chiefs and to counter-raid. From 1830, the Kora turned their raiding to the east because of the tighter control Mzilika-

zi imposed on the north. Sekonyela's exposed position made him vulnerable. Other Southern Sotho chiefs did not escape these attacks, but Sekonyela was the only major chief still living west of the Caledon, his people scattered in small villages rich in cattle. By 1833, when the missionaries arrived, Sekonyela was happy to receive them, hoping they would dissuade the Kora from 'eating him up'

MaNthatisi tried to make peace by arranging marriage alliances for her son with daughters of Moshoeshoe and, in 1831, her people did warn Moshoeshoe of the arrival of Mzilikazi's impi. Sekonyela also granted land to Moshoeshoe's retainers. Moshoeshoe invited him to oversee the circumcision of his son, Letsie, while he went raiding in the south, but Sekonyela's greed overcame him. He not only refused the honour but, when Moshoeshoe left with his troops, he attacked Thaba Bosiu, capturing some of the absent chief's wives and cattle. However, the unhealed initiate youths and old men defended their homes, driving off the Tlokwa. Thereafter, Moshoeshoe built up his strength until he could retaliate. The dominant theme of the internal history of the Southern Sotho for the next twenty years was this conflict between Sekonyela and Moshoeshoe, and ended only in the total destruction of Tlokwa independence.

Though the Tlokwa were descended from the ancient Sotho lineage of the Kgatla, their ways seemed alien to the Kwena and Fokeng peoples whom they sought to dominate. In addition, Sekonyela's personal behaviour alienated them. In the 1830s headmen admitted loyalty to superior chiefs only to the extent that they needed protection, and in the end it was Moshoeshoe who proved more responsive.

The rise of Moshoeshoe

Although Moshoeshoe rose to prominence more slowly than did Sekonyela, he developed a more durable power base. Unlike either Sekonyela or Sebetwane, he never participated directly in a *Difaqane* horde, nor did he leave the land between the Caledon and the Maluti mountains. Though he suffered attacks by every major marauder, the continual fighting and threats of war worked to his advantage in establishing his paramountcy over the Southern Sotho; conversely, it weakened the aggressors.

Before the wars Moshoeshoe was headman of a minor village of Mokotedi Kwena, a junior branch of the same chiefdom as Mohlomi. In his youth he typically raided his neighbours for cattle. He acquired a name which imitated the sound of a razor, in praise of his ability to 'shave' cattle from his enemies. Before the *Difaqane*, however, he had already accepted Mohlomi's advice to rule in peace and generosity.

He entered the wars shielded by the exposed communities north of the Caledon. By the time the invaders reached him at Butha Buthe, he had already incorporated Lethole, a Khwakhwa chief, who had fled to him for protection. He practised his famous skill as a diplomat by inviting Lethole to accept the superior position because of his status and following, but Lethole admitted his role as supplicator and submitted to Moshoeshoe. Even then, Moshoeshoe granted Lethole separate lands on which to rule his people. Thereafter he received fragments of all the old chiefdoms of the area. Their failure to unite in strength before the wars assured their submission to Moshoeshoe in weakness. However, he still did not appear different from other chiefs. His survival depended more on his insignificance and the remoteness of his settlement than on any tangible act he performed.

The first real signs of his superior judgement appeared with the arrival of the plunderers. Whenever possible, he avoided attacks by volunteering to pay tribute. In the case of Matiwane, the Ngwane army killed a messenger and stole the tribute, but Moshoeshoe persisted by sending a second tribute with the request to become Matiwane's subject in exchange for protection. Matiwane accepted this act of humility and dubbed him his 'Little MoSotho'. To win over his own people, Moshoeshoe explained that since Matiwane could easily have taken all, submission saved their lives, and perhaps left them enough cattle to live off. Later, he freed himself from Matiwane by becoming a tributary of Shaka, and thereby turned the Zulu against his former master.

When the Tlokwa attacked him, Moshoeshoe revealed more of his genius. He first experimented with mountain defences by moving to the top of Butha Buthe and rolling stones on the attackers. Then he bargained with them to try to spare his accumulated seed grain. As a last resort he induced an Nguni plunderer, Sepeka, to fight Sekonyela. While the two militants slaughtered each other at the foot of the hill, Moshoeshoe slipped away and settled at Thaba Bosiu, the most famous retreat in Southern Africa.

There Moshoeshoe grew from an insignificant refugee into the master of an ever-expanding circle of people and lands. He first submitted to the local

owner of Thaba Bosiu, but eventually subjugated him. For some time after his arrival in 1824 he remained subject to Matiwane. Once Shaka had driven Matiwane away, he claimed his vast lands. They stretched across the Caledon as far west as Thaba Nchu. This brought under his control the remnant Ramokhele chiefdom of Moseme and numerous other Hoja fragments hidden in remote places to escape the frequent raids. When the British defeated Matiwane his surviving followers also submitted to Moshoeshoe.

The *Difaqane* rapidly spent itself with Matiwane expelled and Sekonyela settled, but the Southern Sotho still faced Kora raids. Moshoeshoe's growing power enabled him to resist them, but their occurrence assured him the continued loyalty of his subjects.

Broken chiefs needed land and cattle. Moshoeshoe appears to have appropriated to himself a stewardship over vacated land and no one but Sekonyela could challenge his claim. His ability to protect those who sought his aid kept them content, even though they probably ignored his political pretensions. Many chiefs who remained scattered over the land appear to have submitted alternately to Moshoeshoe and to Sekonyela, depending on who supported or coerced them at any moment. Moshoeshoe ultimately offered more aid and thus gained their final submission.

The plunderers had significantly reduced the herds of cattle. Moshoeshoe gained adherents by his success in keeping his herds and increasing them by his own raids. He lent cattle to other chiefs under the *mafisa* system, whereby petitioners received the use of the milk in exchange for tending them. By this means, the offspring provided Moshoeshoe with an increasing source of influence. As Andrew Smith observed, 'All the cattle in the country belong to Moschush and he distributes them amongst his subjects, he receiving the increase, they the milk.'

His generosity produced dependence of the people, but Moshoeshoe freely allowed the chiefs who submitted to him to settle in separate villages, where they ruled without interference and where they followed their own traditions.

Moshoeshoe acknowledged his inferior genealogical position, and always recognised the claims of superior chiefs. In his dealings with Mojakisane, Mohlomi's son, he granted *mafisa* cattle, and placed his brother at Thaba Bosiu under his protection. When jealousy was aroused, he faithfully respected the other party's claims. Even when Mojakisane removed the *mafisa* cattle beyond his lands, where they were stolen by others, Moshoeshoe allowed

Thaba Bosiu as seen in 1834, when it served as the capital of Moshoeshoe's growing state. Its defences were breached by passes such as the Khubelo Pass, defended by Raphuto. Though the lowlands of Lesotho suffered frequent attacks, hills such as this preserved the nation. From Andrew Smith's Journal, 1834–1836.

him to return and granted him more cattle without reproof.

In addition to individual refugees whom he incorporated and groups who settled in separate villages, Moshoeshoe permitted some refugees to squat on frontier lands under his protection, as Sekonyela also did. They accepted his nominal suzerainty in exchange for the use of the land, thereby preserving his title to it until he could profitably use it.

Once Moshoeshoe had secured his position many refugees returned to Lesotho from the Griqua country or the Cape Colony, where they had fled and obtained cattle. Whether these refugees intended to join Moshoeshoe or simply to return to their homes, their return route led them to his lands, and, finding peace, they remained. Thus his following increased dramatically, and by 1840 his population had trebled to about forty thousand in fifteen years.

He used diplomacy with neighbouring chiefs who remained independent. He tried to regularise his relations with the Tlokwa, and MaNthatisi seems to have reciprocated for a time; however, his fundamental antagonism to Sekonyela persisted. They

remained competitors for the dominance of the area, but Moshoeshoe showed superior skill. For example, he shrewdly stole considerable land by having his sons and other adherents feign a desire to escape his control. When Sekonyela granted them land, they promptly rejoined Moshoeshoe. Moshoeshoe eventually prevailed, however, because he and his system provided peace and regularity, and because he exemplified the core culture of the Southern Sotho; Sekonyela did neither.

He succeeded in establishing alliances with chiefs to the north beyond the Tlokwa. Thomas Arbousset, a French missionary, identified five chiefs, including Sekwati, the powerful Pedi chief of the Northern Sotho, who described themselves as 'Moshoeshoe's Men', though this probably meant they were allies, not subjects, as they never accepted direct control.

The dominant chief in the south was Mokuoane of a Nguni clan called Phuthi, and his son, Moorosi, who survived the wars by capturing cattle from south of the Drakensberg. Moshoeshoe learnt of them through one of their victim chiefs. Fearing a strong neighbour on his flank, he sent his brother, Mohale, to negotiate. The Phuthi had just been weakened by a defeat in the south, so Mohale took advantage of this and captured some of Mokuoane's wives and cattle as hostages. Mokuoane then treated with Mohale, regained his family, and made a tributary alliance with Moshoeshoe. The Phuthi remained faithful friends and drew Moshoeshoe into their cattle forays in the south.

Though Moshoeshoe included the Phuthi in his negotiations with the colony, he may have seen himself as spokesman for all the Africans rather than as their ruler. Certainly, Moorosi's behaviour indicated that he regarded himself as independent, though friendly to Moshoeshoe. When pressed, Moshoeshoe disavowed any liability for Phuthi raids. Though the colonial officials regarded this as a deception, it was probably a rueful admission of reality.

In addition to his successful manipulation of traditional forces, Moshoeshoe also faced new relationships with the encroaching white colony. As refugees from the colony began to return, they brought evidence of the superiority of white men's technology. As early as 1832, white visitors arrived at his hill, and he had already captured guns and horses from the Kora. Thus began the new influences.

Moshoeshoe established permanent contact with white people when the French missionaries—Thomas Arbousset, Eugene Casalis and Constant Gosselin—accepted his invitation to join him in 1833. He settled them at Morija with two of his sons so that his sons could learn from them and protect them. When he became satisfied of their worth, he called Casalis to settle at Thaba Bosiu, where he became a trusted adviser and diplomatic agent of the chief in his dealings with the white men, who soon began to settle near his country.

The missionaries added more strength to Moshoeshoe. They opened stations along his western border, thereby acting as a buffer against the Kora and the Boers and strengthening his claim to those lands. Each subordinate missionary united his efforts with the original group near the capital, and thus centralised further the authority under the chief. This also worked with his allies, Moorosi and Moletsane, where it had the further effect of spreading a common dialect. Present-day Phuthi and Taung admit that they use the Fokeng pronunciations taught in mission schools.

By combining a secure retreat with astute political acts, and wealth in cattle, Moshoeshoe united most of the Southern Sotho. He appears to have obtained the submission of those whom he could dominate, to have accepted the alliance of those whom he could not, and to have submitted, at least nominally, to those whom he could not resist. He used time and circumstances to consolidate his power. As his son, Nehemiah Moshoeshoe, observed, 'The paramountcy was created by the disturbances of the Fetcani', the wandering hordes.

Moletsane, chief of the Taung, carried on a personal vendetta against the Seleka Rolong throughout the Difaqane.

Moletsane and the Taung

Moletsane was the last major leader of a plundering horde to settle down in Lesotho. In 1836 the French missionaries induced him to leave Philippolis, where he had found refuge under Adam Kok, and to settle at Beerseba under the Rev. Samuel Rolland. By then he had only 150 followers. Two years later he and his missionary migrated back towards his old country on the Sand River. The Boers forestalled him by settling there, so he remained at Mekwatleng with the permission of Moshoeshoe. Many other Taung and Hoja who had refused to join him on his wanderings joined him there, having already fallen under Moshoeshoe.

Thereafter, Moletsane remained under Moshoeshoe as an ally in the emerging land conflict that arose between him and the Boers and the Seleka Rolong, who had migrated to his frontier at Thaba Nchu from the Tswana country. He seems to have retained freedom in his internal affairs, but he supported a common foreign policy. With Moletsane's return, the Southern Sotho paramountcy achieved the character which it would carry into the national era.

Rebuilding Tswana Chiefdoms

The *Difaqane* bred more lasting devastation for the Tswana than even that experienced by the Southern Sotho. As with the latter, the Tswana entered the wars segmented into numerous autonomous chiefdoms. However, they failed to unite either during the wars or after. They suffered more continuously and over a longer period from the intrusions, and they permanently lost their heartland, first to the Ndebele, and then, when the Ndebele fled north, to the Boers, who annexed it before the Tswana could return.

No Tswana chief organised a predatory band comparable to those of Moletsane or Sebetwane, though such bands incorporated Tswana refugees. However, individuals and groups of Tswana under their own chiefs had to vacate their traditional lands. Nevertheless, despite severe losses, most chiefdoms survived, frequently with new chiefs or regents replacing their murdered leaders. Often they settled in temporary retreats far from their homes, under the protection of Griquas or European missionaries. The reaction of the Tswana may be divided into two classes—those who revived with alien support, and those who retained traditional modes.

Tswana Societies under Alien Influences

Before the wars European missionaries had already begun to settle among the south–western Tswana, the Tlhaping. By the end of the wars missionaries of the London, the Wesleyan and the Paris Evangelical societies all contributed to the survival or restoration of Tswana communities. Often their contribution was mainly to defend the people from attacks, or to salvage refugees fleeing from the battles, but occasionally they impinged directly on the form a new polity adopted.

The London Missionary Society arrived among the Tlhaping in 1816 before the wars began. There was little progress made, however, until the *Difaqane*, because the Tlhaping refused to settle down. Robert Moffat's participation in the defence of Dithakong improved his reputation, and thereafter he and his colleague Robert Hamilton settled permanently at Seoding ('New Kuruman') where abundant water permitted gardening. The Tlhaping preferred land more suitable for grazing, and the continued threats of wandering hordes and *Bergenaar* marauders kept them uneasy, so they moved about regularly. Then, in 1825, Mothibi, the senior chief, moved permanently near Philippolis under the protection of Adam Kok's Griquas. However, Mahura, his brother, chose to remain with his following near Kuruman until 1835, when he migrated to Taung on the Harts River.

At the Kuruman River a small section of Tlhaping remained, but the missionaries continued to be a magnet for the dispossessed people, their following being identified as mainly refugee Tlharo, Tau, Rolong, Kwena and 'Bashutas'. As a refuge, the Kuruman settlement proved important to the

Kuruman, Robert Moffat's mission station, from Robert and Mary Moffat *by John S Moffat.*

Tswana, but as a political force it had little success.

The Paris Evangelical Society had a similar experience. They first entered Tswana country at the suggestion of the London Missionary Society with the intention of working amongst the Ngwaketse. The wars of Mzilikazi forestalled that, so, in 1831, they tried to settle at Mosega with the Hurutshe. Soon they too fled. While the Hurutshe fled to Taung, the missionaries founded Mothitho, nearer Kuruman. Not until they settled under Moshoeshoe in Lesotho did the French missionaries become a political force.

The Wesleyan Methodist Missionary Society probably had the most far-reaching influence on a Tswana society during the wars. The missionaries Samuel Broadbent and Thomas Hodgson met the Seleka Rolong people in 1823. From that date they remained intimately related to that people despite the repeated attacks which caused them to become a homeless band of wanderers for many months. The missionary presence at the Seleka town preserved it

The eye of Kuruman. This abundant fountain provided water for Robert Moffat, trained as a gardener in Scotland, to establish the most durable missionary base amongst the Sotho peoples. From R. Moffat: Missionary Labours and Scenes *(1842).*

from an attack by the survivors of the battle at Dithakong. After Moletsane had directed repeated attacks against the Seleka in 1824, the missionaries obtained Griqua aid. But the Griquas did not believe that Sehunelo the Seleka chief had been attacked, so they fined him a large herd of cattle. Later, the missionaries established Sehunelo's innocence and persuaded the colonial government to force the Griquas to repay part of the fine which they had imposed. Hodgson even visited Moletsane, the main antagonist, and convinced him that he should stop his raids if the Rolong did not retaliate. Even though he failed to get Sehunelo's concurrence and, as a result, the Taung savaged the Rolong further, the Wesleyans remained the Seleka Rolong's faithful companions as they wandered homelessly.

Finally, the missionaries induced a portion of the Seleka to settle on the southern bank of the Vaal River at Platberg (called Mothana-wa-pitse by the Rolong) by August, 1826, and brought greater peace and prosperity to them than they had known for three years. Gradually, as the fragments of the Seleka returned to their chief, the village grew to about 8 000 inhabitants. So successful were they that they attracted refugees from across the Vaal, from the other sections of the Rolong who had fled from Mzilikazi's range in the north-west. The Rolong

made peace with the Griquas and Kora living at Daniels Kuil and Boetsap, and the missionaries established a new station at Boetsap.

Moroka succeeded Sehunelo as chief of the Seleka. The new chief faced persistent drought, which defeated his efforts to support the growing population. From 1831, James Archbell, their new missionary, had proposed seeking a new location to settle. In 1833 he overcame the reluctance of his parent society and the chief. He explored westwards to the Modder River, which was largely deserted. There he found a small community of Ramokhele Taung under a chief named Moseme hiding atop Thaba Nchu, a flat-topped hill which dominated the vista. As described by Archbell, Moseme received him well:

'He was greatly pleased, that at length, white people had compassion on them, and were about to save their scattered remains. I shall be glad to see you and your people, and shall join you. The whole land is before you. The Bastards [who were represented in Archbell's party] I respect. They never committed any depredations upon us. The Borolongs I know they always come to buy our corn. Come to us as soon as you can. If you do not come soon you will not find one of us, for commandos are coming every day in search of our children.'

When asked if he would sell suitable land to the missionaries, he replied, 'Why should I sell a thing that is of no use to me . . . If you give me anything I shall take it, but your particularity makes me almost feel that you have no design of coming to this part.'

This meeting occurred on 21 May 1833. In June the French missionaries passed Thaba Nchu on their way to Moshoeshoe, and by November the Wesleyans arrived with their Rolong charges after their own 'Great Trek'. (Fig. 11.) By the beginning of 1834, Archbell reported a population of 7 000 on the new land, including 2 000 of the Taung. When the Griquas and Kora arrived, the Wesleyans arranged for three more settlements to the west of the Caledon. All four stations were procured by written agreements signed by the missionaries, their chiefs, and Moshoeshoe or Sekonyela as claimants to the land. The transfer of land at Thaba Nchu was explicitly made to the society and not to the Seleka.

From that time forward the Wesleyans served as practical as well as spiritual guides to their host. Moroka apparently never became a Christian, though the missionaries remained hopeful, but his dependence upon them for the preservation of his land in his growing opposition to Moshoeshoe is clearly apparent from the correspondence he entered into for the next twenty years. He never preserved

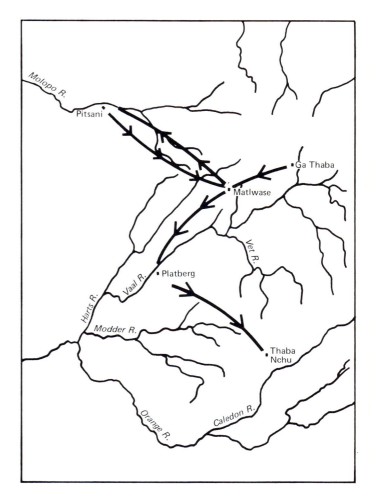

fig. 11 *The wanderings of the Seleka Rolong, 1822–33. The Seleka Rolong were unique among the Sotho in having literate observers accompanying them throughout their wanderings during the Difa-qane. This map illustrates their experience and is an example of the experiences of many of their kinfolk.*

the independence of action that Moshoeshoe did with the French missionaries, or that Sekonyela did with the Wesleyans. That fact may explain the re-migration of the other Rolong chiefs from Thaba Nchu once Mzilikazi had deserted their old lands, and why Moroka remained at Thaba Nchu, far from his traditional homelands.

American and German missionaries also entered the region north of the Orange River during the reconstruction period, but they had no direct effect on the rehabilitation of Tswana chiefdoms. The American missionaries directed their efforts towards Mzi-

A medicine man administering a charm to Rolong warriors going to battle. Opposite, the medicine man blowing a counter-charm towards the enemy. From Andrew Smith's Journal, 1834–1836.

likazi in 1836 and 1837. Before they could influence him to ameliorate his treatment of Tswana subjects, the trekkers drove him off and carried the missionaries back to safety. The Germans attempted to work with the Kora at Bethany on the Riet River, but though they persisted, they did not exercise much influence.

A discussion of alien influences on the Tswana must include their experience with the Griquas. The value of the Griqua settlements as a refuge is evident in the reports of the missionaries at Griqua Town and Philippolis, which stated that the majority of the inhabitants there were either Tswana or Southern Sotho. Nicholas Kruger, a Griqua who testified at the Bloemhof hearings on land claims in the dimond fields, confirmed this, asserting, 'People of various tribes came our way, and are still doing so—such as Baralongs, Batlapins, Baruchees, Banoaketse, Makhatla, Bakkalagari, Matabelelus, and many Basoutas and Damaras.'

That the refugees viewed their status as temporary can be shown in the case of Moletsane, who left Philippolis for Beerseba, and Lepui, the Tlhaping chief, who moved to Bethulie with his followers, as soon as peace returned to the Sotho lands.

This supportive role of the Griquas had only limited impact on the Tswana. Though Berends mounted large commando attacks on Mzilikazi, he never reclaimed that land, and as refuges the Griqua towns served only temporarily; nonetheless, they provided succour and the possibility of survival for many. They had little part in the actual reconstruction of the Tswana chiefdoms. The Cape Colony, though more removed, played a similar role.

Mzilikazi's occupation of the central highveld assured that the Tswana would either succumb and be relegated to the status of herders of Ndebele cattle, or would be forced to flee. His practice of denuding a belt around his settlements accentuated the problem. Some Kgatla and Kwena chiefdoms chose the first course and remained intact on their lands, then reclaimed them at the end of the wars. More powerful chiefs, especially in the west, generally tried to resist and then had to flee. Often, before Mzilikazi occupied an area, he imposed tribute on a chief. The Ngwato, Ngwaketse and Hurutshe suffered in that way. The Rrapulana Rolong became Mzilikazi's ally in his fight with Moletsane, but after several raids, they preferred to flee to Thaba Nchu.

Only the Tlhaping and their neighbours in the far south-west escaped Mzilikazi's control.

When the Ngwato were attacked, they fled north and west. Driven by Sebetwane, they fled from Serowe to Kutswe and then further. When they tried to return to Kutswe, Mzilikazi drove them off again. The Ngwaketse, judged the strongest Tswana chiefdom before the wars, successfully resisted the *Difaqane* hordes twice, but suffered the loss of their chief, Makaba II, in his battle with Sebetwane. Later, when Mzilikazi arrived, other Tswana chiefs, jealous of his power, enticed the Ndebele to attack his people. They broke and fled to the Kalahari Desert where the Ndebele could not reach them. These examples illustrate the reaction of the Tswana to the wars.

The loss of life amongst the Tswana, as with the Southern Sotho, and the disruption of villages, has received wide publicity, and rightly so, but this may have been exaggerated by the frightened frontiersmen who encountered the fleeing refugees. Explorers and settlers who rolled their wagons northward after the wars frequently told of crunching skulls under their wagon wheels, of burnt and abandoned villages and of the ascendancy of the lion on the veld, but the extent of the destruction remains a question. George M. Theal, the distinguished historian, per-petuated a story of twenty-eight chiefdoms which 'disappeared, leaving not so much as a trace of their former existence', but his observation appears to have originated in an account by an anonymous missionary which identified the names, locations and populations of '28 tribes of 384 000 souls dispersed and destroyed, and whose destruction cannot be attributed . . . but from the mere native restlessness and ambition'. An examination of the names, however, reveals that many were merely sections of major chiefdoms which did survive. That some chiefdoms did cease to exist, and that all suffered extensive losses, is undoubtedly true, but frequently they remained intact, and merely fled to more secure areas until the hostilities ended. Even when a chiefdom was destroyed, not all its members were necessarily killed, of course.

The first reaction of the Tswana to the expulsion of the Ndebele by the Boers was to attempt to reclaim their patrimony. Some succeeded because the Boers were yet too few to occupy all the vacated Ndebele lands, even though they claimed them by virtue of their conquest. The Hurutshe of Moilwe, the Ngwaketse and the Rolong could also claim their lands by right of their own reconquest, since they had assisted the Boer commandos. The Hurutshe and the Rolong also obtained concession from

the Boers, and Moilwe obtained his grant from Hendrik Potgieter. The Rolong, at the time of the battle, lived at Thaba Nchu, and had formed a major part of the commando, and Matlaba, the chief of the Rrapulana Rolong, had served as guide for the Boers.

When peace came, only the Seleka Rolong remained at Thaba Nchu. The other Rolong settled temporarily near the present site of Potchefstroom, and then the Tshidi returned to the Molopo River, while the Rratlou stopped at Khunwana. When the Ngwaketse attempted to reoccupy their old lands, they were divided. By the time they reunited, the Boers had consolidated their position and required them to pay taxes for the use of their old lands. Many Tswana chiefdoms which remained intact found their way back to the general area of their old homes, but often under conditions which led to dissension with the Boers for generations.

The wars with traditional peoples had come to an end with the expulsion of the Ndebele. The Southern Sotho and Tswana would both face a far more formidable and lasting adversary with the arrival of the advance columns of European settlers in the Great Trek.

Four major Tswana settlements retained their traditional character into the twentieth century. Above left: Mochudi Kgatla village in 1919; below: Kanye Ngwaketse village in 1919. Above right: Molepolole Kwena village in 1919; below: Serowe Ngwato village in 1934.

4

Transitions

WILLIAM F LYE

The expulsion of Mzilikazi and his Ndebele kingdom from the highveld lands of the Tswana marked the end of one disruptive era of alien intrusion, but it introduced an even more pernicious variety. Not that the Tswana and Southern Sotho had never known Europeans. Explorers, traders and missionaries had visited them since 1801, and missionaries had settled in their midst from 1817. Nonetheless, those early contacts remained few and scattered, and certainly had not threatened the life style of the people. In fact, Europeans' horses and guns assisted the Tswana in several battles of the *Difaqane*. At least the Tlhaping chief could attribute his independent survival to the presence of his missionary, Robert Moffat, who befriended Mzilikazi. Sotho refugees had become even better acquainted with whites as a result of straggling southward from the holocaust of the *Difaqane* to serve as 'apprentices' on white farms until they could safely return home with fabulous tales to share with Moshoeshoe. Even renegade whites who joined the dissident Griquas in their plundering excursions left their mark. Nevertheless, no intensive European presence had yet challenged the Sotho people by 1835. The European claim of Ndebele domains changed that rapidly.

The Boer Intrusion

The new wave of immigrant Afrikaner pastoralists posed a more threatening challenge to the Sotho mode of life than anything which had preceded it. These new pastoral migrants were descended from those who had trekked from the Cape of Good Hope ever since the inception of that settler colony centuries before. Successive waves of 'trekboers' had sought to claim a birthright in the thirsty lands of the interior, each generation claiming new 'loanplaces' of 6 000 acres beyond their fathers' lands. By the 1820s these frontiersmen grazed their sheep and cattle on the banks of the Orange River. Drought, the perennial plague, gradually pushed from the west to threaten even these newest ranges by 1827, thrusting the trekkers in a new wave of migration over the river into the Griqua lands around Philippolis. At first they returned annually to their more permanent homes south of the river, but gradually they spread further and further afield over the northern lands in permanent dwellings. By 1833, some amongst them had penetrated to the Caledon valley and even to the court of Moshoeshoe.

Though this natural extension of the trekker frontier loomed ominously for the future of the Sotho, these casual visits never seriously worried them until 1835. Abruptly, after 1835, circumstances changed for all the peoples of the interior. The natural expansion of the European colony was replaced by an entirely new white invasion. The 'Great Trek' was on. The new 'Voortrekkers' differed from their precursors in their intentions and methods. These new migrants had severed their ties with the mother colony, and had fled northward in search of lands where they could establish their own independent state.

By 1837, nearly 5 000 Voortrekkers had fled their country and had become vagrants and squatters north of the Orange, hoping to continue a life style which they had evolved, free of interference. What they ignored was the degree to which their intrusion interfered with the continuation or restoration of the Sotho life style, far older than their own.

The first Voortrekkers intended to lay claim to lands in the distant north, in the Zoutpansberg, or in Natal, where they could escape contact with their new British rulers, and where they could acquire access to the outside world in the east. The direction of their migration followed the old trekboer routes across the Orange River and along the sparsely settled lands west of the Caledon. They quickly concentrated at Thaba Nchu, where the Seleka Rolong of Moroka had recently settled with their Wesleyan missionaries. Though this was intended as a staging point, they soon spread over the surrounding land.

Conquest of the Ndebele Domains

As the Voortrekkers continued their spread northward across the Vaal, Mzilikazi's scouts spied their arrival, unannounced and without permission, along routes so frequently traversed by Kora, Griqua and Zulu raiders of the Ndebele. Alarms at the Ndebele camps sent impis rushing towards them. In August 1836 these impis destroyed a Boer hunting party and a Voortrekker encampment along the river. The remaining Voortrekkers laagered at a hill just south of the Vaal near the Rhenoster River, which soon gained notoriety as 'Vegkop', the 'Hill of the Fight'. A powerful impi from the Ndebele towns arrived there on 19 October to challenge their arrival, but the guns of the Europeans repulsed them despite repeated efforts to break the defences. In the end the Ndebele retreated homeward with 4 600 head of cattle and 50 000 sheep for their trouble, but leaving behind 430 of their soldiers dead or dying on the field. Soon thereafter, Moroka aided Andries Potgieter, the Voortrekker leader, by sending oxen to retrieve the Boer wagons and return them to Thaba Nchu, where the survivors received kind treatment.

Shortly after the battle at Vegkop, a new party of Voortrekkers under the leadership of Gerrit Maritz arrived at Thaba Nchu to reinforce Potgieter's band. The expanded party organised a commando of 107 Europeans, 40 Griquas, 5 or 6 Kora, 60 Rolong and a few Tlokwa under Sekonyela. Matlaba, chief of the Rrapulana Rolong, acted as guide, having served under Mzilikazi until his recent defection. The commando travelled northward on 2 January 1837 for over 500 kilometres, until they reached Mosega, the Ndebele town, on 17 January. They arrived at a time when the Ndebele soldiers were absent, and only the old men attempted to defend the town. The invaders killed about 400 of the Ndebele, scattered the rest, burnt the town, and captured about 7 000 head of cattle. They also retook the wagons which the

A cattle boer's outspan. From Andrew Smith's Journal, 1834–1836. *The long history of trekking by the cattle boers of South Africa prepared them to face the challenge of the new frontier country that they entered when they crossed the Orange River on the Great Trek.*

Ndebele had captured from the hunting party. The only casualties for the invaders were three Rolong.

Not satisfied, the Voortrekkers mounted a second commando led by Potgieter and Piet Uys, which set out in November to renew their attack on the Ndebele. This time they pressed on to the Ndebele capital, eGabeni. In their battle, which raged for nine days, the Boers and their African allies drove back the enemy with great carnage until they finally broke and fled across the Limpopo River to begin their own trek in search of more secure lands, beyond the reach of their Zulu, Griqua and Voortrekker attackers.

With the expulsion of Mzilikazi and his Ndebele followers, the Voortrekkers had thus acquired, by right of conquest, a claim to all the lands of the central highveld. They had neither a clear understanding of the boundaries claimed by Mzilikazi or actually settled by his people, nor did they possess sufficient numbers of migrants effectively to occupy or control all they claimed. Their definition of their conquest encompassed virtually all the land north of the Vaal and south of the Limpopo Rivers from the Drakensberg in the east to the Kalahari in the west. They also claimed to have freed all the Africans resident within that vast area from Ndebele thraldom,

and, therefore, to have acquired mastery over them as their own subjects.

The lands were extensive and the Voortrekkers were few individuals in an unknown country. As the Boers tried to make good their occupancy of farms generously sufficient for them all, the Tswana chiefs found little difficulty finding space for their own resettling. The Voortrekkers concentrated in distinct areas: especially between the Orange and Vet Rivers, between the Vet and Vaal, and north of the Vaal in the Potchefstroom district.

Several Tswana chiefs could legitimately disprove any claim of Voortrekker overlordship, having remained independent of Mzilikazi during his reign in their midst. These included important chiefdoms, such as the Tlhaping, the Ngwaketse, the Kwena and the Ngwato. Others quite clearly fell under the definition of Mzilikazi's subjects and, hence, of the Voortrekkers. These included the Hurutshe, the Ratlou Rolong and two major branches of the Kgatla. The latter had submitted to Voortrekker rule by the time of the Sand River Convention (1852), in which Britain recognised an independent trekker republic north of the Vaal. To submit meant to provide labour for the white farms, to pay taxes to the new government, to sue before the trekkers' raad for the title to their own lands, and to submit to the white man's law.

The trekkers continued their efforts to gain control over the western Tswana chiefs for many years. Even after the British recognised their independence as the South African Republic in 1852, they still attempted to force the submission of the Ngwaketse of Gaseitsiwe and the Kwena of Setshele. They particularly resented the presence of David Livingstone as the missionary to the Kwena because of his virulent propaganda against them. Setshele's continued refusal to supply labourers, coupled with his grant of sanctuary to the Kgatla chief, Mosielele, whom the Boers claimed as a vassal, finally led Commandant P E Scholtz of Marico to organise a commando against him. He attacked Setshele's village of Dimawe, trampled his fields, scattered his subjects, and captured over 200 women and children, whom he took back to work on the farms as 'apprentices'. In the same raid, Scholtz proceeded northward to Kolobeng, Livingstone's mission station, which his men ransacked, destroying Livingstone's books, medicines and surgical supplies, and stealing his furniture and personal belongings and hunting supplies which he had stored for a party of Englishmen who were travelling to the north. On their return to their farms the commando turned on Montshiwa, chief of the Tshidi Rolong, whom they had recently required to submit, for failing to join in the commando.

Despite the violence and threats against the Kwena and their neighbours, these chiefs maintained their independence. They thus confined the westward expansion of the Great Trek, preserving a vital link with the north for the Cape Colony. They also provided a window on the Afrikaners' behaviour towards their African subjects, which served their critics in the Cape Colony and at the Colonial Office and the London Missionary Society headquarters in London. Following the commando raid, the Boers expelled the L M S missionaries from the area under their control.

The Voortrekkers and the Southern Chiefs

The Voortrekkers in the area south of the Vaal River at first treated their African neighbours well. They were refugees in an unfamiliar land, and they intended only to pass through the area to the west of the Caledon River in order to reach lands in the north or in Natal, as far removed from the British colony as possible. Only after their early efforts aborted did many trekkers view the southern lands as a permanent home.

In 1833 the region extending to the west of the

Boer commando turning out. Etching by W Syme, 1858.

Eugène Casalis and (right) Thomas Arbousset, two pioneer French Protestant missionaries who demonstrated their value to Moshoeshoe so convincingly that the great chief allowed them to establish colleagues in many stations throughout his country.

Caledon River appeared to be nearly depopulated. The *Difaqane* and the succeeding unrest had blunted the southward migration of the Sotho and had driven the pioneer occupants of the area to seek protection in remote valleys or on defensible hills. As the trouble diminished, the French Protestants and the Wesleyan missionaries competed for the loyalty of the chiefs, and exacerbated the relations between the chiefs resident in the area.

Refugees intensified the pressures on the area even further as they learned of the restoration of peace in their home country and flocked back to settle under the established chiefs, especially Moshoeshoe, who dominated the routes from the south. The rivalry for dominance over the area between Sekonyela and Moshoeshoe added to the strains and contributed to the opportunity the Europeans needed to establish themselves on the land.

In their first contacts the Voortrekkers treated their hosts with great respect. They were few in numbers, and they only desired temporary grazing rights and a staging area. The chiefs, particularly Moroka at Thaba Nchu, freely granted their wish because their only experience with white men had

been with the missionaries and occasional traders or hunters who made no serious demands on them. Their needs seemed reasonable and easily filled, and their weapons would surely add protection should the unrest of the recent past revive. No titles to the land were requested, and none were granted, with the exception of the case of Makwana, a chief of the Taung, who lived north of the Vet River, who reportedly 'sold' part of his land, contrary to traditional custom, for forty-nine head of cattle.

The trekkers concentrated at first around Thaba Nchu, the new village of chief Moroka. His Rolong people befriended the immigrants, assisted them in their difficulties with Mzilikazi's impis, and joined with them in their commandos against him. The only disturbing incident in the relations between the Africans and the immigrants at this early stage resulted from Piet Retief's negotiations with the Zulu king, Dingane. Just before Retief had reached the Zulu kraal, Sekonyela's men had raided the Zulu cattle posts and captured large herds of animals. Dingane attributed the incident to the immigrants because the Tlokwa had arrived on horseback firing guns. He required the trekkers to return the cattle as proof of their innocence. Retief undertook the task, knowing the unsavoury reputation of the Tlokwa chief. He obtained an interview with Sekonyela at the Wesleyan missionary's station, and when he arrived, detained him in handcuffs until his people paid a ransom of the Zulu cattle. His accomplishment was noted by Dingane's representative, and may well have been a factor in the reaction the Zulu chief expressed in calling for the death of Retief and his men, calling them 'sorcerers'. Much is made of the perfidy of Dingane in killing the Boers, little of Retief's betrayal of his supposed friends on the highveld. His Sotho neighbours might well have taken note.

As the trekkers drifted on towards Natal, they usually left their grazing stations to newly arriving trekkers, who continually poured out of the colony. Even though no ownership was implied by the initial grants of grazing rights by the chiefs, the transfer of those rights from Boer to Boer gradually diminished the original understanding and replaced it with an assumption of title to the land, though Moshoeshoe, at least, consistently refused the claims or to accept any payment or to sign any documents which the trekkers might offer. Gradually this situation intensified the feelings between the migrants and their African hosts, particularly Moshoeshoe, because he claimed most of the area through which the trekkers passed, as heir to the claims of the ancient Sotho chiefs. As the opportunity for independence in Natal diminished for the Voortrekkers with the British annexation of that country, they returned over the mountains. Though most of them persisted in their effort to escape beyond British influence, others found less cause to trek on with the loss of Natal, and squatted permanently with trekboer kinsmen on the lands claimed by Moroka, Sekonyela and Moshoeshoe.

Immediately before the arrival of the trekkers, the chiefs beyond the Orange River had hosted Dr Andrew Smith, the leader of a major exploratory expedition, who came with symbols of the friendship of the British governor, Sir Benjamin D'Urban. The governor had already negotiated a treaty of friendship between the colony and the Griqua of Andries Waterboer at Griqua Town in 1834, and with other chiefs to the west, in order to stabilise the northern border of the colony. Smith was commissioned to establish friendship with the African chiefs beyond the frontier by offering those who were well disposed medals and cloaks and looking-glasses. The missionaries who laboured with the chiefs all concurred in that plan and encouraged their chiefs to participate. Though nothing tangible was signed, with the exception of a formal treaty between the representatives of Mzilikazi and the governor, all the southern chiefs regarded themselves as allies of the British by accepting the tokens.

As the trekkers began to claim permanent title to the lands they grazed, particularly in the triangle formed by the Caledon and Orange Rivers, Moshoeshoe heeded his missionary advisers and relied on his friendly relations with the colony to obtain relief, inasmuch as the trekkers were legally British subjects. For several years the colonial government threatened the migrants with punishment if they interfered with the Africans, but took no action. Then, in 1843, Sir George Napier, the new governor, followed through and signed a formal treaty with Moshoeshoe, as he had with the Griqua of Adam Kok, in which the chief agreed 'to be a faithful friend and ally of the colony', and 'to preserve order in his territory; to restrain and punish any attempt to violate the peace of the frontier of the colony by any people living within his country, or by any people from the interior who may attempt to pass through the territory for the purpose; and to seize and send back to the colonial authorities any criminals or fugitives from the colony'. The governor, on his part, agreed to grant Moshoeshoe £75 annually in either arms and ammunition or in money as the chief desired.

In the treaty the boundaries of Lesotho were defined explicitly for the first time: 'The territory of the chief Moshesh is bounded from the west, from the junction of the Caledon with the Gariep [Orange] rivers to the sources of those rivers near the Bouta Bouta; on the south, by the Gariep River, from the junction aforesaid; on the north, by a line extending from about 25 to 30 miles north of the Caledon River, excepting near to its source, and at its junction with the Gariep, where the lands of Bethulie and the territory of Sekonyela come close upon its northern bank.'

Strict boundary lines were unfamiliar to the Sotho. Moshoeshoe expressed the traditional concept by stating, 'My lands are where my people live.' The formal delimitation of the treaty posed a new problem for the Sotho. The line encompassed the heart of Moshoeshoe's domain, but its western limit cut through those lands granted by him and by Sekonyela for the use of the Wesleyans and their Rolong, Griqua and Kora charges, and recognised the independence of Sekonyela on lands which Moshoeshoe regarded as the hereditary home of his Kwena clan. He sought, through his missionary, Casalis, to obtain the recognition that his rights extended to all the lands he had granted for the use of the Wesleyans, while they countered by seeking recognition as independent claimants of their lands equally worthy of treaties for their chiefs. These counter-claims split the Africans and their respective missionary societies at the very time they needed to unite in defence against the encroachment of the

Chronology of Major Events Affecting the Tswana and Southern Sotho in the Nineteenth Century

1821	*Difaqane* commenced by Hlubi invasion of Tlokwa.
1823	Mzilikazi fled to land north of Vaal River.
1823	Battle of Dithakong.
1824	Moshoeshoe occupied Thaba Bosiu.
1825	Matiwane (Ngwane invader) defeated Hlubi.
1833	French missionaries settled with Moshoeshoe; Seleka Rolong settled at Thaba Nchu.
1834–5	Andrew Smith treated with leading Tswana and Southern Sotho chiefs.
1835–6	Trekboers settled on the highveld.
1843	Napier Treaty established boundary for Moshoeshoe.
1848	Sir Harry Smith annexed territory between Orange and Vaal Rivers.
1849	Major Warden further contracted Lesotho boundary.
1852	Sand River Convention between Britain and Transvaal. Boers attacked Livingstone's station.
1854	Bloemfontein Convention.
1861	Moshoeshoe requested British protection.
1865–6	Treaty of Thaba Bosiu carved up Lesotho.
1868	Governor Woodhouse annexed Basutoland.
1871	Basutoland was incorporated into self-governing Cape Colony. Britain annexed diamond fields. Keate established boundary for Tswana.
1877	Britain annexed Transvaal Republic.
1877–8	Tswana and Griqua rebelled.
1880	Transvaal War.
1880–1	Gun War in Basutoland.
1881	Pretoria Convention established boundary between Tswana and Transvaal.
1882	Stellaland and Goshen were founded in Tswana land.
1884	London Convention established boundaries for Tswana. Germany annexed South West Africa. British resumed control over Basutoland. Orange Free State annexed Thaba Nchu. British Bechuanaland was proclaimed.
1885	Bechuanaland Protectorate was proclaimed.
1890	Bechuanaland Protectorate was extended northward.
1899	Anglo–Boer War began

lands. He relied entirely on negotiations with his new ally, the colony, and directly with the Boers to preserve peace.

Leonard Thompson makes a convincing argument that Moshoeshoe and Casalis created by their defence of Sotho land claims an ideological basis for uniting the diverse peoples of Lesotho into a single unit, 'a historical charter, legitimising the King and the Nation and the bonds between them'.

The inexorable encroachment of the Boers, especially in the triangle from the junction of the Orange and the Caledon Rivers, posed the most serious threat. In some cases, the grants of grazing rights continued the expectation that the occupants were transient. In others, trekkers persuaded individual Africans to sell their land without the authorisation of the king. Finally, in October 1844, Moshoeshoe travelled through the area publicising his intent that all land exchanges between his people and the settlers were null and void. In the meantime, the Voortrekkers, with their trekboer kinsmen, had also encroached on the lands of the Griqua around Philoppolis, where they had precipitated a conflict.

In an attempt to resolve the Griqua problem, the new governor, Sir Peregrine Maitland, called all the chiefs from beyond the Orange together at Touwfontein, in Griqua country, in June 1845, and there negotiated a plan to divide the lands of the Griqua and of the Sotho into 'alienable' and 'inalienable' parts. The former would be available for purchase by white occupants, the latter would be returned to the Africans at the end of the current leases. After lengthy deliberations over the alternatives, the Sotho king agreed in October to allow permanent white occupation of the area to the west of a line between Commissie Drift on the Caledon and Buffel's Vlei on the Orange. He complied with this plan in order to end the conflict which threatened his security. Accompanying this settlement was the understanding that revenues from land transactions would go towards paying for a resident agent of the colony to settle disputes and to keep the 'British' settlers in line. With this settlement the period of the Great Trek may be said to have ended for the Caledon area.

settlers. Of course, the trekkers also opposed the treaty, as they had all intrusions of British influence north of the Orange River. They particularly resented the implications of being placed under the jurisdiction of African chiefs. Nonetheless Moshoeshoe made no attempt to expel anyone from his

Mission Influence

The physically violent assaults on the life style of the Sotho overshadow the more subtle, but nonetheless fundamental, changes which occurred during the latter half of the nineteenth century. Whether they retained the semblance of political autonomy, as in 'Bechuanaland' and 'Basutoland', or fell under the conquest of a Boer republic, all Sotho communities responded to attacks on their political, social, cultural, economic, and even psychological life.

During that period the Sotho peoples restructured their political forms, including the increased incorporation of aliens, the consolidation into increasingly large chiefdoms, the break-up of traditional clans, and the imposition of alien, and sometimes hostile, rule over them. Traditional warfare ended, but even more destructive wars between them and technologically advanced enemies ensued. They experienced the contraction of their lands and the intensive occupation of lands from which they were expelled and the exploitation of newly discovered resources. A cash economy was introduced and dependence upon migrant labour in mines and cities increased. Traditional crafts gave way to cheap manufactured goods, but people gained ingenious new utensils, tools, weapons, crops and techniques. Of all the introductions, perhaps the most fundamental was Christianity, which challenged traditional relationships, substituted new values and, especially, contributed literacy and literature by which the new religious and secular knowledge penetrated every village. These transitions illuminated Sotho life during the remainder of the century.

The Arrival of the Missionaries

As has been shown, Christianity reached the Tswana even before the end of the *Difaqane*, primarily through missionaries of the London Missionary Society (1816) and the Wesleyans (1823). The L M S concentrated its activities amongst the western Tswana chiefdoms beginning with the Tlhaping. The antagonism of the Boers dating back to the pre-trek restricted them to the west, but that concentration produced, particularly in British Bechuanaland, one of the most widely christianised areas of Africa.

Robert Moffat may be the most important missionary in Southern African history. He settled permanently amongst the Tlhaping in 1821. His influence led many other chiefdoms to accept missionaries. In Britain he influenced others to take up the work, including David Livingstone, who followed him to Africa and opened a path for missionaries, traders and settlers into the heart of the continent. Moffat's career extended for fifty-four years, mainly at Kuruman, first among the Tlhaping, who proved unreceptive, and then among whatever refugees settled with him to escape the wars. While his career was unusually long and

David Livingstone began his career as a missionary for the London Missionary Society amongst the Tswana, but his political interests soon embroiled him in conflict with the Boer settlers of the frontier.

productive, many others who followed him gave equally dedicated service.

The Methodists started with the Seleka Rolong in 1823, and followed their destitute hosts until they finally settled at Thaba Nchu. Their pilgrimage lasted until 1833, but it finally placed the Rolong in a strange land where the missionaries had an unusual influence over them. In the end, the Wesleyans became the most successful mission society in Southern Africa in terms of numbers of converts.

When the L M S evacuated Shoshong as the result of the Boer attack in 1852, and because Livingstone had begun his explorations, the Ngwato chief, Sekgoma, invited the trekkers to send a missionary to fill the void. They sent Hermannsburg missionaries from Germany in 1858. Though internal troubles within the society cut short their work, the L M S soon returned to open stations with the five main chiefdoms of what became the nation of Botswana. Thereafter, from 1864, the Hermannsburg missionaries entrenched their Lutheran gospel in the

'Bechuana reed dance by moonlight', from David Livingstone: Missionary Travels and Researches in South Africa *(1857).*

Western Transvaal amongst the Kwena who remained under Afrikaner rule. Other societies also taught the Tswana before the end of the century.

The Southern Sotho remained remote from missionary influence throughout the wars, though refugees drifted into stations amongst the Griqua and Tswana as well as in the colony. On their return they told Moshoeshoe about missionaries. In 1833 a wandering preacher arrived at Thaba Bosiu en route to the Zulu, but failed to make an impact because he did not know the Sotho language. That same year a Griqua traveller told Moshoeshoe of the benefits of missionaries, so he sought to buy one with cattle. Twice he made an offering only to have it stolen by marauders. Nonetheless, when his request reached the French missionaries passing through Philippolis they regarded it as a divine calling. Moshoeshoe allowed them to develop a string of stations which tied his people to him in yet another way. Roman Catholics, Anglicans and Methodists also settled in Lesotho and they eventually outnumbered the French Protestants.

After faltering beginnings by the L M S pioneers with the Tlhaping, African chiefs generally welcomed missionaries, though some subjects opposed their coming. A friendly reception, however, did not assure easy evangelisation. In the case of Kuruman, no convert accepted baptism for twelve years. Normally conversions came slowly, and then often only to lesser members of the community. Even those chiefs who sought out missionaries frequently refused baptism.

Many chiefs clearly welcomed missionaries in order to gain material advantages. They hoped for defence and for new technology by which they could build a better life. Nonetheless, such practical considerations do not minimise the respect which the missionaries frequently received for their selfless service.

The Impact of Christianity

The primary objective of the missionaries was to convert Africans. That goal may be viewed statistically or qualitatively. Statistically great variations exist, but government census reports, which record the people's own declaration, provide a consistent measure of their success: by 1911, the first census of the Union of South Africa, one-fourth of all Africans declared themselves Christian. That grew to 49 per cent by 1936, to over 66 per cent by 1960, and to more than 79 per cent by 1970. Those figures include the entire nation, but the Tswana and Southern Sotho are among the most widely christianised people. Figures for Lesotho confirm that today over 80 per cent of the people are Christians. Botswana is much less christianised, perhaps because the missionaries concentrated on the Tswana living in lands which are now part of the Republic of South Africa.

Other measures reveal the intensity of christianisation which occurred in the nineteenth century. Du Plessis, who wrote an assessment of missionary work, found that in every missionary society working amongst the Tswana and Southern Sotho, African teachers predominated by the end of the century. As early as 1840, Molema, brother of the Tshidi Rolong chief, adopted Christianity at Thaba Nchu, and, even when he returned to lands near the Molopo River, he continued worshipping with the small band of converts, and attempted to proselytise his kinsmen. Mission reports abound with similar stories.

Though most of the early chiefs resisted conversion, they generally accepted missionaries in their country, and frequently assisted them in building churches and schools. Their sons, however, often became converts. A remarkable example was

This hand press, carried to the frontier by ox cart in 1833, was used by Robert Moffat at Kuruman Mission Station to print the books he needed to carry out his mission to the Tswana. The first Bible ever published in the Tswana language issued from this press in 1857.

the conversion of Kgama of the Ngwato, who remained faithful for sixty-four years, firmly entrenching Christianity amongst his people. Setshele, the Kwena chief, readily accepted baptism in 1848, but was later suspended. He nonetheless sought readmission, and regularly supported his missionaries.

From the beginning, the L M S, P E M S and Wesleyans incorporated Africans as teachers. By 1863 the French in Lesotho had appointed indigenous evangelists. That fortuitous decision preceded the expulsion of the missionaries by the Boers in 1866. When they returned at war's end their evangelists delivered to them a thriving church, including several hundred candidates for baptism. Thereafter, they founded a school to train teachers, catechists and evangelists, and increasingly shared leadership. By 1891, they ordained their first black minister, and in 1898 created a national assembly (Seboka) including the local ministers, to govern the church.

Reluctant chiefs opposed Christianity because the missionaries undermined their authority. The missionaries also attacked traditions, such as the payment of bride-price at marriage, polygamy, leviratic marriages of widows, male (and especially female) circumcision, ritual murder, sorcery, rainmaking, and drinking intoxicants. Some even opposed dancing, harvest festivities, and all types of 'revelry'. Whatever success they had in abolishing such practices weakened the cohesiveness of Sotho culture. Despite this, the Kgatla retained polygamy; *diretlo*, or ritual murder, persisted in Lesotho; and Africans still widely exchanged bride-price.

Although in some ways they were destructive, the missionaries also brought tangible advantages. Perhaps most comprehensive were literacy and education. From the start they founded schools, which remained the basis of local educational systems. The missionaries learnt the local languages in order to teach, and in 1819 the first missionary to the Tswana, James Read, produced a small spelling-book that his colleagues printed at Griqua Town. Robert Moffat, Samuel Broadbent and James Archbell had all translated teaching materials by 1826. Archbell even printed his own language book on the banks of the Vaal, before his people had settled from the wars. The study of the Sotho language became systematic for aliens with the publication of grammars in Tswana by Archbell in 1837 and in Southern Sotho by Eugène Casalis in 1841.

The birth of Sotho literature occurred with the publication of the Gospel of Luke that Moffat translated and assisted in printing at Cape Town in 1830. He then took his own press to the frontier and by

Sekhonyana, baptised Nehemiah, son of the Paramount Chief. He is possibly the first Sotho author to have been published in a magazine of general circulation in South Africa.

1833 had published selections of scripture. He completed the translation of the New Testament by 1838, and the Old Testament by 1857. The Wesleyans at Thaba Nchu established a full-time printer from 1837, the L M S at Kuruman in 1850, and the P E M S at Morija from 1861, all of whom published scriptures, catechisms, hymns and school materials in local dialects.

From 1856, a new phase began in the emergence of Sotho literature. That year the Wesleyan, J D. M Ludorf, began publishing a periodical entitled *Molekori oa Bechuana* (The Tswana People's Visitor). The next year Ashton started a newspaper called *Mokaeri oa Becuana, le Muleri ea mahuku* (The Instructor of the Tswana People and Announcer of the News). These short-lived papers gave place to the French missionaries' *Leselinyana la Lesotho* which, beginning in 1863, survives as the longest continuously existing publication in a Bantu language.

The creation of an indigenous literature began in the newspapers, especially *Leselinyana*, with current news and biographies of converts. As Africans became literate, they also began to write. Pupils at the mission schools reached elementary levels of reading and writing, so several chiefs sent boys to the

colony for further training. Moshoeshoe sent several of his sons to Cape Town from 1844. Tladi (George) and Tsekelo wrote essays on history and customs in Sotho during their stay there in 1858; in 1880 Sekhonyana (Nehemiah) wrote an historical account for the *Cape Monthly Magazine*, entitled 'A Little Light from Basutoland'.

From the beginning the French missionaries showed interest in local history and culture. By 1866 *Leselinyana* was publishing Sotho authors. The most prolific was Azariel Sekese, who wrote several hundred pieces from 1892 to 1925. He also published an account of Sotho customs and proverbs *(Mekhoa le Maele a Basotho)* and an imaginative work called *Pitso ea Dinoneana* (The Meeting of the Birds).

Other teachers and catechists wrote histories and fiction with encouragement from their missionaries. The finest Sotho novelist, Thomas Mofolo, wrote an allegorical novel of traditional life called *Moeti oa Bochabela* (Traveller to the East) in 1908, and followed it with a novel of modern life, *Pitseng*, and an account of Shaka in 1910. Zakae Mangoela compiled a collection of the praise poems of the chiefs of Lesotho and an account of the times of the *Difaqane*. Edward Motsamai published *Mehla ea Melimo* (Times of the Cannibals) and E Segoete *Raphapheng* in 1912 and 1915, recounting the troubles of the *Difaqane*. This literary tradition stimulated by the French missionaries at the turn of the century exceeds the production of any other African culture of the time. Though the momentum could not be sustained, a steady flow of historical and imaginative literature issues from Lesotho from the Morija Press and, more recently, from the Catholic press at Mazenod. As has been noted, perhaps the greatest Tswana author of the period was Sol T Plaatje, a Rolong who edited two newspapers from 1904 to 1914 at Mafeking and Kimberley *(Koranta ea Batswana,* and *Tsala ea Batho:* 'The Tswana People's Newspaper' and 'The People's Friend'). His most important book was *Native Life in South Africa*. In addition to his polemical work, he wrote a book of Tswana proverbs with English translations and a Tswana reader. He ended his career in 1930 with his novel, *Mhudi: An Epic of South African Native Life a Hundred Years Ago*. The literary tradition amongst the Sotho and Tswana is a positive result of missionary endeavour.

The spread of missionaries resulted in the printing of many dialects. The Methodists printed works in SeRolong, SeTlokwa and SeSotho; the LMS in SeTlhaping; the PEMS in SeFokeng, and the German missionaries in SeKwena and in Northern Sotho. They also created their own orthographies.

Donald M'Timkulu berates them for 'immortalising every dialect in print', thereby perpetuating tribalism. In fact, the missionaries were opposed to the proliferation of dialect publications as an impediment to their work. Informants in Lesotho freely admit, regardless of their clan origins, that all Southern Sotho use the national language as preserved by the missionaries from the Fokeng clan amongst whom they first worked. Indeed the missionaries became unwitting exponents of Fokeng speech as they were of Christianity and western civilisation. Although distinctions still exist, the limited printing facilities probably reduced the number which existed when they arrived.

In addition to their political activities, the missionaries' economic contributions included the introduction of new crops and farming methods. They introduced the cultivation of wheat, which became a commercial crop in Lesotho. They also introduced vegetable crops, well-digging and irrigation, and cultivation with the plough. In building their stations, the missionaries taught building trades. The stations became magnets for traders, thus introducing the products of the European industrial revolution, and creating the need for a cash economy. The missionaries also prompted the Africans to accept employment with whites. An indirect outcome of wage labour was the weakening of traditional crafts by taking the craftsmen's time and providing money to procure manufactured goods. Only in remote villages did iron smelting survive the century. Calabash and pottery making and the tanning of hides fared better, but had to compete with manufactured enamel-, tin- and china-ware and blankets.

Assessing the missionaries, S M Molema, the Rolong Christian, suggested: 'Manifestly, however, missionaries were primarily valued by the Batswana and Basotho chiefs—if indeed not by all the Bantu chiefs—for the temporal benefits accruing from their presence. . . . The white missionary was also the chief's principal advisor, interpreter, translater, secretary, diplomatic agent, health officer, mechanical and civil engineer, etc.—all offices and material services necessary and even essential, but secondary to the missionary's main purpose of spiritual regeneration; but services more highly appreciated by the chiefs and the tribes. . . .'

Sectarian conflicts which split the missionaries also divided the Africans. The conflict between the early Wesleyans and the late-arriving Anglicans caused a succession controversy at the death of Moroka in 1880. The broader conflict between Moshoeshoe and Moroka which weakened their resistance to Boer intrusion was intensified by jealousies between the French Evangelicals and the Wesleyans. Within Lesotho, the arrival of Catholics also divided the loyalties of the Sotho. On the other hand, the propaganda and diplomatic campaigns of the P E M S and the L M S led to the establishment of British protection over Basutoland in 1868 and Bechuanaland in 1885.

An assessment of the impact of missionaries must acknowledge both good and ill. They made few personal demands on Africans, and often dedicated long careers with little return. On the other hand, they rejected the cultural values of the Africans and tried to supplant them. They sometimes destroyed more effectively than they built. In any event, they changed the Tswana and Southern Sotho societies fundamentally.

Encroachment on the Land

The Boer intrusion on the highveld continued even after the Great Trek. The fate of the Tswana and Southern Sotho depended largely upon the relationships of the Boers with the British, who reacted erratically, leaving the Africans unsettled for half a century. In 1848, Sir Harry Smith annexed the lands between the Orange and Vaal Rivers. By 1852 the British had renounced all claims north of the Vaal, and two years later returned the Orange River country to the Boers. However, this did not end British interference for they annexed Lesotho in 1868 and the diamond fields in 1871. They also annexed the Transvaal in 1877, only to relinquish it again in 1881. British intrusion became complete when they annexed the Tswana lands in 1885 and the Boer republics in 1901.

For the Sotho and Tswana, this period resulted in severe restrictions on their sovereignty and on their land. The wedge of the Great Trek virtually isolated the Southern Sotho from the Tswana, thus enabling the two Boer republics to deal with them separately. In addition to the major fronts described here numerous lesser chiefs also lost their sovereignty to the Boers.

The most continuous pressure occurred along the Caledon valley. Following the Maitland Treaty in 1845, the Boers continued to infiltrate Moshoeshoe's land. Complaints by him and by the Griqua led Sir Harry Smith to annex all the land south of the Vaal River. He placed a resident at Bloemfontein, Major Henry Warden, who aggravated the problem in 1849 by excising the Rolong migrants and Boer squatters from Moshoeshoe's western boundary. Warden's act officially pitted Africans against each

Moshoeshoe in 1860, on the state occasion of a meeting with Prince Alfred at Aliwal North. Moshoeshoe offered himself as a subject and an ally, in the hope of enlisting British protection.

other as well as against the Boers. When Moshoeshoe rejected this act, war ensued in which Moshoeshoe defeated Warden in 1851. Two years later he also defeated his old foe, Sekonyela.

When the British renounced Smith's annexation, trouble persisted over cattle, grazing rights and squatters. The Sotho defeated the Boers and a new boundary, drafted by the governor, Sir George Grey, gave temporary advantage to them. Nonetheless, the chief sensed the changing circumstances and begged for British protection. His fears were confirmed when cattle raiding and recriminations between the Boers and Moroka and Moshoeshoe and his allies continued without let. Open conflict broke out in 1865 which pressed to the heart of Lesotho. One subchief after another, including some of Moshoeshoe's family, capitulated. Finally, Letsie, the heir to the ageing chief, sued for peace at Thaba Bosiu in 1866, retaining mainly the high, infertile mountain country.

Moshoeshoe regarded the treaty as a truce only.

When his people had gathered their harvest into their strongholds, he resumed war, but the Free State again demolished his power. The aged king again begged for British protection. He might have failed, except that the punitive character of the treaty of Thaba Bosiu and the Boer's act of expelling the French missionaries aroused the British. They annexed Lesotho in 1868, just before the king died. While the belated protection of the British staved off the destruction of the Sotho nation, it never created peace. The Cape colonial administration angered the Sotho, particularly when they attempted to disarm the Africans. Peace finally came in 1884, when the British assumed direct control.

The heartland of Lesotho remained to the Sotho, and the British restored some of the land lost by the Treaty of Thaba Bosiu, but the long series of conflicts ended with the permanent loss of the

fig. 12 The changing boundaries of Lesotho. From 1843 the encroachment of European settlers eroded the land claims of Moshoeshoe until he finally obtained the protection of Britain. This map shows the boundary established by Governor Napier, Moshoeshoe's counter claim in 1843 and the final boundaries of Lesotho as established in 1868.

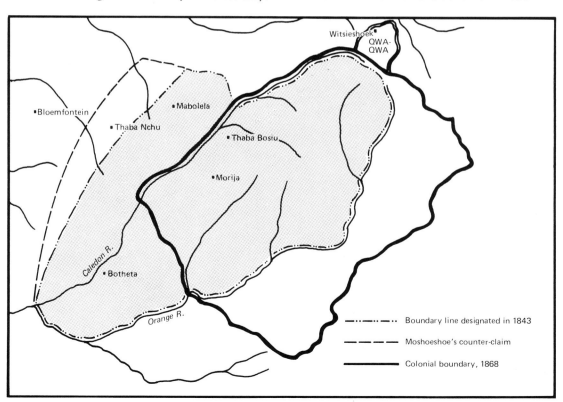

Witsieshoek
QWA-QWA

•Bloemfontein

• Mabolela

• Thaba Nchu

• Thaba Bosiu

• Morija

Caledon R.

• Botheta

Orange R.

— · · — · · — Boundary line designated in 1843

— — — — — Moshoeshoe's counter-claim

———————— Colonial boundary, 1868

favoured lowlands (fig. 12). Moshoeshoe also lost any possible alliance with Moroka, whom he had welcomed to his borders so long before. He also lost the allegiance of his brother, Mopeli, who became subject to the Free State in the land now called Basotho QwaQwa.

Moroka did not profit long by casting his lot with the Boers. Their friendship at first made him more important than his numbers justified and Warden made him independent. However, in the frequent conflicts between the Boers and Moshoeshoe, he regularly suffered raids on his villages and the loss of cattle. In the end, when the succession to Moroka became disputed at his death in 1880, the Free State readily ignored a generation of treaties and friendship and absorbed his country. They who would not be vassals of Moshoeshoe became vassals to their white 'friends'.

The western Tswana chiefdoms fared no better. Those chiefs who remained free after the trek found their lands increasingly pressed, especially after the discovery of diamonds. Though the diamond lands were primarily occupied by Griqua, both the Rolong and the Tlhaping claimed the area north of the Vaal River. R W Keate, Lieutenant-Governor of Natal, arbitrated the issue awarding the south to the Griqua and the north to the Tswana claimants. The Griqua ceded their part to the British in 1871, but the Tswana remained independent. The Transvaal, angered by the decision, allowed their subjects and local officials blatantly to evade it. Some chiefs sought British protection, but others found advantage in siding with the Boers against their kinsmen. 'Treaties' signed by some Tlhaping and Rolong chiefs legitimised Boer intrusion beyond the Keate line. Discontent led some Tlhaping to attack the Europeans amongst them in 1878. Botlhasitse, whose father was killed by Boers, and who had lost part of his land to the Transvaal, led the attack, besieging Kuruman until a volunteer column from Griqualand West relieved it, ending the uprising. Nonetheless, it drew attention to the plight of the Tswana.

When the British annexed the Transvaal in 1877, Africans hoped for peace, but when they relinquished control after the Anglo–Boer War in 1881, their hopes were dashed. The British simply affirmed a boundary between the sides and committed the Boers to respect it by the Pretoria Convention. With the signing of peace, the garrison sent to the Tswana in 1878 was withdrawn, leaving the Boers to police themselves.

A problem for the Tswana and the Sotho was the disposition of the British to leave South African matters to the Cape administration, leaving African affairs in the hands of the settler government. The High Commissioner, who acted for Britain, was at the same time colonial governor. The British also tended to equate good policy with economy, precluding commitments which required treasury expenditure.

Immediately after the British withdrawal troubles recurred. Tswana chiefs divided against each other, not only over the new boundary, but also because of the sides they had taken in the recent war. On the west, Montshiwa of the Tshidi Rolong and Mankurwane of the Tlhaping opposed Moswete and Matlaba, two other Rolong chiefs living in the Transvaal. Fighting began in 1881, but the sides were so evenly matched that Moswete and a Kora ally enlisted Boers with the promise of the lands of their enemies. On the other side, the Cape government, in order to 'preserve strict neutrality', forbade whites to volunteer or to sell ammunition. By early 1882, the attackers had laid waste to Montshiwa's land. The Boers claimed all of his country south of the Molopo River. Mankurwane suffered daily raids until he, too, sued for peace. Both chiefs ceded much of their land to the Boers, in complete violation of the Pretoria Convention. Moswete's volunteers called their conquest Goshen, while the Tlhaping lands became Stellaland; both were proclaimed republics.

The Rev. John Mackenzie hurried to London to advocate British protection for the Tswana chiefs. Paul Kruger, president of the Transvaal, also arrived seeking to revise the Convention, claiming that the boundary split chiefdoms and caused anarchy. Governor Hercules Robinson arrived in time to confirm Mackenzie's arguments. Together they exposed Kruger as trying to perpetuate the trek and to close off the 'road to the north'. The British established protection over the southern Tswana, naming Mackenzie as commissioner and confirming the boundary of the Transvaal.

The settlement failed on the frontier because the two rump republics refused to acknowledge Mackenzie's authority, and both the Transvaal and Cape governments opposed imperial intervention. Rather than fostering peace, the Goshenites raided the Ngwaketse. When Montshiwa tried to stop them, they killed one hundred of his men. To stop anarchy, Mackenzie was removed and Cecil Rhodes, who advocated Cape control, replaced him. Though the Stellaland people accepted his authority on promise that he would honour their land titles, the Goshenites ignored him and conquered even more of Montshiwa's land.

In all their plundering, the men of Goshen miscalculated on one point. They killed a British ally of Montshiwa. British opinion was more aroused over him than over all the depredations the ruffian Boers had committed. To top all, the Transvaal annexed Goshen in defiance of the London Convention. Sir Charles Warren led a military expedition in 1885 to the troubled region and annexed it as the colony of British Bechuanaland, and proclaimed a protectorate over the north. Though the northern chiefs had not been consulted, they generally favoured British protection and cooperated with the new government, which protected them not only from the Boers, but also from the Ndebele in the north. Though neither Montshiwa nor Mankurwane regained their lands, the main losers were those Rolong and Kora who remained under the Transvaal.

The Southern Sotho had early unified as a nation, and the imposition of British rule did not alter that. In the case of the Tswana, they retained separate identity throughout the wars, and British protection did not change them. They remained a collection of autonomous chiefdoms under a common administration for external protection. However, whether the Tswana and Southern Sotho fell under direct rule or under a protectorate, they all lost part of their sovereignty. Nonetheless, traditional loyalties and ways of life persisted in their villages.

Migrant Labour

A third transition which befell the Africans by the end of the century was the imposition of a cash economy and the necessity for men to earn money as migrant workers away from their homes. A major cause was the loss of sufficient land to sustain the traditional means of subsistence. The Africans who were pushed aside kept only the least favoured land, while those who submitted were crowded even more. As the republican governments matured, they imposed taxes on the chiefs for the use of the lands they kept. Whatever the demands, cash came most readily from labouring for the aliens. With the discovery of diamonds in 1866, the modern patterns of migrant labour emerged. By 1878, the Griqualand West administration recruited in the Bechuanaland protectorate for mine labour. Their system of housing the workers in compounds without their families for limited contracts, spread to the new gold mines. By the end of the century 30 000 workers left Lesotho for the mines and railways, and others worked on the farms near their country. While the Tswana possessed more expansive lands for a sub-

sistence economy, by 1898 they too had contributed 2 000 workers to the gold mines. As land became impacted by growing population, labour migration became increasingly important. Its effect on the village life may best be described from the reports of the missionaries in Lesotho in the early 1900s:

'Between sowing-time and harvest there are months of expectation. What have they lived on hitherto and what will they subsist on until the first mealie cobs are available? They began by eating the little they had. Next they bought maize imported from Australia or the United States, paying six to eight times the normal price. They went to work in the gold mines of the Transvaal or on railway construction, more or less everywhere. The money thus earned was carefully sent to Basutoland and served to keep alive the little family which had remained in the village. Blessed gold mines to which even more evil is attributed than they have actually caused and in which, impoverished or ruined by the Transvaal war, Blacks and Whites seek the means of sustenance which they can find nowhere else.'

Again, 'Were the population to continue to increase, the situation would become truly critical within a few years, unless other means of livelihood were provided for the Basuto. They would be forced to emigrate in large numbers to offer their services to the Europeans of the neighbouring countries which are less densely populated, but where their social conditions would deteriorate and where, above all, they would lose their independence.'

Early in this century, the Africans had become significantly changed by their intimate contacts with the Europeans who had settled amidst them and claimed mastery over them in various forms of government. Both the Tswana and the Southern Sotho retained something of their cultural identity and the semblance of autonomy, but they had both altered radically as they entered the modern word.

5

Responses to Colonialism

WILLIAM F LYE

The century opened with the Southern Sotho and Tswana being ruled by five distinct and alien administrations, and evolved through a period of subjugation by aliens and new challenges to their traditional culture. For the first half of the century the prospects appeared to become more and more bleak for all Africans, but by the end of the period a 'wind of change' was formally acknowledged by the visiting Conservative Prime Minister of Britain.

The history of this period involves the African response to the shifting character of European control, and the era of colonial domination proved also to be a period of growing national consciousness of the Tswana and Southern Sotho. As each new contact affected them, they responded in increasingly complex ways. At first the people relied on their chiefs, but as they entered directly into the white environment, resistance took on varied forms. The intent was to preserve or gain back their personal freedom and right to control their own lives. Though these reactions led to the formation of two sovereign nations and two 'homelands' within the South African orbit, they have left a mass of people scattered throughout South Africa seeking freedom in the land of their birth.

South Africa: The African Response

The Tswana who lived south of the Molopo River accepted British rule to restrain the Boer interlopers of Stellaland and Goshen. The Tshidi Rolong dominated the north while the Tlhaping and Tlharo were the major chiefdoms of the south. They fell under British control in 1884 as the Crown Colony of British Bechuanaland. The Governor of the Cape Colony acted as governor over the Tswana through resident officers in each of three districts of Vryburg, Mafeking and Taung. In 1895 the British transferred the territory to the Cape Colony, fulfilling the goals of Cecil Rhodes to acquire direct control over the Africans for the settler colony.

At the time the southern chiefs accepted British control, those in the north—the Ngwato, Kwena and Ngwaketse—accepted British intervention by becoming the Bechuanaland Protectorate. The chiefs retained internal authority but they gained protection against the encroachments of the Transvaal Republic. Over the next decade the Protecto-

rate extended northward to include all of the western Tswana peoples.

To the east the Hurutshe and many of the Rolong, Kwena and Kgatla chiefs had submitted to the trekkers to become integrated into the Transvaal. Though they controlled their internal affairs, they became subject to taxes, labour levies and other laws of the republic, and their lands were reduced leaving them small patches interspersed between white farms. The Seleka Rolong lost most of their land to the Orange Free State when it absorbed them in 1884.

Most of the Southern Sotho remained in Moshoeshoe's state under the administration of Britain after 1884. The rest became landless squatters on European farms or were crowded into the tiny reserve granted to Mopeli, or shared the Herschel District in the south with Xhosa people.

Life in the White States

African interests in the colony and republics were subordinated to the goals of the settlers. British intervention in South Africa during the last century frequently reflected liberal and humanitarian concerns, but the first major issue of the new era, the Anglo–Boer War, clearly reflected the dominant imperial interests. The basic causes were the competition for mineral rights between the Afrikaners and the British and the imperial scramble affecting all Western Europe. Nonetheless, the war was fought on African soil and affected African lives and destinies. Even though the war ignored Africans,

Bechuanaland differed from Basutoland in that no one chiefly family dominated the whole nation. Each chiefdom retained its own ruling family. These three chiefs travelled to England in 1895 to negotiate land concessions. Seated are Bathoen I of the Ngwaketse, Sebele I of the Kwena, and Khama III of the Ngwato.

and by agreement they were not recruited as combatants, they served as auxiliaries, and even as spies, and they lived in the areas and suffered along with their white countrymen.

After the British victory all the Tswana and Southern Sotho fell under direct or indirect control of the British. However, by 1906 both of the conquered provinces received self-government under the same leadership which had subjugated the Tswana in the republics. Then, in 1910, all the settler communities became united in the Union of South Africa with the understanding that the African territories, Basutoland and Bechuanaland Protectorate, would eventually be incorporated.

With the creation of a single government for all the settler territories, the Tswana and Southern Sotho living within them fell under a common 'native policy'. Basutoland and Bechuanaland were excluded. Nonetheless, the Union government repeatedly tried to incorporate them. Prime Minister Hertzog made three attempts between 1925 and 1937, but the British honoured their promise to require the consent of the Africans. World War II delayed action, but after the National Party victory in

1948, Prime Minister Malan petitioned the British declaring that the presence of these 'alien' territories within South Africa's boundaries limited its sovereignty. These pressures continued in 1950 and 1952 with threats that the High Commission territories would be considered foreign country and would be deprived of the special customs and fiscal treatment they received. Prime Minister Strijdom renewed the request in 1954 and 1955, promising to 'treat them as we treat our own'. British resistance was reinforced by a growing sense of African nationalism, particularly by Tshekedi Khama of the Ngwato, who asked for representative government for his people.

In 1955 the Tomlinson Report proposed the development of the African people, including those of the High Commission territories, under the program of separate development or apartheid. If this were not sufficient to discourage union, the departure of the newly proclaimed Republic of South Africa from the Commonwealth in 1961 sealed the fate of transfer, even though Prime Minister Verwoerd asserted, 'South Africa could lead them far better and much more quickly to independence and economic prosperity than Great Britain can do.' However, by then both territories were well on their way to independence.

At the same time that the Union government was trying to incorporate the High Commission territories, they were establishing their rule over Africans within their country. Unification may not have improved the lot of the Tswana and Sotho in the Transvaal and the Free State, but it retarded the rights of those in the Cape. Prior to Union, Cape Africans had access to a common voters' roll with whites by property and educational qualifications. This policy favoured Western-oriented Africans to the neglect of the traditional majority, but it did permit participation in government. After unification, the Cape retained its common roll while the other provinces continued their exclusionist policy. When Hertzog became Prime Minister he ended the common roll. In its place Africans in the Cape could elect three white parliamentarians on separate rolls, and two Cape Provincial councillors. In addition, Africans throughout the nation could elect four senators by an electoral college system and could vote for African representatives on the new Natives' Representative Council, which also had nominated *ex officio* members and served as an advisory body.

Prior to 1913, their reserved lands provided the Africans with a base for economic and political life, but did not confine them. The land laws of 1913 and 1936 closed their right to own lands elsewhere. Territorial partition became the basis for development of South Africa. Africans could enter the white man's areas only on suffrance and squatters could be expelled. The Natives' Land Act of 1913 explicitly limited land for Africans as a means of assuring an adequate labour supply to the European farmers and industries, and to eliminate competition with the poor-white class to acquire land. The preservation of the reserves assured the Africans of a place where they could perpetuate their own culture, but it was not adequate to support them. The injustice of the land allocation of 1913 created one of the earliest oppositions by blacks. The author, Sol T Plaatje, joined other Africans to take their case to Britain. The act designated only about 9,1 million hectares as reserves. Though a study commission recommended adding to the land, the proposal only passed in 1936, permitting an additional 6,2 million hectares to be purchased; much of the released land was not acquired until recently, and still allowed only about 13,5 per cent of the country for the African majority. During the delay in acquiring the land the African population grew rapidly, causing overcrowding, over-grazing, erosion and deterioration of the soil. The 1951 Union census estimated that only 43 per cent of all Africans actually dwelt on the reserves, while 30 per cent lived on white farms and 27 per cent lived in cities and industrial areas. The percentage of Tswana and Southern Sotho was even less.

The new land allocations were not co-ordinated with those in 1913, and fragmented the reserves still further. Even after explicit changes in policy by the current government intending to advance the Africans to 'independence' within their reserves ('homelands'), consolidation attempts have thus far only reduced the number of fragments for the Tswana homeland, BophuthaTswana, to six pieces of land in three provinces of the republic. The tiny Witsieshoek Reserve, now called QwaQwa, can accommodate only a small fraction of Southern Sotho resident in South Africa, while BophuthaTswana claims only one-third of its 'citizens' as residents of the 'homeland'. The larger part of both people are permanently integrated into the labour force of the republic as landless migrants, though the government identifies them as citizens of the 'homeland' where they may never have lived, and requires them to bear identity documents which tie them to those lands.

Labour laws in the republic similarly affected their African citizens and migrants from other countries. The voracious appetite of the mines has grown constantly. At the turn of the century it required

Stakaneng, a section of the sprawling slum north of Pretoria known as the Winterveld. The laid-out township in the foreground underlines the scale of congestion.

fifty-four thousand Africans. By 1936 mineworkers totalled three hundred and eighteen thousand and by 1972, three hundred and eighty-one thousand. By the latter date, only 22 per cent came from within the republic. Over seventy thousand came from Lesotho and twenty thousand from Botswana. Because of the rural dispersion of the Tswana and Southern Sotho residents of the republic, most of them earned their living on white farms nearby.

From the beginning labour laws restricted African workers. The diamond industry established the pattern of migrant labour contracts, which later spread to other mines and industries. Immediately after unification, the new nation passed laws which reserved certain jobs for whites and forbade Africans to strike. With restrictions against organisation and

imported surplus labour wages were kept low. The so-called civilised labour policy of the 1920s sought to improve the living standards of poor-whites at the expense of the Africans. As the country became increasingly industrialised, especially after World War II, that policy faded because industrial work blurred the distinction between skilled and unskilled labour. The full impact of the labour laws and the differential wages, the land reservation system and the suffrage restrictions effectively limited the advancement of Africans: they were doomed to a subservient and temporary status in the 'white' area, and to crowding, underdevelopment and poverty in the reserves.

The erosion of political, economic and social rights for the Africans intensified with the rise of the Afrikaner National Party to power in 1948. The official articulation of their policy was the Tomlinson Commission Report. This report proposed that the only just solution to the unfortunate condition of the Africans was the complete separation of the

Sorghum is one of the staple crops in Lesotho.
Here men do the threshing and women winnow.

Right: Activity at a bus-stop in Lesotho. Buses
are the basic means of transport in Lesotho.

Below left: A typical Tswana domestic scene.

Below right: Severe gully erosion near the land-
mark of Qiloane in the vicinity of Thaba Bosiu.

Transporting and drawing water in Botswana.

Sotho mine labourers at a mine dance competition held at the East Driefontein goldmine.

races. It recognised that the separated areas needed to be developed to provide for the support of the African residents. The logical end of separate development was the complete separation of the African areas as sovereign lands, just as Britain was providing for Lesotho and Botswana. Whether that assumption was fully understood or agreed upon in 1955, the government acted out its theory by granting Transkei 'independence' within that framework in 1976, and BophuthaTswana in 1977. Other 'homelands', including QwaQwa, are heading toward the same goal. The logical outcome of the policy of separate development will be elimination of all African citizens within the republic, as every African will be designated a citizen of his or her ethnic 'homeland' regardless of residence.

On the way to achieving that goal, the entire educational, political, social, and economic structures of the republic have been changed to isolate the Africans from each other as well as from the whites. However, the industrial growth of the nation has rendered separation impractical, for economic interdependence has forced the integration of Africans in every phase of South Africa's development. Nonetheless, that policy has imprinted itself into every aspect of South African life for the past thirty years.

The Context of Opposition

The move to the city or to work on white farms attenuated the links between many African people and their rural areas of origin. At the same time, new perspectives of life were gained, new philosophies introduced, and new associations and organisations encountered. Naboth Mokgatle, for example, in his *Autobiography of an Unknown South African*, relates the evolution of a Tswana worker from the Transvaal. He was born a Fokeng villager and gained his education in Lutheran schools, then he migrated to the nearby farms. Eventually he drifted on to the city where he eventually became a labour organiser and political activist. Finally, he fled the country to escape permanent imprisonment.

In the broad perspective of political awakening, the new Africans began to compete with the traditional chiefs for leadership over the people. Their opposition to pass laws, labour conditions, social restraints and political exclusion began in the cities amongst an urbanised élite, but it eventually infected the villages. Some of the earliest exponents gained their education at Lovedale and Fort Hare, where they mixed with Africans of other ethnic groups, and where they gained a broader national consciousness.

When workers left their villages they became subject to two restraints that provoked their reaction: working conditions and pass laws. When they laboured on nearby white farms they could readily return to their villages, and they were generally dispersed in small groups. But when they moved to the mines or cities they could not easily return, and they found themselves in large groups of mixed backgrounds for extended periods away from home. The laws of the new nation forbade strikes by Africans, but they did permit organisations. After World War I inflation affected living costs, but wages remained fixed at pre-war levels. After 1919 spontaneous strikes occurred, but they were poorly organised and easily suppressed. Nonetheless, workers gained experience and leadership. Perhaps the most important advance was the founding in 1919 of the Industrial and Commercial Workers Union by Clements Kadalie, an immigrant from Nyasaland. Thousands of workers throughout South Africa joined that union or break-offs from it during the next decade until it disintegrated. Perhaps the most significant labour reaction occurred in 1973 when strikes broke out, apparently spontaneously, throughout the Republic of South Africa and South West Africa/Namibia, and which led the government to offer concessions to the workers.

Pass laws existed in South Africa from early Cape days. The trekkers also implemented them in their republics. They became the symbol of white oppression. Resistance to the pass laws became particularly strong when they were applied to women and intruded into traditional villages. The Tswana became involved when the women of the Hurutshe Reserve refused to register for their passes in 1956. Their Chief was deposed and the people reacted with violence, but the government retaliated by house searches, refusal of medical services and the expulsion of children from school if mothers failed to produce the passes. When the Africans protested they were turned back, even by being buzzed by training planes of the South African Air Force. The culmination of opposition by Africans to pass laws occurred on 21 March 1960, when a national campaign was organised by the Pan African Congress. In the Transvaal town of Sharpeville, police fired on an unarmed crowd killing 69 and wounding 180 men, women and children. That incident galvanised world opinion against South African race policies more than any previous event.

An important element in the development of national consciousness was the development of an African press. Mission papers began the process. The first non-mission papers amongst these people were *Mochochonono* (The Comet), published in Basutoland, and the two papers of Sol Plaatje at Mafeking and Kimberley. As political parties emerged they also developed papers to present their views. The first was *Abantu-Batho* (Meaning 'The People' in Zulu and Sotho), published in English, Zulu, Xhosa, Sotho and Tswana by the African National Congress. A contributor and editor to that paper from 1912 to 1931 was the Sotho author D S Letanka.

Independent papers became important with the founding of *Bantu World*. Its success led the Argus group to absorb it in 1963. Even though papers for Africans are most important in the cities, and suffer from limited financing and frequent bannings by the government, they are becoming increasingly important as a medium for encouraging political consciousness.

Political Action

Direct political action emerged amongst the Southern Sotho and Tswana very early. In 1899 the Resident Commissioner of Basutoland, Sir Herbert Sloley, took some chiefs to England to petition for exclusion from any union with the white settler colonies. The major chiefs of Bechuanaland also petitioned for exclusion in 1909.

The most pressing issue for Africans in the new nation was land. The South African Native National Congress (later called the African National Congress) came into being after unification and it took direct action against the Land Act of 1913. It sent delegates to England in 1914 and 1919, including Sol Plaatje, to petition the British government, but failed because Britain had granted the new nation control over internal affairs. Unfortunately for the growing national consciousness of Africans, the land measure tended to isolate them into separate ethnic divisions.

Perhaps a high point in African resistance occurred in 1935 when an All-African National Convention brought together many budding organisations to oppose the Natives' Representation Act which deprived Africans of their position on the common voters' roll in the Cape. They failed in their goal, partly because they became divided over tactics; some advocated direct action while others proposed negotiation and mediation. This division would mark all African political activities thereafter.

The earliest national movement was the South African Native National Congress, which brought together the African élite of all ethnic groups from its foundation in 1912. It advocated a non-racial government, but it relied on legal tactics. Its conservative methods and its willingness to link with other ethnic groups in South Africa led to the formation of the Pan African Congress in 1959. The Communist party also vied for leadership amongst the Africans after World War I, and won limited support during the economic difficulties of the 1930s. National political organisations always came under suspicion by the government. The Communists were outlawed in 1950, and the African National Congress and the Pan African Congress were banned after Sharpeville. These national movements included many followers from the Tswana and Southern Sotho people, but they evolved their own ethnic organisations as well.

The Colonial Era: Basutoland and Bechuanaland

If life for the Tswana and Southern Sotho of the republic was characterised by subjugation to the white minority, life for their kin in the High Commission Territories was characterised by neglect. As one author described Britain's rule in Basutoland: 'They made a wilderness and called it peace.' But while it is easy to criticise Britain's failure to develop the country, this must be tempered by the fact that Basutoland had almost no developable resources. In fact, Britain began to erect erosion-control structures in 1902, and persisted through independence with what has been regarded as a model programme. It should also be pointed out that since independence massive development aid has not solved Lesotho's problem of dependence.

Despite this, the primary policy of the British towards both territories seemed to be to maintain peace, to minimise expenses, and to avoid antagonising their white neighbour. The result was the general decline in prosperity, and the increasing dependence upon labour wages in the Union. The policy of 'Indirect Rule' allowed the traditional rulers to administer local affairs but, as in other cases in Africa, it tended to freeze political structures while undermining their validity. What began as grateful acceptance of protection ended in general hostility to the British protectors.

Basutoland

British protection of Basutoland resulted in rapid population growth. The first census under the British in 1873 counted 127 000 Sotho inhabitants. By 1890, the population had reached 218 000; by 1911, 428 000 and by 1966, one million. This demonstrated stability but the failure of the British to de-

velop the land resources led to problems of overcrowding. A French missionary reported in 1890, 'Soon the country will no longer suffice for its inhabitants: the population increases considerably from year to year; the fallow shrinks in the same proportion and at the same rate as the pastures. More than half the fields have been under cultivation for half a century and are exhausted.'

The people found subsistence increasingly difficult. To supplement the exhausted farms, grazing lands and lands in the remote mountain regions began to be cultivated. Increasing numbers of the men drifted off to labour in South Africa. In the period 1896–8, the Chamber of Mines reported that eleven per cent of their men came from Basutoland (6 000 men). By 1936 that figure had risen to 14,5 per cent (46 000) and by 1972 had reached 18,5 (71 000). In addition, others worked on white farms.

Modern political development can be said to have begun with the founding of a National *Pitso*, or popular assembly, in 1874. This adaptation of the traditional clan meeting provided a forum for the men to participate in decision-making. However, the large numbers involved and the distances to the capital caused the *Pitso* to be more of an opportunity for the Paramount Chief to announce decisions than for him to receive advice on new proposals. These difficulties rendered the National *Pitso* less than successful.

As the colonial government established itself it had limited manpower to impose its will, so local politics fell to the Paramount Chief and to the sub-chiefs. Considerable opposition developed because of the dominance of Moshoeshoe's family, who became a ruling élite over the traditional clan heads. Conflicts between Moshoeshoe's offspring also created problems. Masupha rose in rebellion against Lerotholi, claiming the paramountcy. While this rebellion fitted traditional succession practice in which the claimants would test their support by arms, in the context of the British overlordship Lerotholi easily defeated his opponent, reinforcing the new political order.

Next came the National Council in 1903 as an advisory body to the Paramount Chief. This council met annually from 1908. Though it had limited functions and was dominated by the chiefs, it participated in the opposition to unification in 1909.

Britain assured the Sotho that they would not be incorporated without consultation, and they were granted a new 'Basutoland Council' in 1910 to defend their interests in the event that they did unite with South Africa. The new council consisted of one

Masupha, younger son of Moshoeshoe's great wife, aspired to political importance in Lesotho even before the death of the king. He later rebelled when his brother's son succeeded to the paramountcy.

hundred members, including ninety-four appointed by the Paramount Chief. The council provided criticism and advice on proposed laws, but was dominated by the 'Sons of Moshoeshoe' (see fig. 16).

By 1930 the office of High Commissioner was separated from that of Governor General, giving specific attention to the interests of the Africans. As a result of the Depression and a drought the Sotho became disgruntled with their chiefs, who seemed oblivious of their plight. The British Pim Commission investigated the problems and recommended political reform. Two proclamations in 1936 reformed the courts and gave the High Commissioner control over the appointment of chiefs and subchiefs to avoid the dominance of the Sons of Moshoeshoe in government. Thereafter, other reforms incorporated elected members in the Basutoland Council and the formation of District Councils.

These reforms led to further competition for chiefly powers, and to the revival of the ancient rite of *diretlo*, or ritual murder, in which chiefs doctored themselves with flesh of sacrificial victims to strengthen their power. Such murders plagued Basutoland during the 1940s as the tensions over power reached into many villages. Perhaps the most serious example of *diretlo* occurred in 1939 when Bereng, the eldest son of Chief Griffith, was passed over in favour of his younger half-brother, Seeiso (who nevertheless was senior to Bereng in terms of ranking of houses) and then a year later in favour of his widow, Mantsebo, as regent for their young son. Though Bereng was a Roman Catholic, he was accused of trying to gain his 'rightful place' by practising *diretlo*. In 1949 he was tried, convicted and executed for complicity in murder.

By 1948 the *diretlo* scandal caused the Regent, Mantsebo, to accept the requirement to consult advisers selected from nominees of the Council before making any decision. A National Treasury was also instituted under the control of the High Commissioner, which eliminated the control of revenue by the Sons of Moshoeshoe.

Political complications in Basutoland exceeded those of Bechuanaland, primarily because of the dominance of the family of Moshoeshoe. The first political opposition to the chiefs emerged amongst the budding civil servant and trading class. They organised the Progressive Association in 1903, to oppose the power of the appointed chiefs. They sought the election of representatives on the Basutoland Council. In 1950 they gained the right to nominate one member of the National Council. A more radical organisation *Lekhotla la Bafo* ('The People's Court'), came into being in the 1920s and by 1928 had made contact with the South African Communist Party. It was primarily the work of two brothers, Maphutseng and Joseil Lefela. Though it was suppressed for sedition during the war, in 1950 it too was represented on the National Council by Joseil Lefela. His politics ranged from an extreme left-wing support of the commoners to defence of the Paramount chieftainship.

As Basutoland appeared to be moving towards self-government the first modern parties came into being. The Basutoland African Congress (later called Basutoland Congress Party), led by Ntsu Mokhehle, began in 1952 to oppose authoritarian British rule. The British proposed modest reforms in 1954, but the Congress demanded constitutional talks. The British retaliated by suspending the leaders of the Congress, but this only caused the organisation to become more strident and more popular. Conflict with the Roman Catholics over their domi-

Chief Leabua Jonathan, first Prime Minister of independent Lesotho, remains a man of controversy in Lesotho and in the Republic of South Africa.

nance of politics, led them into a newspaper fight, with the Catholics accusing them of being communist.

In 1958, Chief Leabua Jonathan and G C Manyeli founded the Basutoland National Party to counter the Congress. The new leaders were both Catholics, but they sought to dissociate themselves from the church and to propose 'the ancient democratic relationships of the chief and the people'. They also advocated independence, but at a slower pace. Other parties fragmented from the B C P as the Marema-Tlou Party, which advocated the installation of the prince, Bereng Seeiso, in place of the regent, with the Paramount Chief as Head of State in the emerging nation. The Basutoland Freedom Party also split from the Congress after the first election in 1960 as a conservative reaction. These splinter parties united temporarily as the Marema-Tlou Freedom Party in 1963.

An important stride towards self-rule occurred in 1955 when the Basutoland Council voted to be allowed to make laws for all internal matters. The concept was accepted by the Secretary of State for Commonwealth Affairs and he invited them to submit proposals. They formed a committee which developed a constitutional proposal by 1958. The proposal would have turned over authority to a responsible Legislative Council and Executive Council. They also proposed greater local authority, including treasuries, within the districts. The British responded cautiously, not wishing to antagonise South Africa. Nonetheless, the new constitution was implemented in 1960, but with the reservation that the country could not become completely independent in the foreseeable future.

The limitations of the constitution, particularly those which provided for indirect election to the Legislature, caused the Sotho to become increasingly politicised. In the elections the Congress obtained 73 seats on the District Councils (of 162) which assured them 30 of the 40 elected seats on the Legislative Council. Though the other parties polled 64 per cent of the vote, the distribution left them underrepresented in the legislature. The nominated members helped to rectify that imbalance, and their conservative reaction caused them to appoint an Executive Council favourable to Britain. As one author pointed out, the elected majority thus became the opposition.

The B C P rejected the outcome of the constitution and demanded a constitutional review. When the new Paramount Chief joined the cry for a review and demanded full independence, discussions began in May 1962. The Sotho took their case to the United Nations and to the Afro-Asian People's Solidarity Conference meeting in Tanganyika. The combination of radical demands by the Sotho and the unwillingness of the British to arbitrate every difference between Basutoland and South Africa led Britain to permit the Sotho to advance to responsibility. A new constitutional committee reported their recommendations in October 1963 recommending independence by 1965 and the immediate transition to a 'protected state' rather than a colony. Britain's reluctance precipitated an unusual show of unanimity on the part of the political parties. By June 1964 the Legislative Council had approved the new proposal with modifications and, after lengthy debates in Britain, and a change which would permit the new government to ask for independence within one year after holding elections, the proposal was accepted. When the elections were held in April 1965, party strength had shifted in favour of the B N P because the campaign against the B C P had successfully branded them as radical. The B N P won a plurality of the votes but a narrow majority of the seats in the National Assembly. The day following the election the Paramount Chief was sworn in as 'Her Majesty's Representative' in place of the Commissioner. Political controversies involving the B N P's alleged submission to South Africa delayed a decision on independence, but it was finally granted on 4 October 1966. Independence did not end the political feuds within the new nation of Lesotho. Refugees from South Africa fired political opposition to the government's conciliatory policy towards the republic. When a new election in 1970 gave evidence that the government had lost support, the Prime Minister declared an emergency and cancelled the election, using military force to retain his power.

The conflict between the parties was joined by a conflict between Leabua Jonathan and the King. In 1970 the King went into exile leaving his fragmented powers in the hands of Jonathan's nominee. He returned later that year on condition that he remain aloof from politics. Thus Lesotho gained a precarious independence. Recent pronouncements by the government indicate that Lesotho is shedding its image of being subservient to South Africa, but it remains economically dependent.

The Bechuanaland Protectorate

Although the Tswana people obtained protection in 1885, they did not experience all the difficulties suffered by their Sotho kin. They remained poor and politically retarded but Bechuanaland nevertheless enjoyed several advantages. It is a large, strategically located land, and by the time Britain proclaimed protection over the northern section it was twenty times the size of Basutoland and had a smaller population. Further, its division into several chiefdoms precluded the dominance of a single Paramount Chief and his descendants. Because of its location on the main route north, it enjoyed access to a telegraph system by 1892 and a railway along its entire eastern boundary by 1897. Its greatest problem at first was the threat of incorporation into the South Africa Company. That problem ended in 1896 after the ill-fated Jameson Raid.

The British established 'Tribal Reserves' for the major chiefdoms; the Ngwato, Tawana, Kwena, Ngwaketse and Kgatla in 1899, the Malete in 1909, and the Tlokwa in 1933. Land was also reserved for the Tati Mining Company in 1908 and for European settlers in four districts. The rest of the country became Crown Lands. Even though the country was large, it was mostly arid and, as with Basutoland, the Tswana had to support their growing population by migrant labour. In recent years twenty-five per cent of the men work in the republic.

The Tswana also opposed being incorporated into the Union of South Africa. Their first national political institution was established in 1920: the Native Advisory Council. (A European Advisory Council was established in 1921.) Though the Ngwato chiefdom was the largest, it refused to participate. The Pim Commission also proposed reforms for the Tswana in the 1930s.

Because of political differences Tshekedi Khama, the Ngwato Regent, was suspended from his office in 1933. When the reforms proposed by the Pim Commission restructured the legal powers of the *Kgotlas*, or 'Tribal Councils', Tshekedi Khama and Bathoen II of the Ngwaketse, sued the High Commissioner. A special court held in 1936 declared that Britain 'had unfettered and unlimited power to legislate for the government and administration of

Tshekedi Khama as a young man.

justice . . .' Nonetheless, from 1936, Charles Arden Clarke, as Government Secretary and later as Resident Commissioner, consulted with Tswana leaders. In 1939 he sought Tshekedi's advice and established 'Tribal Treasuries' which allowed the chiefs to fund improvements in education, agriculture and the cattle industry. In 1940 the Ngwato joined the Native Advisory Council, which was renamed the African Advisory Council.

Sir Seretse Khama and the late President Jomo Kenyatta of Kenya. President Khama gave up his royal title, but he won the allegiance of the nation to lead Botswana into independence.

Further troubles burdened the Ngwato when the heir to the throne, Seretse Khama, married a white woman. This was seen by Tshekedi Khama as hostile to tribal tradition, and by the British as hostile to South African politics. Nonetheless, in 1949, the Ngwato *Kgotla* supported Seretse as the rightful chief. The British offered him a pension to renounce his title. He refused and was deprived of his chieftainship and exiled in 1952. Tshekedi was also exiled and the chieftainship suspended. Disorder plagued the Ngwato until Rasebolai, third in line to the succession, was allowed to rule with the title, 'African Authority'.

Tshekedi returned to the African Advisory Coun-

cil as the appointee of the Kwena chief, Kgari. He and Bathoen II there proposed the advancement of Bechuanaland towards self-government, but the British wished to avoid a conflict with the Union government. They did, however, form a Joint Advisory Council in 1951, bringing together the African and European councils. When the Joint Council met it also advocated a Legislative Council.

In the meantime, the Ngwato refused to discuss mineral rights within their land until Seretse and Tshekedi were returned to them. In 1956 the two men became reconciled and they became members of the reconstituted Ngwato Tribal Council. By 1959 the British had committed themselves to self-government for the High Commission Territories. In 1961 the Legislative Council came into being, and the Resident Commissioner became Queen's Commissioner in 1963. A year later the office of High Commissioner was abolished, and the territory moved more quickly towards independence, some months ahead of Lesotho.

For many reasons Botswana achieved its independence first. The Bechuanaland Protectorate appears to have matured its political consciousness by having numerous South African refugees living there. Prior to their coming politicians were drawn largely from the traditional chiefs. Tshekedi Khama and Seretse Khama took the lead. With the announcement of the founding of the Legislative Council in 1960, the first modern party emerged, the Bechuanaland People's Party. This organisation, led by K T Motsete, opposed the nomination of chiefs to the council and also opposed the biracial character of the constitution which gave white settlers separate representation.

Seretse Khama, acting as a private citizen, opposed the radical platform of the B P P by forming the Bechuanaland Democratic Party, based heavily on support from his own chiefdom. His problems with the British had led to his removal from chiefly office, but his return to politics as a private citizen helped him weld together the traditionalists and the political modernists. His opposition to the radical B P P also gained him support from the settlers. When constitutional talks resumed in 1963, his leadership led to the establishment of universal suffrage on a common roll. Whites had to participate in politics through the national parties. The chiefs were placated by the establishment of a House of Chiefs which could discuss their concerns before action would be taken by the Legislature.

When Prime Minister Verwoerd campaigned for the federation of the High Commission territories with South Africa, the Tswana backed the new constitution and it was swiftly implemented. Seretse Khama's Democratic Party won 28 of the 31 seats, and he became the first prime minister. The capital was moved to Gaborone within the new nation's borders, and independence was granted on 30 September 1966. The new nation adopted a republican constitution with Seretse Khama as president. Thus, in less than five years, the Protectorate rose from being a dependency of Britain to full independence within the British Commonwealth, with full membership in the United Nations and the Organisation of African Unity. South Africa accepted the results primarily because of the tact of the new president. Though Botswana has remained dependent upon South Africa economically, and has retained diplomatic relations with it, it has also taken an active role as a 'Front Line State' in the negotiations over the settlement of the Zimbabwe/Rhodesia and South West Africa/Namibia issues.

Thus the long era of political dependency on Britain ended for both Lesotho and Botswana in the same year. That period had permitted them both to escape being completely absorbed into the white-dominated nation beside them. It also allowed them slowly to gain the political tutelage which allowed them to emerge as separate national entities. Unfortunately, it also saw their economic underdevelopment, and their survival increasingly tied to the very nation from which they had so long struggled to remain free.

This historical summary of political developments among the Southern Sotho and Tswana must be viewed in the context of their social structures. The following chapters analyse them and their response to changing conditions.

6

The Political Community: From Tribe to Nation

COLIN MURRAY

Tribe and Clan

The present complex distribution of the Sotho–Tswana peoples reflects, firstly, historical processes of accretion and dispersion that took place as a result of the nineteenth-century wars; and, secondly, the large-scale appropriation of their lands by white settlers, out of which evolved the present boundaries between nation-states and the present division between 'white' areas and black reserves in South Africa. These processes have been described. They are a necessary background to understanding an ambiguity of reference, in practice, between the concepts of tribe and clan. Confusion often arises because members of one political community may describe themselves as all related; while those who acknowledge common descent may in some contexts claim to be a discrete political community.

The difference in principle is quite clear. As used in this book, the term tribe refers to the members of a political community defined by their allegiance to a chief who has authority over a given territory. The term clan refers to people who acknowledge common descent, in the sense that they venerate the same totem (*seboko*). Most totems are species of wild animals. Recognition of the same totem is not however a definitive criterion of common clanship, since some totems have been forgotten and others have been adopted.

The tension of meaning between tribe and clan arises out of the process by which old political communities broke up and new ones were formed. Succession disputes or the competition for resources on the highveld commonly led to conflict within the aristocracy and brought about the secession of one section of the tribe under a junior relative of the chief. The nineteenth-century wars also had the effect of scattering individual clans whose members sought refuge in different political communities. The consequence of these movements is that the ruling families of different tribes are often able to trace their genealogical connections; and people who venerate the same totem, i.e. belong to the same clan, are scattered throughout the highveld in many different tribes. Genealogical connections thus provide clues to the historical links between different communities. They also provide a contemporary framework within which political loyalties are articulated. Accounts of the same genealogies are often at variance with one another, so that the historian must be wary of literal use of them to reconstruct the past. The anthropologist regards them, rather, as 'charters' used to justify existing political arrangements. Those with long memories are sel-

dom disinterested in the contemporary implications of stories from the past.

The internal stratification of the main Tswana tribes reflected a characteristic pattern of political incorporation. The Ngwato political community, for example, comprised the following strata: 'royals' (*dikgosana*), descendants of the chiefs of the ruling family of the Ngwato clan; 'commoners' (*batlhanka*), also belonging to the Ngwato clan but including others who had long been absorbed by it; 'strangers' (*bafaladi*), members of alien or refugee communities who accepted Ngwato political domination; and, lastly, groups of servile status

fig. 13 *Rolong chiefdoms in African reserves (shaded areas) which were formerly part of the Mafeking administrative district in the Cape Province, and which now form the Molopo district and part of the Ditsobotla district of Bophutha Tswana. The map shows the African reserves before consolidation of the 'homeland'.*

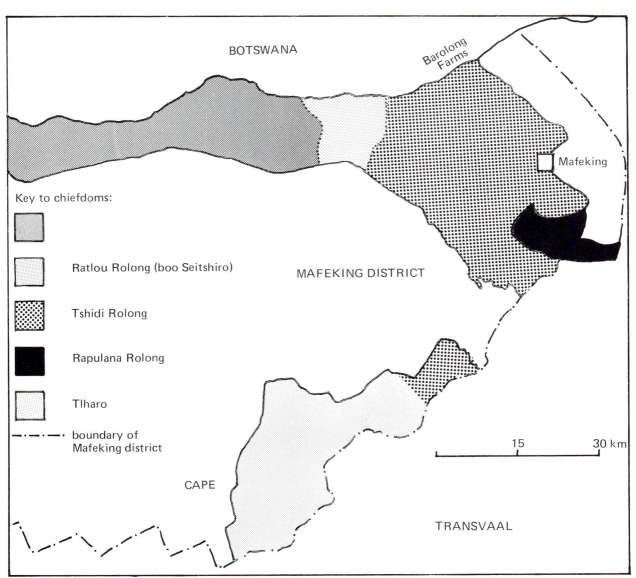

Dispersion: The Example of the Rolong

All Barolong acknowledge their descent from a common ancestor Morolong. They venerate two totems: iron (*tshipi*) and the kudu (*tholo*). But there has been no united Rolong political community since the latter half of the eighteenth century. There are four main branches of the Rolong 'nation', whose founders are all placed on the original Rolong genealogy—namely, Ratlou, Tshidi, Seleka and Rapulana, in that order of seniority. Only the last of these branches today remains a united chiefdom. The others have further sub-divided. The two sections of the Ratlou Rolong occupy areas of land along the northern and southern edges, respectively, of the Mafeking administrative district (see fig. 13). The Tshidi Rolong live in a block of land surrounding the 'white' town of Mafeking. Some of them occupy a part of this area known as the Barolong Farms, which lies across the Botswana border. The latter were in the anomalous position of being citizens of Botswana but of owing political allegiance to the South African chief of the Tshidi Rolong. In 1970 this anomaly was resolved through the appointment of the Tshidi Rolong's junior brother as independent chief of the Botswana section of the Tshidi Rolong, in effect creating a new political community.

The majority of the Seleka Rolong live in the isolated enclave of Thaba Nchu in the Orange Free State. But a small section of them is found in the Tati district of Botswana. The Rapulana Rolong occupy a small area immediately to the south of Mafeking. Most of the Rolong chiefdoms today are incorporated within the independent 'homeland' of BophuthaTswana. But, as may be expected from the processes of fission and fusion that are characteristic of Tswana history, not all Barolong clansmen live in Rolong political communities; while Rolong chiefdoms also incorporate non-Barolong.

known as *malata*, the majority of whom were Sarwa and Kgalagadi: they were hereditary servants attached to the chief and other wealthy or prominent men. Members of all these strata were politically linked to the tribal capital through their attachment to basic residential units known as wards (described in chapter 8), whose heads, either 'commoners' or 'strangers' and ranked accordingly, were directly subordinate to the chief. They were also economically linked to the capital through tribute relationships and the system known as *mafisa* by which cattle were loaned out to people without livestock. Residential patterns correlated with political status both in the capital itself and in the tribal territory as a whole. The capital was clearly divided into royal, commoner and 'stranger' wards, according to the political status of their founders, although the actual membership of most wards was mixed. Within the tribe as a whole, people related to the ruling family were concentrated in the capital; while communities of alien origin were often distributed in outlying settlements.

Thus people of the Ngwato clan, who venerate the duiker (*phuti*), are the politically dominant members of the Ngwato tribe of Botswana. In the 1930s, at the time Schapera conducted his research among them, the tribal population numbered just over 100 000. Only one-fifth of these people belonged to the Ngwato clan; about 23 per cent belonged to other Tswana clans; and there were a further 23 per cent Kalaka (Shona), 13 per cent Tswapong (Northern Sotho), 11 per cent Sarwa and 6 per cent Kgalagadi. In most other tribes, people of Tswana stock constituted a clear majority of the population.

The term tribe properly refers, then, to a political community defined by reference to its chief's jurisdiction. In this sense, Schapera wrote about the eight Tswana tribes of Botswana. The old Tribal Reserves which they occupied are shown in figure 14. According to the *South Africa Yearbook* of 1976 there are fifty-nine Tswana tribes in South Africa, although a special supplement of the *Financial Mail* in December 1977 described BophuthaTswana as a 'nation' of 76 tribes. The discrepancy probably reflects the staggered implementation of South African government legislation leading towards 'independence', in terms of which separate tribal authorities are officially constituted.

By contrast, the independent kingdom of Lesotho may be considered one political community on quite a different scale. All its citizens, who belong to many different clans but who collectively identify themselves as the Basotho of Moshoeshoe after the founder of the kingdom, owe ultimate allegiance to King Moshoeshoe II. This is also true of three communities which retained their own chiefs and, for a long time, semi-independent political status—the Tlokwa of the eastern mountains, the KgwaKgwa in the Butha Buthe district, and the Taung ba Moletsane in the south-west corner of the country. In Lesotho, therefore, the tribe is synonymous with the nation (*sechaba sa Basotho*).

With this partial exception, Sotho–Tswana tribes have not survived as independent political communities. They are all incorporated within modern nation–states. All three national governments have committed themselves, in varying degrees, to the retention of indigenous authorities. But subordination of the traditional political community has taken place in rather different ways in Lesotho, Botswana and the South African 'homelands'. The remainder of this chapter deals with each of them separately.

Lesotho: Too Many Chiefs?

In Lesotho every village or village section has a headman who belongs to the lowest stratum in the chiefly hierarchy. He may or may not be 'gazetted', i.e. officially recognised by the government, depending on the number of tax-payers for whom he is responsible. He is politically subordinate to the chief (*morena*) within whose area of jurisdiction his village lies. This chief in turn owes allegiance to one of twenty-two Principal and Ward chiefs who constitute the upper stratum of the chieftainship. Nineteen of these Principal and Ward chiefs are 'Sons of Moshoeshoe' in the sense that they belong to the senior descent lines of the dominant Kwena aristocracy (fig. 16). The other three chiefs represent communities of Tlokwa, KgwaKgwa and Taung respectively. The apex of the hierarchy is the present King Moshoeshoe II, the senior representative of the Sons of Moshoeshoe. The traditional prerogatives of his office are strictly circumscribed by the limitations inherent in his modern role of constitutional monarch.

The hierarchy of traditional authority is much more complex than this simple model would suggest. This is due to the historical quirks of the 'placing' system. Senior chiefs in the past used to 'place' their sons and other junior relatives in charge of sub-divisions of their territory. The widespread practice of polygyny meant that there were many junior sons and junior collaterals (brothers, cousins and their descendants) with political aspirations to be placed in this way. Each new placing created an additonal level in the hierarchy which the descendants of each incumbent expected to be maintained in perpetuity (see fig. 17). This worked in such a way as to consolidate the power of the Kwena aristocracy, at the expense of the chiefs and headmen of other clans. It also worked progressively in favour of descendants of the first 'house' of Moshoeshoe as against those belonging to junior lines of descent. But the placing system was consis-

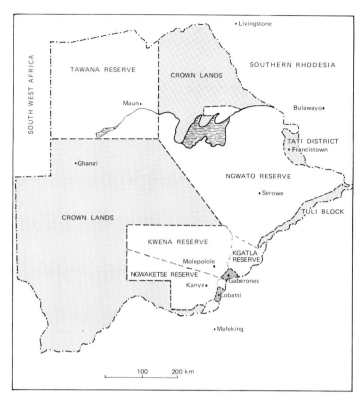

fig. 14   The Bechuanaland Protectorate in the 1930s, showing the principal Tribal Reserves.
fig. 15   The Kingdom of Lesotho.

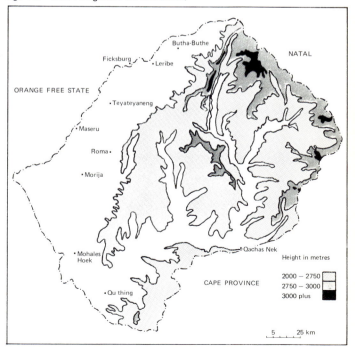

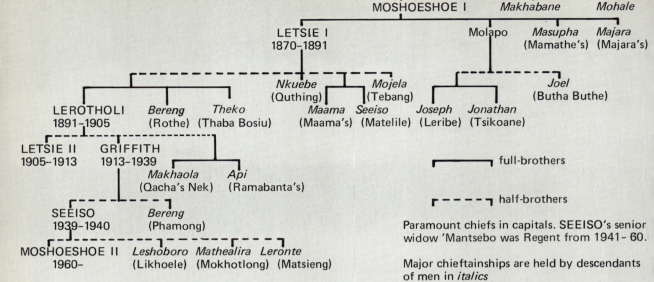

MOSHOESHOE I   *Makhabane*   *Mohale*

LETSIE I
1870–1891   Molapo   *Masupha*
(Mamathe's)   *Majara*
(Majara's)

Nkuebe
(Quthing)   *Mojela*
(Tebang)   *Joel*
(Butha Buthe)

LEROTHOLI
1891–1905   *Bereng*
(Rothe)   *Theko*
(Thaba Bosiu)   *Maama*
(Maama's)   *Seeiso*
(Matelile)   *Joseph*
(Leribe)   *Jonathan*
(Tsikoane)

LETSIE II   GRIFFITH
1905–1913   1913–1939

Makhaola
(Qacha's Nek)   *Api*
(Ramabanta's)

SEEISO   *Bereng*
1939–1940   (Phamong)

MOSHOESHOE II   *Leshoboro*   *Mathealira*   *Leronte*
1960–   (Likhoele)   (Mokhotlong)   (Matsieng)

full-brothers

half-brothers

Paramount chiefs in capitals. SEEISO's senior
widow 'Mantsebo was Regent from 1941–60.

Major chieftainships are held by descendants
of men in *italics*

*fig. 16   Nineteen out of the twenty-two major
chieftainships in Lesotho are held by descendants
of Moshoeshoe and of two of his brothers. Each incumbent of the paramountcy was able to 'place'
his own sons and brothers in senior positions, with
the result that twelve of these chieftainships are
held by members of the house of Letsie I alone.
Relative seniority within the house of Moshoeshoe
involves competitive principles of reckoning. Men
either look 'round about them' vis-à-vis the incumbent paramount, or they look 'backwards' vis-à-vis*
*the four cardinal lines of descent in Moshoeshoe's
first house — those of Letsie, Molapo, Masupha
and Majara. Ian Hamnett, a lawyer and anthropologist, has called these the* circumspective *and* retrospective *principles, respectively. He has explored
the tension between them in practice in his very interesting book* Chieftainship and Legitimacy. *There
is some doubt, for example, whether the second
chief in Lesotho is the junior brother of the present
King or the senior descendant of Molapo.*

tent only with an expanding polity. When there
were no new areas to settle, a new placing could only
be made at the expense of existing placings. In the
first decades of this century, under conditions of increasingly acute land shortage, the continuing proliferation of chiefs and sub-chiefs reached absurd
proportions. A member of the National Council remarked in the early 1930s that 'there are now as
many chiefs in Basutoland as there are stars in the
heavens'.

Reforms were therefore introduced in 1938. Their
effect was to freeze the system to some extent and to
curtail the discretion of chiefs in making subordinate
appointments. From that date, every placing had to
be approved by the central government and an
official gazette of recognised chiefs and headmen
was established. Steps were taken simultaneously to
reduce the number of chiefs' courts, whose operation was cumbersome and inefficient, and thereby to
curtail the judicial functions of chiefs. When the
Basuto National Treasury was set up in 1946, the
recognised chiefs were paid salaries or tax gratuities,
partly in compensation for their loss of income from
court fines and stray livestock.

These reforms induced widespread insecurity in
the lower levels of the chiefly hierarchy. In the first
place, senior chiefs were no longer able to
accommodate the political aspirations of junior
kinsmen. And the establishment of an official
gazette led to a scramble for recognition in which
many headmen were displaced altogether, at the
whim of some senior chiefs acting with the
administration. In the second place, the tax gratuities received by those who were gazetted were
quite arbitrarily assessed, and did not compensate
them for loss of revenue. Many politically sensitive
Basotho realised that the substitution of one form of
income for the other would undermine the account-
ability of chiefs and headmen to their subjects which
was expressed in the Sotho–Tswana proverb, 'a
chief is a chief through the people'. The wave of
'medicine' (*diretlo*) murders that swept Basutoland
in the late 1940s was attributed largely to the insecurity induced by the reforms. Lesser chiefs in-

voked sinister ways of resisting their official eclipse.

Constitutional developments in Basutoland, the circumstances of its emergence as the independent state of Lesotho in 1966 and its political difficulties since that year were described in chapter 5. Suffice it to say here that both the long period of British over-rule and the short period of self-government since 1966 have been characterised by a dualism of power and administrative competence between the traditional hierarchy of chiefs and the central government. The power of the chiefs, as such, has been steadily eroded in recent years, and replaced by that of district administrations. But many of the new élite are recruited from the ranks of the old. Members of the senior Kwena lineage are disproportionately represented in the government and civil service.

The chiefs retain a formal role in the transmission of executive authority between central government and people at the local level. The public gathering or *pitso* convened by a chief at the appropriate level in the hierarchy remains the proper instrument of all official communication, though it is often clumsy and inefficient in practice. Disputes, tax matters, court summons and statutory requirements of all kinds must pass through the formal channels of the hierarchy irrespective of individual chiefs' competence or otherwise in particular matters. Subjected to conflicting pressures from above and below, many chiefs prefer the least offensive course of action and relapse into inertia. In view of this it is perhaps surprising that the Basotho today retain a strong respect for and loyalty towards the chieftainship. The institution embodies a history of which they are justly proud.

The most politically sensitive aspect of the chief's remaining prerogatives is the right to administer titles to arable land. The principle that all land is vested in the nation is fundamental to concepts of land tenure in Lesotho. A chief holds *administrative* title to land in the area of his jurisdiction. He is responsible for allocating arable lands in an equitable manner to those of his subjects—married male taxpayers—who are qualified to exercise *usufructuary* title to land: that is, the right to cultivate and dispose of the product. Such title is not formally heritable.

Under conditions of acute population pressure and declining yields, reform of the land tenure system is one of Lesotho's most intractable problems. Opposition to reform comes not merely from the chiefs who, probably realistically, fear the loss of their last substantial prerogative, but also from commoners, who seldom see any justification for adopting an alternative to a system which, despite its

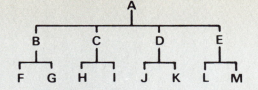

Stage 1: original structure.

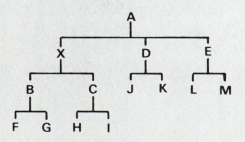

Stage 2: after the placing of X over B and C.

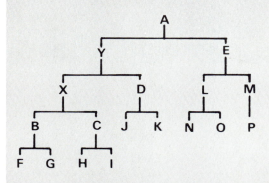

Stage 3: after the placing of Y over X and D.

fig. 17 *The complex effects of the placing system. By the time stage 3 has been reached, F, G, H and I have been reduced to headman status. Their sons will certainly be commoners.*

apparently communal nature, is defined essentially in terms of familiar individual rights. Since independence in 1966 there have been three major pieces of legislation affecting the administration of arable land in Lesotho, and therefore the rights of chiefs. Provision was made in 1967 for the election of a Land Committee to advise each area chief on the administration of land, and in 1973 for a Development Committee whose responsibilities were somewhat more broadly defined. The effective operation of these committees has often been stifled by party political factionalism at the village level. During 1979 Chief Leabua Jonathan's government passed legislation for more radical reform of the land tenure system. This is a measure of the scale of the agricultural crisis, and also perhaps of the government's

A Migrant Worker

Malibo, born in 1933, has worked for twenty-five years at the South African plant for extraction of oil from coal at Sasolburg in the Orange Free State. His wife and family remain behind at his village home in Lesotho. He comes home for fleeting visits four or five times a year, and stays for several weeks at Christmas. Otherwise he never sees his family. His children have grown up in his absence. Here he is seen on twenty-four-hour leave with his second daughter, Palesa, and his youngest son. Below, his elderly and infirm father Mafa, a widower, with his grandson.

94

A Village Headman

Semahla was born in 1914 and died in 1978. During his later years he was ungazetted (unofficial) village headman of Pitse's Nek, in northern Lesotho, and was widely respected for his judicial expertise and political sensitivity. As senior resident member of the Sia family, which first settled at Pitse's Nek before the Gun War of 1880, he had inherited the position of principal adviser to the Kwena chief of the area. Semahla had previously spent most of his adult life working at a clothing factory in the Transvaal, and he had established the right to reside with his family in Natalspruit, Germiston, under Section 10 (1) of the Black (Urban Areas) Consolidation Act of 1945 as amended. Semahla's two sons and one daughter are all married and permanently resident in South Africa. His widow lives in Pitse's Nek with one of her grandchildren. She depends entirely on remittance from her sons.

Below left: A chieftainess in court session at Gabane in Botswana.
Below right: A court case in the village of an area chief in Lesotho.

renewed confidence after years of prevarication over the issue. The law provides for long-term leases of urban and rural land for residence, various classes of business, and charitable and public uses. It also provides for licences to be issued to work agricultural land. The law will be administered by the local Land Committees, with the chief as chairman holding one vote. It is expected to take many years to implement the scheme because of the costs and technical expertise involved in surveying and recording all titles. Urban residential and business land will be registered first, followed by agricultural land proposed by the Minister of Agriculture as 'select agricultural areas'. Other rural areas will not be included for several years. The title to land will remain with the nation, but the licences and leases will be heritable over specified periods—for example 90 years for individual residences.

Botswana:
The Eclipse of Traditional Authority

The main Tswana tribes of Botswana were remarkable for the concentration of power and wealth in the hands of their chiefs. Traditionally, the chief (*kgosi*) was the ultimate source of all authority. He embodied the material and spiritual welfare of his people. As custodian of the land, he controlled its distribution. The prerogatives of his office—tribute, court fines, his command of labour and regulation of grazing—enabled him to accumulate vast numbers of livestock. Schapera reports that in 1932 the Kgatla chief owned 'about 5 500 head of cattle, one-seventh of the tribe's total holding'. He was also receiving annually 1 200 bags of sorghum from his tribute fields, 30 head of cattle in stray stock and from 20 to 40 head of cattle in court fines.

Subject to the advice of his counsellors, the chief decided questions of public policy, introduced legislation and judged all serious crimes and disputes. He regulated the sowing and harvesting of crops. He was responsible for making rain on behalf of the tribe. The British administration left tribal procedures largely intact, except that they gave official support to the chiefs when it was deemed necessary to maintain public order. Many Tswana and administrative officials felt that this enabled some chiefs to abuse their power, since the people no longer had effective recourse to the traditional sanctions of removal of an unsatisfactory chief from office or of moving themselves out of his area of jurisdiction. In one commentator's view, 'the whole 80 years of British rule up to 1965 can be regarded as a period of chiefly autocracy intensified and corrupted by Brit-

ish overrule'.

This may be an extreme view. But there is no doubt that the chiefs remained the most powerful forces in local government until 1965. In that year, with independence imminent, elected District Councils were established. A series of subsequent legislation steadily eroded the chiefs' authority. For example, responsibility for administering and registering title to land was from 1968 vested exclusively in Land Boards, under the control of the District Council. The chief is himself an *ex officio* member of the board, but the new arrangements have inevitably qualified his pre-eminence. Similarly, the district administrations have also assumed responsibility for supervising local development initiatives, through Development Committees elected at village level. This has led to some conflict with chiefs who oppose what they regard as the subversion of their traditional prerogatives. Some office-holders retain considerable influence through their manipulation of the new channels. In general, however, competition between chiefs and representatives of the educated élite in the district administrations remains a major source of conflict.

In the interests of developing a national as opposed to a tribal political consciousness, the government has sought to replace the power of the

chieftainship with that of representative bodies elected on party political lines. If chiefs wish to participate in national politics they must first relinquish their office. In 1970, frustrated by the erosion of chiefly power, the Ngwaketse chief Bathoen II resigned his hereditary office in order to contest the election as leader of the opposition Botswana National Front. He defeated the incumbent Vice-President Quett Masire. This illustrates the strong hold that chiefs retain on the loyalty of their people. The President himself, Seretse Khama, is aware that much of his popular support derives from his traditional position as head of the Ngwato ruling house. Thus the polarisation of tribal and national sources of authority has potentially ominous consequences for the political stability of Botswana.

Another important trend has been observed in some Tswana areas, which is partly related to the decline in chiefs' authority. An increasing proportion of the population is settled at the outlying arable 'lands' rather than concentrated in the villages. The Tswana are well known for their traditionally large settlements. But this concentrated settlement pattern has always been associated with seasonal movement between the village (July to October) and the lands (November to June). Wealthy cattle-owners also had to establish a third base, a cattle-post. For

A member of Lesotho's paramilitary defence force, the Police Mobile Unit, plays a home-made herdboy's instrument in an informal moment during the opening of the Thaba Tseka district headquarters in the mountains of Lesotho in March 1980.

political reasons, chiefs actively resisted the tendency for some of their subjects to remain at their lands throughout the year. But there is considerable recent evidence—for example, an increasing number of new, relatively small settlements—that a higher proportion of people than in the past now live permanently at their lands and cattle posts.

This trend reflects the decline of chiefs' centralised authority; the increasing scarcity of arable land; and the greater distances, and consequent transport costs, involved in seasonal movement. The provision of permanent water supplies in some areas may have facilitated the process of dispersion. On the other hand, expansion outwards may be officially discouraged in future because it is easier for the government to provide educational, health and welfare services to a concentrated than to a dispersed population. The tribal capitals have expanded in population owing to the development of government infrastructure and associated employment opportunities.

fig. 18 The Botswana government stresses the importance of full consultation of the people in planning and carrying out development plans. This drawing is from a booklet in Setswana and English which was widely distributed in order to explain the purpose of the National Migration Study conducted in 1978 and 1979.

Thus there are various different population movements taking place in Botswana. It is not easy to assess the magnitude of the trends in the country as a whole because of difficulties in comparing the 1964 and 1971 census results. In particular, owing to the pattern of seasonal movement, it is unknown what proportion of people in 1964 were actually resident in the villages where they were registered as politically affiliated. It is hoped that a National Migration Study conducted in 1978 and 1979 will provide some of the answers.

The 'Homelands': Jigsaws that Do Not Fit

Two-thirds of the Sotho–Tswana as defined in this book come from the Republic of South Africa but nominally belong, in terms of South African government policy, to the 'homelands' of BophuthaTswana and QwaQwa. What are the consequences for them of the implementation of this policy?

The policy is explicitly committed to working through indigenous authorities. But the tribal chiefs are merely part of an imposed administrative superstructure that has no popular legitimacy. The anthropologist John Comaroff has argued, on the basis of his study of the Tshidi Rolong chiefdom near Mafeking, that the effect of the policy in practice has been to eliminate the political processes—of popular consultation and of factional competition for office—that gave the institution of chieftainship its vitality and its central importance. Thus the policy of separate development has retained the *form* of chieftainship but profoundly altered its *substance*.

The key to understanding the consequences of the policy for the South African Tswana and Southern Sotho therefore lies in an investigation of the administrative superstructure itself. The most devastating aspects of the policy in practice are those relating to citizenship, land and the compulsory resettlement of the African population on a massive scale. Here the two sets of figures to which we referred in chapter 1 are directly relevant. They help us to understand why Pretoria's grand design for ethnic purity is a tragedy and a gross injustice for hundreds of thousands of people.

In 1976 there were over two million Tswana of South African origin (see fig. 5). But only 736 000 of them (35 per cent) were resident in their 'homeland' of BophuthaTswana. The remaining 65 per cent comprised a small number of temporary migrants normally domiciled in the 'homeland', and a very large number of Tswana who had no connection with it and were permanently domiciled elsewhere. Yet, in terms of the Status of BophuthaTswana Act of 1977, all of these people became 'nationals' of BophuthaTswana on the attainment of 'independence' on 6 December 1977, and all of them automatically lost their South African citizenship. The Act is both sufficiently vague and sufficiently comprehensive in its provisions to allow effective sole discretion to the South African government in determining who is and who is not a Tswana citizen in this sense. Apart from criteria of birth or residence in BophuthaTswana, these provisions include persons who speak a language used by members of any tribe which forms part of the population of the 'homeland'; and persons who are related to any member of that population, or who have identified themselves with any part of that population, or who have culturally or otherwise associated with any member of part of that population.

Tswana resident in 'white' South Africa bitterly resent the unilateral deprivation of their South African citizenship and the implied threat to their right to live and work in the 'white' areas. The correspondence columns of the African newspaper *The World* during 1977 were filled with letters expressing anger over what was perceived as a fundamental injustice. With independence for BothuthaTswana imminent in December 1977, urban Tswana were not consoled by a ministerial statement that the existing rights of Tswana in 'white' areas would not be forfeited, with the exception of their citizenship. Ironically, the minister had already given an assurance that preferential treatment in employment contracts, housing and other matters would be given to Africans who 'sought a healthy relationship' with their 'homelands'. Co-operate in your compulsory alienation, he seemed to be saying, in order to protect your interests in a foreign country.

Much of the anger was directed against Chief Minister Lucas Mangope for his readiness to initiate independence despite failure to resolve the two major issues of citizenship and land consolidation. Despite strongly worded public statements during 1977 Mangope could not soften the South African government's attitude on either issue. It emerged that the 1975 consolidation proposals, by which BophuthaTswana would consist of six scattered fragments (see figs. 19 and 20), represented the 'final' limits of Pretoria's willingness to negotiate. A feature article in the *Rand Daily Mail* of March 1977 was headed 'The jig-saw that won't fit'.

The rationalisation programme outlined in the 1975 consolidation proposals has involved the forcible removal of vast numbers of people in order to excise 'black spots' from 'white' South Africa and to remove black tenant farmers and squatters from white-owned land. Even before these plans were announced South African officials admitted that as many as half a million people had been subjected to forced removal in this way, in the process of creating the 'homeland'. During the year April 1976 to

A Short Guide to the Politics of Ethnic Citizenship

The ethnic population associated with a particular 'homeland' does not necessarily coincide with its actual population. There are two aspects to this lack of 'fit': particular ethnic populations are found in 'white' areas as well as homelands, and some homelands have ethnic minorities nominally associated with other homelands.

The diagram gives a schematic representation of this lack of fit for any one homeland, H. (The term 'domicile' includes de facto residents and absent migrants.) The population categories in the numbered boxes may be described as follows:

1. Some members of the ethnic population nominally associated with H are domiciled in 'white' South Africa, and may have no connection with H.

2. Other members associated with H are domiciled in homelands other than H, and may likewise have no contact with H.

3. Some members associated with H are actually domiciled there.

4. However, some of the population of H belongs to other ethnic populations than the one associated with it.

Thus people in categories 2 and 4 belong to ethnic categories other than the one officially associated with the homeland in which they are domiciled. They experience an acute dilemma. Either they can attempt to secede and identify with another homeland, in which case they risk forced removal; or they can accept citizenship of the homeland, in which case they may be discriminated against in terms of jobs, services, etc.

The diagram helps to explain the apparent resurgence of 'tribalism' in the homelands, as a result of the presence of ethnic minorities whose future political status is uncertain.

The populations with which we are concerned may be classified both by (a) ethnic identity and by (b) place of domicile.

(a) ethnic identity	members of the ethnic population officially associated with H			members of other ethnic populations
POPULATION	1	2	3	4
(b) domicile	'white' South Africa	other homelands	H	

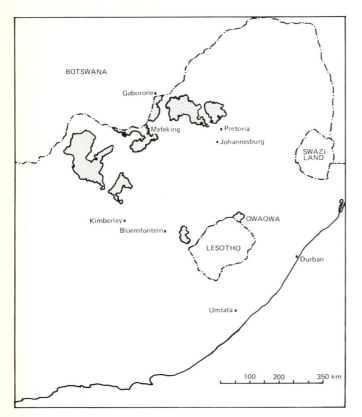

in the area than the census had shown.

These non-Tswana minorities in Bophutha-Tswana were alarmed by Chief Mangope's strident expression of Tswana nationalism in respect of business facilities, jobs and social services. Their anxiety as to their future was reflected in a series of incidents during 1976 and 1977. Firstly, Chieftainess Ester Kekana and 60 000 Ndebele followers objected to the compulsory use of the Tswana language in their schools and proposed instead to join the North Sotho 'homeland' of Lebowa. They had been using the Pedi language, since no books were available in Ndebele. Secondly, many residents of the Winterveld, a vast sprawling slum near the homeland towns of Mabopane and Ga-Rankuwa, north of Pretoria, registered a request to break away from Bophutha Tswana. During 1978 many people in this area were harrassed by Bophutha Tswana police, on grounds of being illegal squatters. Thirdly, three Ndebele chiefs near Hammanskraal, also north of Pretoria, formed a separate regional authority with the intention of joining the Ndebele Territorial Authority, which was to become the tenth 'homeland'. Later the Kekana faction also chose to join this Authority. At the end of 1978 12 000 Ndebele at Majaneng who wished to join the new Authority were given an ultimatum either to take out Bophutha Tswana citizenship by February 1979 or to leave the territory. They were intimidated by Chief Mangope's threats to stop the payment of pensions and teachers' salaries and to prevent Ndebele from being employed in the industrial centre of Babelegi. In the face of these threats the Ndebele withdrew their opposition. There remain fears that they will effectively be second-class citizens in Bophutha Tswana.

During April and May 1977, at Maboloka in Bophutha Tswana, near the town of Brits, a series of violent clashes took place in a community of Southern Sotho known as Bataung ba Maboloka. About twenty deaths resulted from fighting between supporters of Chief Philemon Tsajoa, a member of the Bophutha Tswana legislative assembly, and supporters of his uncle Mr Solomon Lyon, who did not recognise the former's leadership. Ostensibly the dispute concerned the Zion Apostolic Faith Church's 4 800 morgen of land in Maboloka which

March 1977 some 17 000 people were removed from the Transvaal and the Cape Province into Bophutha Tswana. And the process continues. All these people were deprived of their homes, many also of their livelihoods. Many have been dumped in barren wastelands without adequate water, shelter, food or work. They live in squalor, hunger and degradation. The human misery caused by such removals is recorded in Cosmas Desmond's book *The Discarded People*.

We have so far looked at only one aspect of the problem of citizenship: the question of the status of Tswana who live and work outside the 'homeland'. Another extremely important aspect is the status of ethnic minorities within the homeland itself. In addition to the 736 000 Tswana resident in Bophutha Tswana in 1976, there were some 300 000 people of non-Tswana origin. In other words, 41 per cent of the *de facto* population of the homeland were 'foreigners' in terms of government policy. This figure is likely to be an under-estimate. In 1975 a semi-official publication acknowledged that, as a result of the considerable migration of people from other 'homelands' to the districts north of Pretoria, there were probably far more non-Tswana residents

BOTSWANA

Mafeking

TRANSVAAL

Rustenburg■

Babelegi■

Brits
Ga-Rankuwa
Rosslyn■
Pretoria■

Johannesburg

■Kroonstad

■Welkom

ORANGE FREE STATE

■Kimberley

Bloemfontein■

Thaba Nchu

LESOTHO

Mr Lyon had bought on behalf of the Southern Sotho people, including the Tsajoa family. It emerged that the real issue between them was over independence. Chief Tsajoa's supporters wished to remain within BophuthaTswana; while those of Mr Lyon wished to secede and to join Basotho QwaQwa. Lyon was deported to Lesotho following charges of being a foreign black. Tsajoa was arrested in May and charged with murder. A sectarian conflict was also involved. Some of the violence took the form of a confrontation between the Zion Apostolic Faith Mission Church, supporting Lyon, and the Zion Christian Church, supporting Tsajoa. Press reports in May 1977 described Maboloka as a desolate and unhappy place.

BophuthaTswana is not the only 'jig-saw that won't fit'. In 1976 there were more than one and a half million Southern Sotho (or Seshoeshoe, in official parlance) of South African origin (see fig. 5). In terms of official policy, all belong to their 'homeland' of Basotho QwaQwa—a tiny, barren and mountainous area (see fig. 21) which is bounded

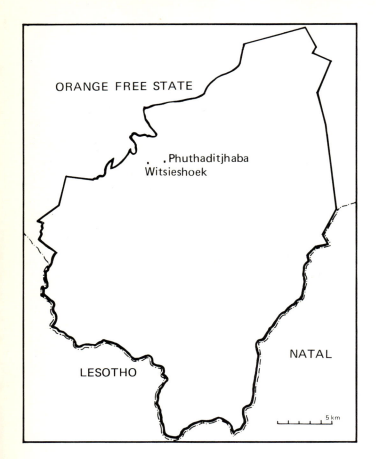

fig. 21 Basotho QwaQwa. Nestling beneath the towering peaks of the Drakensberg, the 'homeland' is barren and grossly over-crowded, with a population density exceeding 1 000 persons per 2,5 square kilometres.

by Lesotho to the south and west, Natal to the east, and the Orange Free State to the north. Chief Minister Kenneth Mopeli has rejected the option of independence but said in 1978 that it might be considered if the size of the homeland were increased to half of the Orange Free State. This aspiration is not taken seriously by the South African government. The homeland is appallingly over-crowded.

There are few reliable figures for the *de facto* population of Basotho QwaQwa, which was recorded as 24 000 in the 1970 census. At that time this figure represented less than 2 per cent of its nominal citizens or *de jure* population. The *de facto* population had risen to an estimated 96 000 by 1976. But press reports in early 1977 suggested an even higher figure of 180 000, which was accepted as more realistic. This rapid rise has been attributed to a

large-scale exodus from the Orange Free State of poorly-paid farm labourers and their families. Attracted by substantial increases in mining wages during the 1970s, these labourers wished to take up mine contracts, but they could not leave their families on the farms if they no longer worked there themselves. Therefore they moved to the homeland. Forced removals of black labour tenants and squatters have also contributed to the mass influx into QwaQwa, as employment on the white farms has steadily declined with increasing mechanisation. The *de facto* population of QwaQwa by 1980 was estimated to be 300 000.

Many more Southern Sotho 'nationals' live in other homelands than their own. In 1970, for example, there were more than 100 000 in the Transkei and approximately 27 000 in BophuthaTswana. The QwaQwa cabinet declared Transkei Independence Day in October 1976 as a day of mourning for many thousands of Southern Sotho of the Herschel and Maluti districts who were not consulted about their future status and feared oppression by the Xhosa majority. The Southern Sotho majority resident in the BophuthaTswana enclave of Thaba Nchu, otherwise occupied by Seleka Rolong, also expressed their wish to join the QwaQwa homeland. Inter-tribal conflict flared over the issue of whether BophuthaTswana should cede some land to QwaQwa to accommodate the Southern Sotho of Thaba Nchu. In May 1978 large numbers of Sotho at Thaba Nchu were arrested by BophuthaTswana police on charges of illegal squatting. It was also alleged that the BophuthaTswana authorities were forcing Southern-Sotho-speaking children to be educated in the medium of Tswana, thus violating an agreement between the two 'homelands'.

These incidents represent an apparent resurgence of 'tribalism'. In fact they reflect the anomalies and contradictions of the South African government's own policy. Tribalism cannot be explained simply as a survival of ethnic rivalries from the wars of the nineteenth century. It is, instead, a result of official

102

attempts to put large square pegs into small round holes. Conflicts which take the form of ethnic rivalries arise directly out of the citizenship issue and the political uncertainties generated by it. Far from constituting a logical expression of 'national' identities, as the *South Africa Yearbook* claims, the Citizenship Act has nurtured the seeds of violent confrontation. The official motto of each 'homeland' is a variation on the theme 'Unity is Strength', but the policy of separate development is a hollow mockery of this. This is why many Africans regard it as a fraudulent attempt to divide and rule, to deprive black people of basic political rights in the country of their birth. This is why, also, the independence of the Transkei, BophuthaTswana and Venda is not internationally recognised.

Internally, the policy exposes and exacerbates conflict along tribal lines within the rural constituencies of the homeland leaders. Externally, it exposes what might be termed a credibility gap between the homeland leaders and their urban constituents—those who live and work in 'white' areas but who stand to lose their South African citizenship on the attainment of 'independence'. Their interests lie in full political, economic and social participation in South Africa as a whole. These are the contradictions which the homeland leaders face in striving to make sense of their 'sovereign independence'. There are no signs of their resolving them. On the contrary, to the extent that Mangope and others pursue policies of ethnic nationalism, they may be seen as playing the game the South African government's way. For the majority of the South African Tswana and Southern Sotho, who are the pawns in that game, the grim reality is a sharpening of political and economic oppression.

From Kromdraai to Onverwacht: South Africa's Internal Refugees

During the 1970s, a large settlement of 'squatters' developed to the north of the railway station at Thaba Nchu in the Orange Free State (see fig. 20). Because of its historical association with the Seleka Rolong, a branch of the Tswana, Thaba Nchu itself is an enclave of BophuthaTswana, but the population of the Orange Free State is predominantly Southern Sotho.

The area where the squatters settled became known as Kromdraai. It had been demarcated as grazing land, but thousands of people moved there apparently because plots had been fraudulently 'sold' to them or because they had been led to believe stands would be allocated to them. According to a press report, 'It is the rejected who come to Kromdraai—those who can no longer work, those who cannot 'fix up their passes'—from the small dorps and farms all over the Free State. The authorities of Thaba Nchu (in BophuthaTswana) do not want them and say they must go to their own place—QwaQwa. But QwaQwa is far away and overcrowded already . . .' By 1978, the population of Kromdraai was estimated to be more than 38 000. They were living in poverty and squalor, in shacks roughly constructed from mud bricks or corrugated sheeting.

The issue developed into a confrontation between politicians of BophuthaTswana and QwaQwa respectively. One indignant correspondent, presumably Rolong, wrote from Welkom to the Bloemfontein *Friend* in 1976: 'We find today that Sotho people who never lived in Thaba Nchu before go to Thaba Nchu when they are no longer wanted by their White masters on the farms or are expelled from the urban areas. Why don't they go to QwaQwa? Must Thaba Nchu take more than it can accommodate? For those who are refused permission to stay and those who are not satisfied the best thing is to go. We simply cannot cater for people who are not our subjects.' Some people from Kromdraai were indeed removed to QwaQwa. The QwaQwa Minister of Education complained that Southern Sotho in Thaba Nchu were discriminated against in respect of work permits, residence rights and language of instruction in the schools. In turn, he was accused of interfering in the affairs of BophuthaTswana. The squatters of Kromdraai were regularly harassed by the BophuthaTswana police as illegal 'foreigners'.

Early in 1979, a land swap was arranged by which 25 000 hectares of compulsorily purchased land in the Free State would be used both to enlarge the Thaba Nchu enclave and to create a Southern Sotho city to the west of it, which would become another section of QwaQwa. Removal of the Kromdraai squatters to the area known as Onverwacht began in May 1979 and was completed by December of the same year. People were provided with numbered toilet stands and had to build their own accommodation from whatever materials they were able to obtain. Most of the shacks are haphazardly constructed from corrugated sheeting and they are extremely hot in summer and bitterly cold in winter. People were also forcibly removed from other areas of Thaba Nchu; and they poured in to Onverwacht from the farms and the small towns of the Free State. Within a year, the new settlement of shacks and tents, which became known as Botshabelo, the Place of Refuge, stretched in every direction almost as far as the eye could see. Most families are grossly overcrowded. Some men commute daily to work in Bloemfontein. Very many others are unemployed. The daily necessities of life are expensive. Nevertheless, people express some relief because they are no longer subject to arbitrary arrest and intimidation by the BophuthaTswana authorities.

Meanwhile, Kromdraai has reverted to bare hillside, scrub and grazing. Only the graveyard remains, and rusting upturned vehicles are scattered across the veld.

7

Kinship: Continuity and Change

COLIN MURRAY

The Structure of Small Communities

In 1934 and 1935 Schapera pioneered a method of describing the residential structure of the Tswana ward, the minimal political community. He chose two wards for the purpose: one in Mochudi, the principal settlement of the Kgatla tribe; the other in Serowe, the principal settlement of the Ngwato tribe. These wards had 106 and 95 inhabitants respectively. Both wards exhibited a characteristic horse-shoe or roughly circular shape, with homesteads arranged around a common cattle-pen and the ward meeting-place (*kgotla*) where cases were discussed.

Twelve out of the sixteen household heads of Rampedi ward, in Mochudi, belonged to segments of an agnatic 'core' lineage: that is, they were all related in the male line to the founder of the ward, one of the senior men who accompanied Chief Kgamanyane in 1871 when the Kgatla migrated from the Transvaal and established a settlement in Mochudi. Contrary to expressed Tswana norms, three out of those twelve were women. Three of the four remaining household heads were related to the core lineage in other ways. One had been adopted by his mother's brother as a child; two were men who had married women belonging to the core lineage and had established their homesteads, again contrary to the norm, in the ward of their wives. The fourth was a 'stranger'. Mean household size was 6,6 persons. But the households varied considerably in size and composition: they included basic nuclear families, single-parent families, families with children from various marriages, and more complex three-generation families.

Schapera used these studies to establish the characteristic structure of the Tswana ward. It contains households belonging to segments of one or more agnatic lineages, whose constituent families are either closely related to the headman or otherwise related. There may also be 'strangers' who, over time, establish ties of kinship and marriage with the original ward members. By definition the ward is a political unit, subordinate to the chief. Yet, at this level as at the tribal level, a tension may be observed between the identity of the ward in this sense and the identity of ward members in kinship terms. Even non-related ward members may speak of them-

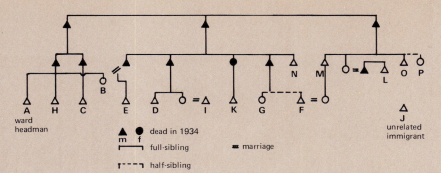

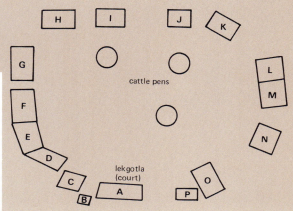

fig. 22 Rampedi ward in the Kgatla capital of Mochudi, 1934, showing the lay-out of homesteads and the genealogical relationships between household heads.

selves in terms which suggest to outsiders that they are related. The structure of the ward at any given time reflects the history of its emergence as a political unit and also the processes of the developmental cycle—the expansion, splitting and contraction of households—which take place within its constituent families over time.

The contemporary interest of Schapera's investigations lies in two points. Firstly, he established a method by which such basic units of social structure could be compared with those characteristic of other Southern African peoples. The method was applied, for example, in Basutoland in the 1940s by Hugh Ashton and Vernon Sheddick, who conducted separate surveys of the composition of small communities. Secondly, Schapera provided a base-line of reliable information on particular communities from which subsequent developments could be traced in detail. A time-depth of this sort is invaluable but very seldom available to anthropologists. The opportunity to trace subsequent developments in this case was taken up by Simon Roberts, in the course of an investigation of Tswana customary law. He carried out a second survey of the Mochudi ward in 1973, nearly forty years after Schapera's original work.

Roberts found that Rampedi ward had expanded considerably in size. In 1973 there were thirty-three households, with a population of approximately 300 people. No fewer than twenty-six household heads, of whom two were women, belonged to the same agnatic core lineage. Its original structure was still discernible through the relationships between these household heads, and a number of marriages had taken place between different branches of this large family. The comparison showed that most men still set up homesteads in their own ward; that women move to their husband's ward on marriage; and that many marriages are still contracted locally. These observations led to the conclusion that 'the basic agnatic character of the grouping has proved durable over time'.

Yet Roberts also found the following features: firstly, a high rate of individual mobility, in the sense that many people who nominally belonged to the ward were absent, mostly as temporary labour migrants to South Africa—so that a survey undertaken at a slightly different time would have revealed a somewhat different resident population; secondly, a high proportion of adult women (40 out of 73) who had never married; and, thirdly, a high proportion of children (65 out of 162) born to such women. Schapera had found in 1934 that four out of six unmarried women (out of a total of 26 women of marriageable age) had borne illegitimate children. He regarded this as a 'striking illustration of the extent to which premarital sexual relations are practised'. Much more striking to the modern observer is the substantial increase between the years 1934 and 1973 both in the number of unmarried women and in the number of children born to such women.

This trend is also obvious elsewhere in the periphery. It is reflected in a form of household com-

A midday break in the fields from the exhausting work of threshing wheat: a scene in the foothills.

position that is reported to be very common in other parts of Botswana, in Lesotho and in Bophutha-Tswana: the three-generation household which includes a daughter or daughters with children. For example, 75 out of a sample of 150 households in Lesotho contained three or more generations, which gives an indication of the extent to which children are brought up in the households of their grandparents. More particularly, more than half of the linking parents in the middle generation were women; less than half were men. This reflects the fact that while men usually establish independent households on marriage, unmarried women, or women who return to their own homes following marital failure, seldom set up independent households. They remain within the household of their parents or widowed mother, but may continue to bear children. The frequency of 'matrifocal' households of this kind reflects the instability of conjugal relationships and even, from the point of view of some women, their redundancy.

The nuclear family form (a man, his wife and their children) still embodies the traditional aspiration of a married couple to 'build their own house', that is to establish an independent household. But there is little point in identifying the nuclear family as the basic unit of analysis in circumstances where thousands of husbands and wives are forced to live apart; where conjugal relationships are insecure and unstable; where many women have to find their own livelihood, either by going out as migrants themselves, or through activities such as beer-brewing in the informal sector; where many households are headed by widows or managed by women in their husbands' absence; and where many children are reared by their grandparents because their mothers or their parents are absent on migrant labour. A contradiction inheres in the attempt to maintain nuclear-family integrity under these circumstances. A man's absence as a migrant labourer is a condition of his family's survival. But his absence also undermines the conjugal stability from which his family derives its identity.

A survey of 73 households in one village in northern Lesotho gives some indication of the demographic consequences of oscillating migration (see fig. 23). In October 1974, when the survey was carried out, the *de facto* population of the village—those people actually present—was 294. The *de jure* population—*de facto* residents plus absentees—was 361. Mean *de jure* household size was 4,95 persons and mean *de facto* household size was 4,03 persons. Thus nearly one in five household members was absent. However, the mean figures obscure two distinct modes, at two and six persons, in the frequency distribution of *de jure* household sizes; and also the uneven distribution between households of absentees—almost all migrant workers in South Africa. Two-thirds of the *de jure* households contained one or more paid employees, defined in a sense that includes contract miners temporarily 'resting' at home. The remaining third of households had no direct access to a wage income. There were 42 male household heads, of whom 20 were absent; and 31 female household heads. Thus women were effective household managers in 51 out of 73 households. Further, 46 of the households had no resident adult male (more than 17 years old).

Changes in family structure are directly related to these circumstances. More than thirty years ago, in his book *Migrant Labour and Tribal Life*, Schapera drew attention to the impact of large-scale oscillating migration on family life amongst the Tswana. He showed, for example, that the repetitive absence of men undermined family self-sufficiency, in that the rural household could no longer produce enough food for its own requirements and became dependent on a cash income from external sources. It also undermined family cohesion, in that the enforced separation of spouses often led to divorce or deser-

tion and neglect, and the absence of fathers caused indiscipline on the part of the youth and a lack of respect towards their elders. On the other hand, Schapera noted that a wife 'enjoys a relative freedom to which she was not formerly accustomed, and the husband may find on his return that she will no longer submit so readily to his authority'. Other observers have pointed out that the concentration of earning-capacity among younger men allowed them to establish economic independence of their fathers, for example through the purchase rather than the inheritance of livestock. In this way it subverted the traditional balance of authority between the senior and junior generation, in favour of the latter.

Meanwhile, increasing general dependence on migrant earnings and the continuing decline of the domestic agricultural base have tended to concentrate income within migrants' own households. A survey of 82 Basotho mine recruits in 1976 found that only 9 per cent of their total cash earnings from their previous contract had been distributed outside their own household, mainly in the form of bridewealth (*bohadi*) transfers to their in-laws and of transfers in cash and kind to their own parents. But approximately one-third of all rural households have no migrant member in paid employment and therefore have no direct access to migrant earnings. Poverty is concentrated in small female-headed households in particular. There is mounting evi-

NUMBER OF
HOUSEHOLDS

fig. 23 *Histogram showing the frequency distribution of* de jure *members per household (X-axis) among 150 households in Lesotho, 1974.*

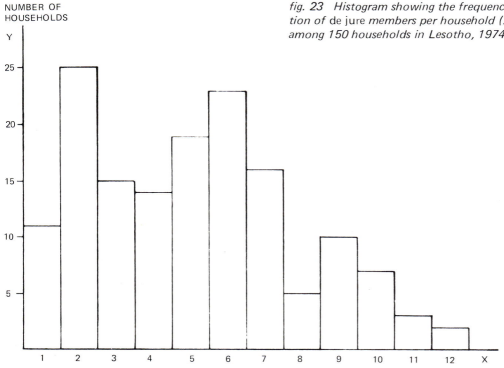

MEMBERS PER HOUSEHOLD

Some Family Histories

'Malimakatso, a widow, sits at home with one of her grandchildren. She has three surviving children of her own: two daughters married in neighbouring villages and a married son who is a regular migrant on the gold mines at Welkom, Orange Free State, but has recently established his own household in Pitse's Nek. The stories of three other members of 'Malimakatso's household illustrate the irregularities which arise out of the circumstances of oscillating migration. Teronko is the son of the sister of 'Malimakatso's husband Saki, who died in 1975. Teronko was brought up in his mother's brother's household because his mother was never married; he is also a regular mine labourer at Welkom. 'Mamosa (shown at the age of fourteen in 1974) had been abducted as a young girl from her mother in Soweto by 'Malimakatso's elder sister, then working in Johannesburg, and brought up in Lesotho as if she were a daughter of the family. 'Mamosa was married in March 1980 to a miner from Teyateyaneng. Teboho (shown, in 1974) was 'given' to 'Malimakatso, under circumstances which remain obscure, during her own years of absence at work in the Republic. He went through initiation school in 1974, took his first mine contract in 1975 and married shortly afterwards. By 1980 he was on his third mine contract and he had transferred a sum of R360 to his wife's family in bridewealth instalments, representing six 'cattle' towards establishing rights of paternity over his two young children. The family are all recently converted Jehovah's Witnesses.

'Mamoroesi was born near Butha-Buthe, northern Lesotho, in 1897, at the time when many cattle died of rinderpest. She was married in another village but, when her only child Moroesi was seven years old, she quarrelled with her husband because of his excessive drinking, and returned to her parents who had moved to Petrus Steyn in the Orange Free State. She then spent eight years working as a domestic servant on a white farm in Botswana, and her speech still occasionally reflects this experience. She returned to her marital home in Lesotho in about 1933, during the savage drought which the Sotho remember as the Great Dust. She has remained a widow since her husband's death at about that time.

'Mamoroesi's daughter Moroesi has spent most of her adult life in Middelburg, Transvaal. She has four daughters, whose paternity is in dispute. The eldest of them, 'Mamataba, was 'spoilt in the yard' (became an unmarried mother) in Middelburg. Her son Senki works for a construction company in Johannesburg but for many years regarded 'Mamoroesi's household in Lesotho as his home. In 1971 he married a teacher's daughter who bore him two children; but in about 1976 she left the rural household because, she claimed, Senki was no longer supporting her from his wages in Johannesburg. Senki has since married another woman and established his own household else-where in the village.

In the photographs 'Mamoroesi is seen sitting, in 1974 and 1980 respectively, with Senki's two young children from his first marrige—her great-great-grandchildren—and with her great-grandchildren Nthabiseng and Jaabo, who were born in Middelburg, Transvaal, to another of Moroesi's daughters, 'Mamataba's half-sister. Nthabiseng and Jaabo came to live in 'Mamoroesi's household in 1974. They attend a local primary school but their mother does not visit them. She is now married to a Pedi man in Middelburg.

dence that the 'extended family' no longer provides adequate security for the elderly, the sick, the unemployed and the very poor.

In summary, then, we have seen that studies of Sotho–Tswana rural communities illustrate processes both of conservation and of change. On the one hand, we have evidence of a relatively stable agnatic structure which endures through several generations. On the other hand, we have evidence of high rates of individual mobility, conjugal instability, illegitimacy, desertion and the break-up of families. The significant inference to be drawn from this is that study of the structure of small communities, defined in terms of the relationship between household heads, does not of itself indicate the qualitative disruption of family life that takes place over time. For the changes in kinship relations that we have described are quite consistent with the persistence of the agnatic structure of small communities as assessed in terms of genealogical relationships between household heads. Indeed, far from being contradictory in their implications, both the conservation and the change are rooted in the political economy of the labour reserve. The stability of residential alignments in many areas of the periphery is directly related to the severity of South African influx control and of land shortage. A man does not have the effective option either to move with his family outside the labour reserve, or to move away from his home area within the reserve, since he is even less likely to be allocated land elsewhere. On the other hand, the instability of conjugal relationships, the haphazard patterns of child-rearing and the high rates of illegitimacy are all largely attributable to the circumstances of migrant labour.

Marriage with Cattle

Marriage with cattle is deeply rooted in the Sotho–Tswana tradition. According to the customary law, various transactions between the families of a man and a woman are necessary to constitute the relationship 'marriage'. The most important of these is the transfer of a certain number of head of cattle from the husband's family to the wife's family. This is known as *bohadi* in Lesotho, *bogadi* among the Tswana and bridewealth in the anthropological literature. In the Sotho–Tswana idiom, 'the child belongs to the cattle'. This means that, where *bohadi* or *bogadi* cattle have not passed, the mother is not properly married and the child remains filiated to its mother's father or brother.

Otherwise, the man who 'took out' cattle to marry the child's mother is recognised as the legal father. In principle, the transfer of paternity rights was permanent. In the past it even survived the death of the husband, through the custom of *kenelo*, the levirate, by which a widow was incorporated into the household of a junior kinsman of her husband, and any children she subsequently bore were still regarded as belonging to the dead man.

Estimates of *bohadi* transferred in nineteenth-century Lesotho varied from ten to thirty head of cattle. Wealthy men were able to marry many wives. The P E M S missionaries recognised the fundamental character of the custom and its connection with the practice of polygyny. They alleged that bridewealth made marriage into a commercial transaction that was incompatible with the spirit of a Christian union; that it kept women in a state of perpetual subjection; and that it led to endless litigation over the rights involved—control over women and their children. The Society vigorously expressed its opposition to bridewealth in evidence submitted to a Cape Governor's Commission in 1872 on the *Native Laws and Customs of the Basutos*. Marriage with cattle, it insisted, was so intimately connected with traditional social life that, were it abolished, heathenism would 'crumble away and cease to exist'.

Bohadi proved remarkably resilient in the face of moral and economic pressures: on the one hand, the indignation of the missionaries; on the other hand, the loss of most of the cattle in Basutoland as a result of the great rinderpest epizootic that swept down Africa in 1896. A Casalis commented on this in a letter dated July 1897: 'If only it could have killed marriage by cattle! Alas no! they are so fond of their cattle that they will continue, as in the past, to marry women with cattle even if they have none. The letter goes on to explain how the Basotho devised marital mortgages by counting stones as surety for future instalments of *bohadi* cattle. Basotho today cite twenty cattle, ten small stock and a horse as the conventional expectation in bridewealth negotiations. Although the expectation is seldom fulfilled in practice, there is enough recent evidence of substantial bridewealth transfers in cattle, small stock, cash and other media of exchange to justify the conclusion that *bohadi* remains as strong a custom today as it ever was in the past (see fig. 24). Yet the structural conditions of high bridewealth in the latter part of the twentieth century are very different from those that prevailed in the middle of the nineteenth century.

The persistence of bridewealth is by no means uniform. *Bogadi* has in fact been formally abolished for over fifty years among the Ngwato and Tawana tribes of Botswana. The Kgatla chief Lentswe abolished the practice in about 1897, in response to missionary pressure and also to the loss of cattle caused by rinderpest. Although *bogadi* continued to flourish in secret, its formal abolition led to confusion and instability of unions. So the custom was restored again after fifteen years, when the tribe had again accumulated cattle. Meanwhile Lentswe had induced the authorities of the Dutch Reformed Church to regard bridewealth as a registration of marriage rather than as a form of wife-purchase. His successor the regent Isang reinforced the transfer of *bogadi* as an indispensable condition of a valid marriage.

In his famous study of Kgatla family life, *Married Life in an African Tribe*, Schapera recorded that the average transfer of *bogadi* per marriage in the 1930s was three head of cattle. Roberts noted forty years later, in his survey of the Rampedi ward in Mochudi which we described above, that the amount of bridewealth was becoming standardised, at two head of cattle or their monetary equivalent of R40. Kgatla still stress two elements necessary for a proper marriage: the tender and acceptance of engagement gifts, and the presentation of *bogadi*. However, Roberts has argued from case material that failure to conform to these requirements does not necessarily affect the validity of a marriage or prevent the husband from being recognised as father to the children of the union. Rather, what is important is formal recognition of the union by the families concerned.

There is often a discrepancy of this kind between what people say in the abstract and what the courts determine in particular cases. We can infer two things from this. One is that it is important to distinguish two ways of trying to define marriage. The other is that we have to investigate the nature of the judicial process.

One way of trying to define marriage is to look at *jural* criteria, that is, at the various rights and duties which people associate with particular transactions. The other way is to look at the evidence for a *conjugal* relationship. The simple criterion of 'living together' which would normally be used here is inadequate where the husband is away for long periods at work. So it is necessary to use other criteria, such as the regularity of remittances, letters and visits home; whether household decisions are jointly taken, and so on. The question of a child's paternity in Sotho–Tswana customary law is resolved by the courts with reference to the jural criteria which constitute a valid marriage. But the need to make such a resolution generally arises retrospectively, usually in circumstances of conjugal breakdown. These circumstances will also be taken into account. The point here is that the protagonists to a dispute are able to invoke witnesses and to select and manipulate evidence relating to the 'facts' of a particular situation in such a way as to favour their interpretation of the case. The judicial process, in other words, involves competing and retrospective *constructions* of events. It does not simply determine outcomes by imposing 'what the law says'.

Returning migrants in Maseru driving home cattle bought in South Africa.

One Hundred and Fifty Years of Bohadi *in Lesotho*

Then . . .

In the unsettled circumstances of the post- *difaqane* reconstruction period, Moshoeshoe and the other senior chiefs of his lineage were able to accumulate livestock through raiding. They exploited their differential access to cattle in two ways: through the practice of polygyny, which facilitated the expansion of the dominant Kwena lineage; and through the attachment of clients called *bahlanka*, typically dispossessed refugees, by providing *bohadi* cattle for their marriages and by lending out cattle to them under the *mafisa* system. High rates of *bohadi* at this time ref ected the fact that control of livestock was the key to the expansion and consolidation of Kwena political patronage.

Writing in 1885, one of the P E M S missionaries explained the connection between polygyny and marriage with cattle. 'Marriage is so much a matter of speculation in this country, that a chief will often marry a woman with no other object than to present her to such and such of his subjects who may be too poor to buy one himself, but on condition that the latter's children will belong to him. Thus it is that numerous natives claim the title of sons and daughters of Moshoeshoe, without having any other bond of relationship with the late chief of the Basuto, than his payment of their mother's *bohadi*. They are called by a rather significant name: *bana ba dikgomo* (the children of the cattle).

'Thus it is that "marriage by cattle" leads to polygamy. In a pastoral country where the herds constitute the principal wealth of the inhabitants and where, moreover, this wealth is the basis of power since, as the Basuto are at liberty to dispose of and to give themselves to the chief whom they prefer, he will have the most subjects who will best know how to attract or retain them with his presents; it follows that the more wives one has, the richer and the more powerful will one be. Provided a man has the means, he will scarcely hesitate to treat himself to such profitable luxury; therefore, while the fairly well-to-do natives content themselves with two or three wives, while the rich and the subordinate chiefs permit themselves a larger number, the great chiefs have twenty, thirty, eighty, a hundred, whose huts often form a village around their lord's residence.'

The Sotho–Tswana attach importance to the establishment, on marriage, of an independent 'house'. A man has as many houses to administer as he has married wives; and each house has well-defined rights, as against other houses, relating to domestic provision, access to land and livestock, and the inheritance of property. The administration of property is governed by the rule 'houses do not eat each other', which precludes the transfer of assets from one house to another except with the permission of the heir and of his mother in each of the houses concerned. The passage cited above makes it clear that a chief's control over the receipt and disposition of bridewealth cattle effectively determined the rank order of the houses established by his successive marriages, and thence the distribution of succession rights. Thus disputes between half-brothers over succession to office commonly turned on evidence relating to the marriages of their father to their respective mothers.

These provisions of the customary law are subsumed under the *house-property complex*, which is generally regarded as the key to Southern Bantu kinship systems. But the features which sustained it—polygyny, wealth in livestock and eligibility for succession to office—were characteristic of the aristocracy, not of commoners.

Now . . .

Circumstances today are very different. Economic security in the labour reserve is above all a matter of establishing claims on the labour and earning-capacity of legitimate dependants within the rural household. High levels of bridewealth in Lesotho, the most acutely dependent of the labour reserves, are a key element in this strategy. 'Receivers' of *bohadi* bargain the receipt of livestock or their cash equivalent against the prospective loss of the economic services of their daughters or of *their* children; 'givers' of *bohadi*, who are usually migrants, transfer substantial sums in order to validate their marriages in terms of the customary law and to establish legal paternity over their children. It is by no means unusual for a young man from Lesotho to return home from a mine contract and to pay out a lump sum of hundreds of rand in cash to his in-laws.

Bohadi is therefore a mechanism by which migrants invest in the long-term security of the rural social system, and by which rural kin constitute claims over absent earners. It sustains relationships both within the household which consists of a migrant and his dependants, and between households in the rural area. The irony of the system is that migrant labour, which is the means by which Basotho find the cash to establish legitimate marital relationships, is itself the largest threat to marital stability by enforcing the separation of husband and wife for repetitive periods of indefinite duration. Therefore high levels of bridewealth are not inconsistent with high rates of conjugal instability and a high proportion of unmarried women.

fig. 24 Marital transactions in Lesotho. Because these transactions are usually distributed over a long period of time it is sensible to regard marriage as a process in time rather than as a single point of transition between the unmarried and the married state.

FROM HUSBAND'S KIN	FROM WIFE'S KIN	SIGNIFICANCE
sheep of *kwae*		to 'receive' the wife when she first arrives at husband's home
cattle: either 6 *matshediso*		compensation enforceable in court for elopement, abduction or 'spoiling' a girl
or 6 *lenyalo*		where there is previous agreement between the families, the payment is regarded as evidence of serious intention to marry
7 *ho supa mohwehadi*		to 'point at one's mother-in-law' — some say this is a gratuitous insult; at any rate the payment achieves nothing, it shows that the husband 'is merely playing'
8 *ho thea bohadi*		to 'lay the foundation' of the marriage
10 *ho phetha hloho*		to 'complete a head': to establish beyond question filiation of children to the husband's family
	ho hlabisa bohadi: — slaughter of ox — provision of feast	feast provided for husband's family by wife's father, timing by agreement, to mark receipt of ten or more *bohadi* cattle and to fulfil the marriage contract
	sheep of *kwae*	to mark first formal visit of husband to wife's natal home
	ho phahlela moradi	to 'pack for' one's daughter: clothes and household goods provided for the wife by her parents for use in her marital home
ho kgaola bohadi		transfer of such additional cattle as are necessary to complete the number specified in the original agreement

The Agnatic Family, the Kindred and the Mother's Brother

Ethnographers of the Sotho–Tswana stress three aspects of the kinship system. The first is the special relationship between mother's brother and sister's child. The second is the absence of a rule forbidding marriage between clan or lineage members. The Sotho–Tswana do not prohibit marriage with close kin (except immediate relatives), as the Nguni people do. Indeed, they express preferences for marrying cousins. The third aspect is the difficulty of determining what kinship groupings are significant above the level of the individual household.

These three aspects are all inter-related and, moreover, cannot be understood independently of Sotho–Tswana political systems.

In 1861 Eugene Casalis wrote: 'Among the Basutos, the eldest brother of the mother (*malome*) also enjoys special rights over the children. He is understood to replace the mother, whose sex keeps her in a state of dependence. This is a counterbalance to the authority of the father and the eldest son; but it often preponderates to excess, especially in polygamist families, in which great rivalry generally reigns, and where the children have no special affection for their father. It is the special duty of this godfather [i.e. the mother's brother] in common to the whole family to protect the child, and to purify it by means of sacrifices. When the right [sic] of circumcision is performed, he makes his ward a present of a javelin and a heifer: he also defrays in part his marriage expenses. In return for all this, he is entitled to a share of the spoil taken by his nephews in war, of the game they kill, and of the cattle that comes into the possession of the family at the settlement of the nieces. It often happens that these uncles fill the office of prime minister and regent at the court of the chiefs.'

There are many hints in this passage of the importance of the true *malome*, the eldest mother's brother. In Lesotho the bridewealth animals received by the *malome* from the marriage of his sister's daughter are known as *ditswa*. This word also refers to boils or eruptions on the skin which it is believed that only *malome* can cure. Some Basotho explicitly link the two senses. They say that the *malome* is entitled to claim his share of the bridewealth as recompense for his active solicitude for the personal welfare of his sister's children. A further custom was specifically noted by the French missionary and ethnologist Henri Junod, who visited Basutoland in 1915. Famous for his earlier classic study of the Moçambique Tsonga in *The Life of a South African Tribe*, Junod described his findings in Basutoland in the second English edition of that book, published in 1927: 'On the death of the nephew, the maternal uncle inherits all his "filth", i.e. all the property which he has constantly touched and which is covered with the exudations of his body.' Personal property is distinguished from estate property, which passes lineally within the nephew's own house.

Thus the essence of the special relationship between mother's brother and sister's child is its mutual warmth and the personal nature of the obligations associated with it. These attributes clearly distinguish it in the abstract from the relationship between close agnates which, as Casalis rightly observed, is characterised by tension and potential rivalry. This difference and the problem of its interpretation gave rise to a notorious controversy in anthropology which still has its own place in the teaching of the subject at undergraduate level.

On the other hand, Junod, a scrupulous and perceptive observer, also remarked that 'the tendency of the Sotho system seems to be to lessen the difference existing in other tribes between the father's family and the mother's family'. Here we have an apparent paradox. Father's relatives and mother's relatives are often not distinguished in practice. A Dutch anthropologist who worked recently in Bokaa, an outlying community in the Kgatleng district of Botswana, expressed this tendency as follows: 'As a general rule, paternal kin *who do not belong to ego's ward* are merged with his maternal kin as one single undifferentiated kindred and *they do not fulfil any functions* which set them apart from maternal kin' (our emphasis). She went on to describe the kindred as a network of relatives on both sides, referred to as *masika*, which is mobilised to attend the rites of passage in the individual's life cycle—birth, initiation, marriage, burial. She suggested that this is a more important kinship grouping than the lineage in Tswana society. Yet Tswana retain a conceptual distinction between paternal relatives, *ba ga etsho*, and maternal relatives, *ba ga etsho mogolo*.

As we have seen, the Tswana conceptualise ward membership in lineage terms, although some members are related in other ways. It is significant that the anthropologist we have just quoted referred to paternal kin outside the ward, who are not directly involved in local-level politics; and that her study was conducted at some distance from the centre of power in the Kgatleng at Mochudi. Both these facts are relevant to a resolution of the apparent paradox to which we have drawn attention. For the resolution lies in an investigation of marital strategies and of the political processes of competition for office. The following argument requires an understanding of kinship algebra—the particular preserve of the anthropologist. It is best explained with the help of diagrams (see figs. 25, 26 and 27). There are two aspects which we have to consider.

The first aspect derives from the logic of the house-property complex. As we have seen, polygyny and sibling rivalry are built into the traditional arrangements by which property and office are transmitted from generation to generation. In principle the rules are clear-cut. The first-born son of the senior house is the legitimate heir. Brothers are always ranked relative to one another: full siblings in the order of their birth, and half-siblings in the rank order of their mothers amongst their father's wives. However, in view of the ambiguities which arise over the problem of defining marriage, there is often scope for argument about which wife was married first, and therefore which house is the senior house. It follows that the characteristic locus of conflict over succession to office is between half-brothers, the sons of different houses. Schapera analysed 91 succession disputes among the Tswana and found a high incidence of conflict between sons of the same father and different mothers.

This reflects the fact that the criterion of eligibility

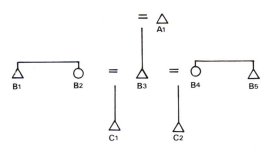

fig. 25. *An illustration of polygyny, and conse-*
quent rivalry between half-siblings. B3 has inheri-
ted the chieftainship from his father A1, and has
married two wives B2 and B4. His sons C1 and C2
are likely to compete for the succession, and each
may expect the political support of his mother's
brother, B1 and B5 respectively.

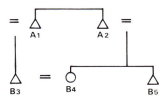

The consequences of close-kin marriage:
fig. 26 *For political reasons, Sotho–Tswana chiefs*
liked to 'marry each other': they preferred to
marry a close kinswoman. Let us suppose that one
of B3's wives, B4, is also his father's brother's
daughter, as shown in the diagram. Then his affines
(relatives by marriage) are also his agnates (relatives
through descent in the male line).

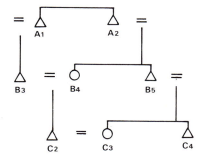

fig. 27 *Let us further suppose that, in the next*
generation, C2 marries his mother's brother's
daughter C3, as Sotho–Tswana custom enjoins him
to do. Then his affines are also his matrilateral kin
(relatives on his mother's side); and they are all,
simultaneously, his agnates. For example, his wife's
brother C4 is also his mother's brother's son (or
cross-cousin, in anthopological terms) and his
father's father's brother's son's son (or classifica-
tory parallel cousin, in anthropological terms).

for succession to office is always agnatic descent.
Since the property-holding unit is the house and not
the agnatic family as a whole, the lineage is a corporate group only in the limited sense that its members
have a direct interest in the disposition of office.
They exercise their influence through the family
council. But every succession dispute clearly articu-
lates the internal structure of the lineage, because
different factions present their arguments in terms of
competing claims of genealogical legitimacy. In this
competition agnates are potential rivals. Mother's
kin, on the other hand, are political supporters.
They are ineligible for office themselves, by
definition. Each protagonist therefore expects to invoke the support of his mother's kin on his behalf.

The second aspect of kinship algebra which it is
necessary to understand is that the habit of marrying
cousins leads to ambiguity in defining the kinship
categories to which particular individuals belong.
Both the Sotho–Tswana, in their language, and
anthropologists in theirs, conventionally distinguish the following categories of kin: *agnates*, who
are kin traced through the male line only, such
as father, brother and father's brother's child;
matrilateral kin who are, as the word suggests, kin on
the mother's side, such as mother's father or
brother, and mother's brother's child; and *affines*,
who are in-laws, people to whom you are related, as
the Sotho–Tswana express it, 'through cattle', such
as wife's father or brother. All these categories of kin
include persons of both sexes. Marrying cousins
confounds the distinctions between the categories,
so that they potentially overlap in ways illustrated in
the accompanying diagrams.

The Sotho–Tswana approve of marriages with
cousins of all sorts. Cross-cousins (children of oppo-
site-sex siblings) are often represented as 'born for
each other'. This preference derives from the relationship of 'linked siblingship' between a brother
and a sister, such that the brother may marry with
cattle from the bridewealth received from his sister's
marriage. He retains a close personal interest in the
welfare of her children to whom, of course, he is
malome. A marriage between his child and her child
in due course is a natural way of perpetuating this
close relationship. According to the Setswana
proverb: 'a sister's child is important at the home of
his mother's people'. Nevertheless, ruling families
exhibited a statistical preference for marriage with
father's brother's daughter, an agnate within the
same lineage and also a parallel cousin (parallel
cousins are children of same-sex siblings). As the
Basotho put it, 'the chiefs like to marry each other'.
They rationalise this preference in terms of the need

117

A number of small but labour-intensive handicraft enterprises have been established in Lesotho. Funded by international agency aid, their main problem is to find suitable commercial outlets.

Basketwork and pottery on sale by the roadside in Botswana.

The Politics of Close-Kin Marriage

fig. 28

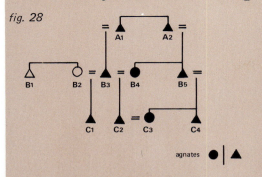

agnates ● | ▲

Suppose that two half-brothers C1 and C2 are competing to succeed to the office held by their father B3. Each invokes the support of his respective mother's kin. C1's mother's brother, B1, is a commoner. C2's mother's brother, B5, on the other hand, is an agnate and also a member of the ruling group, by virtue of B3 having married his father's brother's daughter, B4. Let us further suppose that C2 has married his mother's brother's daughter C3. His wife's brother C4 is both a matrilateral kinsman and an agnate, as shown in fig. 27. The political rewards for C2 of successive close-kin marriages (his father's and his own) lie in the possibility of neutra-lising potential opposition from another agnatic line within the ruling group, and indeed of converting C4's line from agnates into matrilateral kinsmen and therefore political supporters. The logic from C2's point of view is that if you keep on marrying your agnates, who are potential rivals, you can hope to transform them into 'mother's brothers' and rely on their political support. By the same logic, of course, C4's people may wish either to endorse their conversion from agnates into mother's brothers or to resist it, depending on whether they retain any realistic expectation of competing for the office themselves. Correspondingly, the marriage of C2 and C3 may be defined *either* as a marriage between cross-cousins *or* as one between agnates. In descriptive terms, she is both C2's mother's brother's daughter (a cross-cousin) and his father's father's brother's son's daughter (a classificatory parallel cousin). Which construction of the relationship prevails at any one time is the outcome of a political struggle. On the basis of his study of succession disputes among the Tshidi Rolong, John Comaroff concluded that particular classifications of kin are not simple and immutable statements of biological fact. Rather, they 'represent statements of the political relations between the respective parties at a given time. As such they are distinctly mutable.'

to preserve dynastic integrity and to maintain large transfers of livestock in bridewealth within the politically dominant stratum. Some commoners condemn the practice on the grounds that the individuals concerned share the same 'blood'; whereas, in the idiom of folk genetics, cross-cousins are of different 'blood'.

Close-kin marriages may serve a number of strategies. They may be used to create and maintain a political alliance between different agnatic families. They may also be used to weld together different branches of the same agnatic family. Schapera's precise and detailed work on Tswana close-kin marriages has shown that a high statistical frequency of father's-brother's-daughter-type marriage among royals (chiefs, their sons and sons' sons) is best explained in terms of a strategy of reinforcing social ties between different, potentially hostile, branches of the royal line as the heads of these branches are progressively dispersed through the creation of new wards. Adam Kuper has summarised this argument for the Sotho–Tswana as a whole. The purpose of such marriages is to convert 'tense and competitive relationships in the ruling group into relationships of affinity and, later and more particularly, matrifiliation, which can be mobilised more readily for political support'.

By contrast, cross-cousin marriages are relatively more important among commoners because, being unable to compete directly for office, they have no particular advantage in cementing agnatic alliances. Rather, their political interests lie in creating ties of affinity with the ruling group, which become matrilateral ties in due course. They may exploit these connections in advancing their own political careers. Hence a *malome* is well placed to become principal adviser to the chief, or 'prime minister at the court', as Casalis put it. From the point of view of members of the ruling group, men belonging to different houses are distinguished precisely by their different matrilateral ties. In the competition for office, therefore, a man whose matrilateral kin also belong to the ruling group has a political advantage which is often decisive. The history of succession struggles in Lesotho and among the Tswana clearly illustrates this point.

We are now in a position to summarise the results of this analysis. The identity of the agnatic lineage derives from its collective interest in externally defined political rights. If there are such rights, the effective boundaries and internal structure of the lineage will be readily discernible in the context of

factional competition over the succession. This structure is not immutable but susceptible to redefinition depending on the outcome of the competition. Comaroff has shown that the winner 'fixes' the genealogy so as to legitimise his accession. If there are no such externally defined rights, it is unlikely that the lineage will emerge as a significant kinship grouping, in a sense that transcends local residential ties, since it lacks the necessary corporate interest.

Whether or not lineages are identifiable in this sense, individual Sotho–Tswana have significant kin on both father's side and mother's side, who congregate on occasions such as marriages and funerals, 'family' celebrations and feasts for the ancestors. The identity of the lineage in its political context is by no means incompatible with the observation that, in other contexts, paternal relatives and maternal relatives are not effectively distinguished. Instead, they merge to constitute what anthropologists call an ego-centred kindred. It is hardly surprising that modern studies of the Tswana emphasise the importance of the kindred as against the lineage, in view of processes of political decentralisation and demographic dispersion that have already been described. Correspondingly, as may be expected, there has been a marked decline in the frequency and importance of close-kin marriages.

Nevertheless the ideological construction of the role of *malome* is directly related to the fact that a mother's brother, by definition, is a political

Lesotho Airways operates regular flights to the more inaccessible mountain areas.

supporter, whereas an agnate, by definition, is a potential rival. The clear distinction between them, in the abstract, is not qualified by the fact that an individual may be, descriptively, both an agnate and a mother's brother. For in these circumstances a political struggle takes place in which the individual is effectively construed as one or the other. Under modern conditions the coincidence of kinship roles occurs for a very different reason than close-kin marriage. A high illegitimacy rate means that for many children their *malome*, mother's brother, is also their quasi-father, and they may be brought up in his household. In this case the conceptual distinction between father's kin and mother's kin does not arise.

It is interesting nevertheless to consider how women's children are incorporated into their mother's agnatic family. Sotho–Tswana custom would require formal arrangements to incorporate such children and their ratification by the family council. The evidence suggests that, where eligibility for succession to office is at stake, senior agnates whose interests would be threatened thereby seldom ratify such arrangements. Where succession is not at stake, the jural status of women's children is not sufficiently important to justify their formal incor-

poration into the lineage. Women's children, therefore, are just as important as any other units of human labour in strategies of household management. But they cannot expect to compete effectively with men's children in contexts where jural membership of the lineage is of wider political relevance.

Inside a hut in Lesotho.

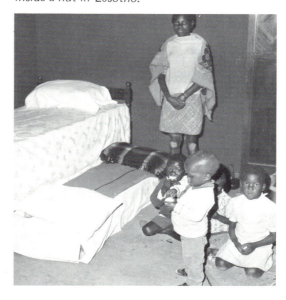

8

Ritual Practice and Belief

COLIN MURRAY

Rain-making

All the Sotho–Tswana peoples traditionally believed in the capacity of their rulers to invoke the rain. Their chiefs employed a powerful doctor as a sort of public health official whose duty it was to provide protective medicines for the village and, if called upon to do so, to summon rain. For both purposes he required a special knowledge of the strongest medicines, and he worked in conditions of the strictest secrecy, for the rain medicines were said to be spoiled by contact with anyone who had had sexual experience. Hence the doctor and his assistants had to abstain from sexual activity throughout the period they were engaged in making rain. Otherwise, communion with the ancestors of the ruling family would be confounded by carnal indulgence; and they would refuse the rain.

In Lesotho there were two communal rituals which, it is said, could be relied upon to bring rain. One was called 'pursuing the little porridge stick', in which the girls from one village would raid another village to capture the porridge stick from the chief's place and carry it back to their own village. If they succeeded in doing this, rain clouds would gather immediately. This rite was still being performed in the Leribe district of Lesotho in 1973–4, at times when the sun 'stood still'. There were no obvious consequences. It was regarded rather as a game. The other ritual was a communal hunt for specified animals, which was organised by the men and which appears to have died out in the 1920s. In most areas Christian congregations have now assumed the obligation of arranging collective prayers for rain, in times of drought.

The problem of succession to the Kgatla chieftainship in the 1920s and 1930s, a period of tribal unrest, was closely connected to the question of competence to make rain. The old chief Lentswe transmitted his knowledge of rain-making to his heir Kgafela. But the latter died in 1914. Lentswe then passed it on to Kgafela's sister Kgabyana, clandestinely, because he suspected that Kgafela's junior brother Isang would usurp the chieftainship if he knew rain medicine. Lentswe became incapacitated in 1920 and died in 1924. Isang became regent because Kgafela's eldest son Molefi was too young to assume office. Grumbling began among the Kgatla as a result of a bad drought in 1926 and Isang's acknowledged inability to make rain. Increasingly unpopular, Isang made way for Molefi in 1929. There followed a period of bitter rivalry between Molefi and Isang, which divided the tribe into opposing factions. Kgabyana, Kgafela's sister, had never transmitted her knowledge of rainmaking to Molefi, because of the unsettled political circumstances in Mochudi. Molefi proved unable to make rain; and he was in any case suspended from office in 1936 for misconduct.

Meanwhile Schapera, the indefatigable ethnographer, discovered from Kgabyana what had happened to Lentswe's rain-making instruments and medicines. As a result of the political quarrels which ravaged Mochudi in 1934, she felt it necessary to dispose of the instruments and was persuaded by Schapera to deposit them in the ethnological museum of the University of Cape Town. Thus a long tradition came to an end. Schapera has however written a very detailed account of all that he learned from Kgatla and other informants in his book *Rainmaking Rites of Tswana Tribes*.

One of the most potent medicines used in rainmaking was the fat of a large and powerful snake named Kgwanyape, which lived in a pool on the top of Modipe hill not far from Mochudi. This is obviously the same snake known to the Basotho generically as *khanyapa* and sometimes explicitly identified as the python. It is also associated with deep pools, which for this reason are regarded by Basotho as repositories of sacred power. It is prominent in various guises in Sesotho symbolic life. It emerges from an erosion ravine at a critical point in the initiation of girls, where it is known colloquially as 'child of the deep waters'. It appears vividly in dreams as an agent of the dreamer's ancestors; and it plays a very common, indeed stereotypical, part in the experiences of people who have been, as the Basotho put it, 'gripped by the spirit of the ancestors' (described below). Encounters with the snake are also a recurrent motif in Sesotho oral literature.

The Ancestors

The Sotho–Tswana traditionally recognised a supreme being, *Modimo*. In order to distinguish the original Tswana concept from the one adopted by missionaries to convey the idea of a Christian God, the Tswana theologian Gabriel Setiloane has referred to *Modimo* as It rather than Him. A remote though pervasive spiritual force, *Modimo* is closely associated with natural phenomena. The essence of mystery, It evokes a sense of awe. It represents the

The spectacular Maletsunyane waterfall (192 m high) at Semonkong, Lesotho. The first recorded visit to the falls was that of Father Le Bihan, a French Catholic missionary, in about 1882. A large snake is reputed to inhabit the pool at the bottom.

ultimate source of man's well-being, but is not directly involved in the affairs of the living. Its influence is mediated through the ancestors, *badimo*, and the Sotho–Tswana direct their ritual activities towards the *badimo* rather than to *Modimo*. The words share the same root *-dimo*, although its basic meaning is controversial. Significantly, they belong to different noun-classes.

The *badimo* are not at all remote. Otherwise glossed as 'our grandfathers and grandmothers of old', they take an active interest in the welfare of their living descendants. In everyday conversation the *badimo* are always referred to in the plural, never in the singular. But when pressed to do so, people can usually identify the individuals whose presence they experience, most commonly in a dream. They are close relatives on both father's side and mother's side. In abstract from particular experiences, however, the *badimo* are generally represented as ancestors in the male line, in contexts such as funerals, where the identity of the agnatic lineage is stressed in order to define the hierarchy of seniority among the living.

The most common manifestation of the *badimo* is a complaint, transmitted in a dream, 'We are hungry, give us food'. In response to this the dreamer will take steps to arrange a 'feast of *badimo*' to propitiate them. This involves the slaughtering of an animal, either a beast or a sheep, and the brewing of sorghum beer. Members of the family are invited, and friends and neighbours attend, generally in proportion to the quantity of meat and beer available. The 'owner' or his representative make a formal announcement of the purpose of the feast, and a prayer is often spoken. Sometimes a migrant miner will arrange a feast spontaneously, without prompting by the *badimo*, in order to give thanks for a safe return home; or someone who wishes to initiate an enterprise—a new business, or building a house—will seek to invoke 'good luck' in the same way.

Active members of Christian congregations are often diffident about an explicit offering to the ancestors, because of a legacy of church prejudice against 'heathenism'. But there is no doubt that most Sotho–Tswana, who are nominally Christians, continue to believe in the importance of their obligations to the dead. Should they repudiate them, they may be sharply reminded of them by the mystical capacity of the *badimo* to inflict illness or misfortune. Stories circulate of the way in which Christians who resist a diagnosis of ancestral interference are ultimately brought to heel. Some elements of custom, such as initiation and a form of affliction which we describe below, are incompatible with practising Christianity. But there are few contradictions at the level of belief.

A feast for the ancestors can be interpreted in various ways. In its own terms, it is an expression of reciprocal goodwill, usually arranged in response to a nudge from the *badimo*. It is a matter of propitiating the dead and of securing 'good luck'. More prosaically, any feast worthy of the name requires the slaughter of an animal and many other expenses which must be met largely out of cash earnings. Ritual obligations are expensive and therefore they are also relevant to an investigation of inter-

household income transfers. From a sociological perspective, we have to relate the incidence of such feasts to household strategies of investment and social control, and to the distribution of the necessary economic resources at any one time.

Otherwise, occasions of communion with the ancestors are generally associated with events in the life cycle of individuals. What follows is a brief description of the more important of these, from the cradle to the grave.

A pregnant woman is in a condition of 'hotness' in which she is peculiarly susceptible to the malice and gossip—'bad breath' in the Sesotho idiom—of neighbours. For this reason she remains in seclusion until some time following the birth of her child, whose 'coming out' is then celebrated by a ritual nowadays known as *pitiki*. A sheep or goat is slaughtered, and thanks given to *Modimo* and the *badimo* for the birth of the child.

In the past both boys and girls were initiated, after puberty, into adulthood. Amongst the Tswana initiation was a prelude to the formation of tribal age-regiments. Men's regiments, under the command of a member of the ruling family, were called upon to perform military service; and they were summoned as a labour force when some large public work had to be carried out. Women's regiments also had cer-

The 'coming out'. A public celebration of the in-itiates' new status as marriageable women. Some of them wear the gall bladders and stomach fat of animals as they process slowly through the village.

The boys chant their own praises, carefully re-hearsed, wearing the blankets, pins and other small gifts from admiring friends and relatives.

tain communal tasks. Loyalty to regimental age-mates cut across kinship and local political affiliations. Nowadays men are reluctant to carry out public duties of this kind without payment. This is another indication of the decline of chiefly authority. The elaborate series of initiation rites known as *bogwera* for boys and *bojale* for girls have all but died out. Schapera observed in the 1930s that, of the Tswana tribes in the Bechuanaland Protectorate, only the two smallest, the Tlokwa and the Malete, still performed them. The Tshidi Rolong still arrange the *bogwera* today, though it is no longer directly controlled by the chief.

Initiation schools for both boys and girls are still held in parts of Lesotho. Hugh Ashton, the principal ethnographer of the Basotho, reported that they were becoming rare in the 1930s except among the Tlokwa in the eastern mountains. But he appears to have exaggerated their demise. I observed several boys' and six girls' initiation schools in the Leribe district in 1973–4. A group of about ten to fifteen boys, between the ages of 13 and 17 or so, is re-cruited by the 'owner' of the school, who has obtained permission to hold it from the area chief. They spend a month or more in preparation for the lodge, gathering firewood and learning songs. There follows a period of two months or more in seclusion in the mountains, at the beginning of which they are circumcised. During this phase of transition, the boys use a special vocabulary and learn the secret songs called *dikoma*, which they will never thereafter reveal, on pain of madness, to any-one who has not himself been initiated. They also compose the praise songs that each of them will re-cite at the public 'coming out' ceremony back in the village.

Girls' initiation involves three stages. The first lasts for about a month, during which they are smeared with black clay and do not appear in public at all. They are enclosed in a special hut in the village. Immediately before they enter this state of seclusion, the mysterious *motanyane*, the big snake otherwise known as 'child of the deep waters', appears to the girls from a deep ravine—an experi-ence women describe as awesome. The second stage also lasts for about a month. They are smeared with

white clay, and go about in a group performing elaborate songs and dramas which they have learned. A common theme of these is parody of male behaviour. They also sing *mangai*, special initiation songs which contain didactic elements but whose allusions are often obscure. The third and final stage is the 'coming out' when, glistening with red-brown ochre, the girls process slowly through the village. This ritual series transforms girls into mar-riageable women. In one school in 1973, however, no less than seven of the group of eleven initiates were married women, and two of these were grandmothers. They had been Christians afflicted by their ancestors and instructed to go through in-itiation school as part of the resolution of their illness. This reflects an explicit connection between initiation and the attainment of true Mosotho identity.

Marriage is the next step in the life cycle, although it is sensible to regard marriage as a process in time rather than as a single point of transition. The Basotho say, '*bohadi* never ends'. In this context the most important of the series of transactions which constitute marriage in Lesotho is the feast of *tlhabiso*, which fulfils the marriage contract. After ten or more *bohadi* cattle have been transferred the man's family will press the woman's family to 'smear them with fat'. The woman's father must slaughter an ox and provide a feast for those who have married his daughter. The meat is divided between the two

Varieties of adolescent experience: right, school-boys at a gymnastics display in Lesotho. Above, herdboys on the mountainside in Lesotho; the two on the right are recent initiates.

families. It is very churlish of him to refuse to do this, in spite of the fact that if he lacks a suitable beast of his own it may cost him R200 to buy one (1980 prices). The expense is prohibitive but failure may expose the family to mystical sanctions. Resentment at delay may be expressed by the ancestors on either side: both sets are hungry for their rightful portions of meat. The married woman herself, the only target available through whom ancestors on one side can exert moral pressure on the other side, may be the hapless victim of this form of mystical attack.

The other outstanding obligation in respect of the *badimo* is that of providing a 'blanket' for a dead person. This is the skin of the beast which relatives should slaughter in order to 'accompany' the deceased on his or her way to the abode of the *badimo*. A departed spirit for whom no such feast has been held will wander in limbo and return to haunt the living with the complaint, again transmitted in a dream, 'Where is my blanket? I am cold'. After the period of mourning, a sheep should be slaughtered to remove the pollution which attaches to close kin following a death in the family. In a widow's case, the 'filth' symbolised by the mourning clothes is said to derive from the 'sweat' of sexual congress and of co-operative labour in the fields. The cleansing ritual takes place at the widow's natal home. She must be washed with a solution of the sheep's gall in water. Her head is shaved, her nails cut and her mourning clothes burned. Her brother or another close relative must provide her with new clothes. Whatever the circumstances, this ritual should not take place in summer but in winter, after the crops have been reaped, for 'what provokes the frost is the mourning clothes'. Similarly, the personal property of the deceased should not be distributed in the summer growing season, lest the crops be spoiled by hail.

Affliction: Its Diagnosis and Resolution

Illness and misfortune are often attributed to the mystical interference of the *badimo* because the living have neglected moral obligations of the kind described above. Occasionally, they are also attributed to *boloi*, which the Sotho–Tswana regard as the manipulation of medicines for evil purposes. The sociological interest of these phenomena lies in the process by which they are diagnosed and the steps that are taken to resolve the problem.

The nature of the problem is identified in one of two ways: either the sufferer experiences the *badimo* directly in a dream; or he consults a specialist who divines the reason for the illness or misfortune. There are various methods of divination, of which the most common is the use of a set of divining objects *(ditaola)* whose 'falls' the specialist interprets. Whatever the technique, effective divination requires communion with the ancestors. Some doctors use snuff to 'clear the wits', the more easily to achieve this communion.

Traditional doctors are very diverse in their methods of practice, their knowledge of herbal and other medicines, and the extent to which they incorporate elements of 'western' diagnosis and treatment. Basotho distinguish them by reputation rather than technique. They say that many are charlatans who exploit the credulous by charging ridiculous fees for minimal service. Only a few have genuine skills. Although there is no rigid division, most doctors fall into one of two categories: 'hornless' doctors, on the one hand, who specialise in the use of herbs and roots and may divine, but learn all their skills through apprenticeship to another doctor; and doctors known as *bakoma*, on the other hand, who are specialists in divination and claim their knowledge through revelation from the ancestors rather than by instruction from another.

We can now describe a form of mystical affliction to which we have already referred in passing. Some people experience symptoms that have nothing to do with neglect of their moral obligations or the malice of their neighbours and kinsmen. The symptoms are fainting fits, bad dreams, prostration, abrupt and noisy belching and spontaneous shuddering. They may occur sporadically; but often

A woman inhaling snuff. A common stimulant, it is also used in divination.

they are persistent. The victim will discover, either through dream-revelation or through consulting a doctor, that he or she has been 'gripped by spirit *(moya)* of the ancestors', and must undertake a prolonged curing ritual, to tame the offending *moya* and to enter the company of *bakoma*. This ritual is a standard cultural response. A doctor is appointed to administer the instructions of the ancestors, the most important of which is churning a frothy mixture of red and white medicines. A white goat is slaughtered, and the victim must wear white beads. The frothy medicines and the 'whiteness' of the other objects turn the 'madness' of *moya* into the 'vision' of a special relationship with the ancestors. A few victims of *moya* turn professional, as it were, and become *bakoma* doctors who are qualified to conduct the curing ritual for other victims.

In the 1930s Ashton observed a striking preponderance of female victims of *moya* over male victims among the Tlokwa of eastern Lesotho. Recent evidence is more equivocal but it does seem that women are more vulnerable than men to being 'gripped' by *moya*. Ashton ascribed this to the 'dullness' of women's lives. But the problem of explanation is much more complex than this. Affliction by *moya* may reflect the anxieties for women that arise out of loneliness and economic insecurity. It may be, also, that men have similar anxieties but that other means of resolution are available to them. For example, men are responsible for the moral conduct of relations with the ancestors. Women are not directly so. Their differential moral responsibilities may affect the cultural logic of diagnosis.

One Belief, Many Churches

Most Sotho–Tswana today are nominally Christians. Most also continue to revere their ancestors. Having grown up in an environment where Christian and indigenous sources of belief have been integrated for so long, people seldom bother to interpret the two theological traditions independently. The most recent detailed study of Sotho–Tswana religious activity and belief was carried out by Jean Comaroff in a community of Tshidi

A Sotho doctor examines his divining 'bones'. These objects, which include bone, stone and shell, have been collected from various parts of the country over a considerable period of time.

An Anglican service at a mission in Lesotho.

Rolong in BophuthaTswana. Her impression was of a widespread uniformity of belief, albeit eclectic and inconsistent, underlying an institutional diversity of religious affiliation. In other words, people believe much the same, but they belong to many different churches.

The proliferation of churches began as a reaction to political domination. Africans proved unable to resist the military power of the whites, but they developed an alternative form of resistance through rejecting white religious institutions. Many Africans opposed Christianity outright on the grounds that it implied rejection of their own culture. Many others gradually accepted the teachings of the missionaries. However, some of those who did become Christians resented their inferior status within the mission

churches, and left in order to found new churches in which they could express their Christian faith under their own leadership. This form of rebellion, which was permitted even when political domination was complete, became known as the 'Ethiopian' movement. It was inspired in part by the appearance in South Africa of black American ministers of the African Methodist Episcopal Church. Such churches developed most strongly amongst the Zulu, Swazi and Northern Sotho. A minor incursion occurred at Hermon in Basutoland in 1875, and in the Tswana country at Taung in 1885. But the Ethiopian movement generally made little progress amongst the Southern Sotho and the Tswana, partly

A group of girls undergoing initiation in Lesotho. They wear beaded masks known as masira. At this stage they are known as bale and perform songs and dramas in public.

An independent-church healing rite in Soweto. Many Sotho–Tswana belong to independent churches with congregations in rural and urban areas.

Weaving at Mazenod Mission.

A parade in Maseru to celebrate the birthday of
King Moshoeshoe II.

The main shopping centre in Gaborone.

perhaps because the P E M S and the I M S opposed settler intrusion on behalf of their respective African communities; and partly because, in any case, there developed vigorous competition for adherents among the orthodox Christian denominations. For example, the success of the Roman Catholic church in Basutoland in the twentieth century may be seen in part as a reaction against the earlier dominance of the French Protestants.

At the turn of the century independent churches began to assume a new form. 'Zionist' or 'Spirit' movements emerged which not only rejected the hierarchies of foreign origin in which the Ethiopian churches had remained, but incorporated traditional African beliefs and practices under charismatic prophet leaders. Some of these movements, such as the Zion Christian church of Bishop Edward Lekganyane, the St Paul Apostolic Faith Morning Star movement and the Zion Apostolic Church, have significant congregations in Lesotho. But the majority of Basotho, as the accompanying table shows (fig. 29), profess allegiance to one or other of the three dominant mission churches—the Roman Catholic, the Lesotho Evangelical (which evolved from the P E M S) and the Anglican. All have Africanised their ministries to some extent. These differences of religious affiliation are also associated with political alignments. The Catholic hierarchy has prominently identified itself with the cause of anti-communism, through its weekly newspaper *Moeletsi* (Adviser), and is in more or less overt alliance with the ruling Basutoland National Party. The fortnightly *Leselinyana*, on the other hand, published at Morija by the Lesotho Evangelical Church, is more closely identified with the views of the opposition Basutoland Congress Party.

The Tswana generally resisted separatism in the early period. Chief Khama of the Ngwato, for example, who was deeply influenced by Christianity, refused to deal with the leaders of independent churches. When they first entered Bechuanaland in 1899, they obtained some success among the Ngwaketse, but their movement was politically suspect because they came from South Africa. Small independent church congregations exist in Botswana today, but their greatest influence, among both the Tswana and the Southern Sotho, is in the towns and cities of South Africa.

It is important to remember that there are two sides to the acceptance, and two sides to the rejection, of orthodox Christianity. On the one hand, the new theology involved subservience to alien institutions. But mission schools also proved a training ground for many of the present generation of nationalist leaders. On the other hand, the independent Zionist churches allowed an opportunity for the free expression of Christian faith in an African idiom. But many regard them as a 'blind alley' in terms of their potential for realising political aspirations.

Jean Comaroff's study, referred to above, offers a detailed example of contemporary religious expression in one Tswana community. She identified three types of church. Type A consists of white-affiliated churches, such as the Methodist and Roman Catholic. Type B are African independent churches, which have no white affiliations but are structured formally along the same lines as white mission churches. Examples of these are the African Methodist Episcopal Church, and the Presbyterian Church of Africa. Lastly, type C incorporates manifestly syncretistic churches, whose organisation and ideology show the influences both of white fundamentalist churches and of African tradition. These churches have more elaborate names, such as the Full Witness Apostolic Church in Zion, and the St John's Apostolic Faith Church. They are otherwise characterised as Zionist, in which 'ancestral veneration, dance and instrumental ritual are incorporated and validated in Christian terms'. For example, the 'holy spirit' *(moya)*, one of the Trinity, 'grips' people in an idiom very similar to the traditional form of mystical affliction by 'spirit of the ancestors' which we described above.

In 1970 there were fourteen type A churches, with a total membership of 6 154 people in the chiefdom; nine type B churches, with 1 271 members; and no less than thirty-three type C churches, with a membership of 3 750. Jean Comaroff stressed, however, that only just over 50 per cent of adults in the population of the Tshidi Rolong chiefdom were registered church members; that formal membership of a church implies neither regular participation nor exclusive attendance at that church; and that individuals may move from one church to another

fig. 29 Church affiliation in Lesotho, according to the 1966 census.

CHURCH	NUMBERS	PERCENTAGE
Roman Catholic	328 793	38,68
Lesotho Evangelical	206 340	24,27
Anglican	88 631	10,43
other Christians	71 238	8,38
non-Christians	155 011	18,24
TOTAL	850 013	100,00

without difficulty. Type C churches had the highest proportion of members of low economic status and educational attainment. Despite the other churches' image of greater respectability in these terms, Comaroff found a tendency for individuals to drift from type A to type B to type C churches in the course of their religious careers. She also found that non-Tswana immigrants congregate in the Zionist churches; and that sometimes ethnic polarisation occurs in which church membership and activity are used by a minority to articulate resentment against the ethnic majority. This recalls another example of factional conflict of this kind, in the community of Southern Sotho at Maboloka, which was described in Chapter 6.

Zionist churches throughout Southern Africa are characterised by their proliferation of leadership roles, their predominantly female congregations, their endemic tendency to split, and their preoccupation with healing. They play a very large part in the everyday lives of their members. Meetings

A Zionist independent-church congregation meeting in a Johannesburg suburb on a Sunday afternoon.

often last a whole weekend. Periods of rhythmic dancing and singing, accompanied by drumming, alternate with rhetorical elaborations by the leader of biblical texts which he knows by heart. He conducts the meeting through a series of climaxes and 'rest' periods which leave participants exhausted and emotionally drained. There is a profound sense of community and of spiritual intensity. Another extremely important aspect of these churches is their formation of self-help agencies and women's groups, which serve to counteract to some extent the endemic insecurity of those who experience socio-economic deprivation.

The Contemporary Economic Predicament

COLIN MURRAY

9

The Roots of Underdevelopment

The purpose of this chapter is to outline the contemporary economic predicament of the Tswana and Southern Sotho peoples. In order to do this, we have to transcend not only the ethnic boundaries which divide the Sotho–Tswana from other African peoples, but also the international boundaries which divide the three nation–states in which they live. The reason for this is that the inhabitants of Lesotho, Botswana, BophuthaTswana and Qwa-Qwa depend for their livelihood, to a greater or lesser extent, on the export of labour to 'white' South Africa. The focus of our analysis is therefore the regional economic system of Southern Africa as a whole, identified by reference to the concept of a labour market.

The labour market in question is loosely but conveniently defined in the emotive prose of the Transvaal and Orange Free State Chamber of Mines in 1951: 'They come on foot, on horseback, on bicycles, by dug-out canoe, by lake and river steamers, in lorries, by train and some even by air. They come from as far afield as 2 000 miles. They come from all points of the compass—from the peaceful hills of the Transkei, from the lion country of the Bechuanaland bush, down the broad reaches of the Zambezi, from the tropical shores of Lake Nyasa and the mountain fastnesses of Basutoland. They come, too, in their thousands from the hills and valleys of Portuguese East Africa, from the rocky uplands of Sekukuniland, the tangled swamp country of the Okavango delta and the green hills of Swaziland. From these far corners of Southern Africa men from more than 100 tribes are attracted every year to the Witwatersrand by the magnet of the mining industry.'

This relationship of dependence is deeply rooted in the structural conditions under which Africans from all parts of the sub-continent were incorporated into the regional economic system. The analytical framework appropriate for investigating these conditions is the relationship between the industrial core and the rural periphery, as it has evolved through time. The industrial core refers to the mining and manufacturing industries in 'white' South Africa. The rural periphery refers to the African reserves within South Africa—the 'homelands'—and to the foreign countries from which black labour has been drawn, on a vast scale, to meet the needs of the industrial core—above all, Malawi, southern Moçambique, Botswana Lesotho and Swaziland. The relationship between the industrial core and the rural periphery is one of fundamental imbalance. Capital accumulation has taken place in the core areas at the expense of the peripheral areas. In simple terms, this means that spectacular economic growth in 'white' South Africa has been accompanied by increasing poverty in the black periphery. The standard of living of inhabitants of the periphery has steadily declined in the last hundred years, a process which may be described as *underdevelopment*. At different periods in different areas, a largely self-sufficient peasantry was transformed into a rural proletariat. The interested reader may wish to pursue the evidence for this transformation in the sources listed at the back of the book.

Development and underdevelopment are two sides of the same coin. In order to understand this we have to look at the regional economic system of Southern Africa as a whole. Nevertheless the presence of international boundaries between South African and foreign sources of labour is of vital significance, as is the isolated and fragmented distribution of the 'homelands' within South Africa. The balance between these sources of supply has changed over time. During the 1970s, various political and economic pressures induced the mining industry to initiate a policy of 'internalising' mine labour recruitment, in order to reduce dependence on foreign supplies and to increase dependence on South African supplies. These pressures were: the dramatic rise in the international price of gold, which allowed wages in the mining industry to rise in such a way as to compete with wages in manufacturing industry for the first time, and therefore to attract black South Africans; internal labour unrest and violence on the mining compounds, attributable to low wages and poor working conditions; and the political uncertainties arising out of escalating civil war in Zimbabwe, Malawi's sudden (and shortlived) ban on recruitment of labour in April 1974, and the collapse of Portuguese colonialism in Mocambique. In December 1973 foreign Africans constituted 80 per cent of the black labour force recruited for mines affiliated to the South African Chamber of Mines, and South Africans constituted the remaining 20 per cent. In December 1978, however, the foreign component was 45 per cent, and the South African 55 per cent (see fig. 30). Most of the increase in the South African supply has been drawn from the 'homelands'. Most of the loss in foreign supply has been borne hitherto by Malawi and Moçambique, although Lesotho and Botswana

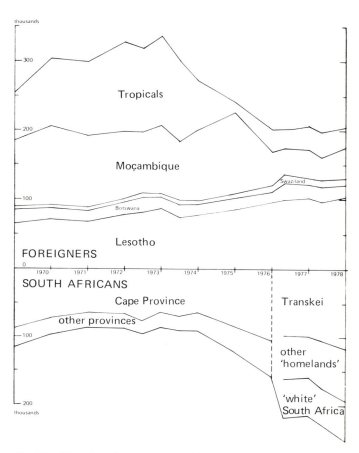

fig. 30 The changing pattern of black labour supply to the South African mines (affiliated to the S A Chamber of Mines) during the 1970s. The most significant change is the increase in the proportion of South Africans and the decrease in the proportion of foreigners. Until 1975 the vast majority of miners in the category 'Tropicals' (areas north of latitude 22° S) were from Malawi. Since 1974, however, substantial numbers have been recruited from Zimbabwe (Rhodesia). Until 1976 South African miners were classified by their province of origin; from 1977 by their origin in the 'white' areas and the ten 'homelands'.

have also suffered to some extent.

Thus from the mining industry's point of view the policy of 'internalisation' has been successful. But a further reduction of employment opportunities available to their citizens would be potentially devastating for Lesotho and at least ominous for Botswana. The internalisation trend has led to the emergence of a relatively favoured 'inner' periphery—the 'homelands'—as against a relatively disadvantaged 'outer' periphery—foreign sources of

A mine compound dormitory in 1946. In many of the older mines conditions have not changed greatly.

supply. But the definition of 'foreign' is a flexible one. The Transkei became 'independent' in 1976, and BothuthaTswana in 1977. Both are potentially 'foreign' in the sense that South Africa will be less inclined than in the past to recognise any obligations towards them. In any case its sophisticated battery of labour controls effectively allows the South African Government to discriminate within the 'inner' periphery in order to bring pressure on 'homeland' leaders to cooperate in the full implementation of the strategy of separate development. In this way unemployment in the peripheral areas may be distributed according to the political convenience of Pretoria. Whatever the policy, the reality is separate underdevelopment.

This is the general framework necessary for understanding the economic problems and prospects of the Tswana and the Southern Sotho peoples. Each part of the periphery, of course, has its

own particular history. In the following sections we look first at Lesotho, as a classic case of underdevelopment, and then at Botswana and BophuthaTswana, representing variations on the theme.

Lesotho: From Granary to Labour Reserve

Lesotho is recognised by the United Nations as one of the poorest nations in the world. It has very few resources other than, in one description, 'water, people and scenery'. Three-quarters of its land area of 30 350 square kilometres is rugged mountainous terrain, forming part of the Drakensberg range. Most of its inhabitants live in the remaining part of the country, the western lowland belt running from north to south. This landscape is dotted with sandstone plateaus and scarred with erosion ravines. Average annual rainfall is about 700 mm, of which most falls in the summer months from October to

March (fig. 31). Its distribution varies greatly, however, both from year to year and within the growing season. Sometimes the young crops are scorched by the fierce heat of December and January, unrelieved by a drop of moisture. At other times, torrential rainstorms carry away metres of good soil. Crops are also subject to damage by hail and, as they ripen, by frost. Agriculture is a risky enterprise.

The acute economic dependence of Lesotho is simply illustrated. In 1976 there were only 27 500 Basotho employed inside the country. Perhaps 200 000 migrants from Lesotho find employment in South Africa, out of the country's total population of one and a quarter million. More than 130 000 men were employed in the mines alone in 1977, supplying a quarter of the industry's complement of black labour. In the short term, the effect of the 'internalisation' policy was to increase the number of recruits from Lesotho, to make up for the sudden reduction from Malawi. However, these jobs were by no means secure. It was estimated in 1978 that the country would have to anticipate the loss of about 40 000 jobs. There is no realistic prospect of Lesotho's being able to accommodate large numbers of its unemployed citizens, since the rate of domestic job creation cannot even keep pace with the natural increase in the labour force. This is a crisis of potentially massive proportions for government and people.

The earnings of Lesotho's migrant labourers far exceed the country's Gross Domestic Product. According to a recent survey, about 70 per cent of mean rural household income is derived from migrant earnings. Only about 6 per cent is derived from domestic crop production. Agriculture does not 'support 80 per cent of the population', as the prime minister asserted in the Second Five Year Plan. It is hardly the 'backbone' of Lesotho's economy to which official sources refer. On the contrary, it is a feeble limb invigorated, if at all, by migrants' cash investments. Even with this investment, most farmers cannot grow nearly enough of the staple grains, maize and sorghum to sustain their own families, let alone the landless and the 6 per cent of the Basotho who live in towns. Today the population of Lesotho is aptly described as a rural proletariat which scratches about on the land.

It was not always so. The French missionaries of the P E M S in 1834 observed a country that was fertile and teeming with game. Following the discovery of diamonds at Kimberley in 1867, the Basotho vigorously responded to the mining camps' demand for food supplies. They exported vast quantities of grain. In 1870, shortly after a devastating

fig. 31   Monthly rainfall and mean daily temperature at Roma, Lesotho, 1972-6.

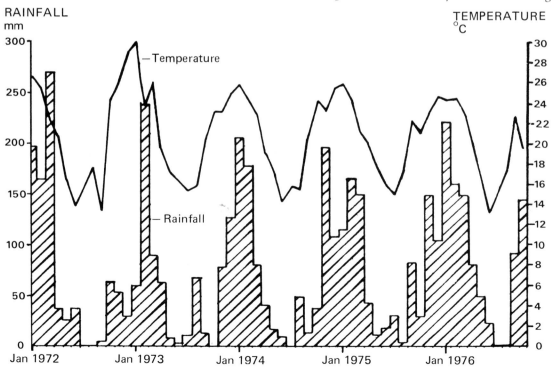

RAINFALL
mm

TEMPERATURE
°C

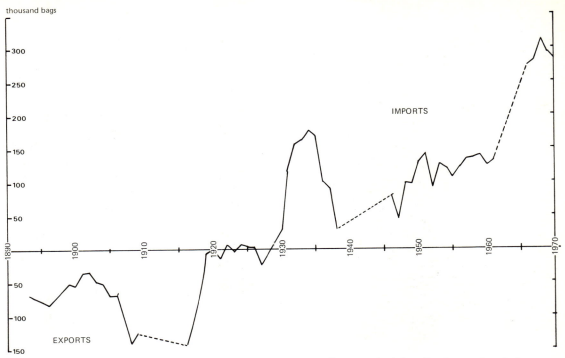

thousand bags

IMPORTS

EXPORTS

fig. 32   Net exports and imports of maize, Lesotho, 1890 –1970. (1) Exports only, 1893-1918. (2) All figures are expressed as 5-year rolling averages. (3) There are no figures available for 1910–15, 1939-45 and 1963-65.

war between the Basotho and the Boer settlers, the *Friend of the Free State* was able to remark: 'Nowhere else in South Africa is there a more naturally industrious nation, as honest and as peaceable as the Basotho.'

The period of prosperity was short-lived. The economic history of Lesotho in the last hundred years is a story of its transition from the 'granary of Southern Africa' to an impoverished labour reserve which imports basic foodstuffs. The reasons for the transition are manifold and complex. They include population growth, scarcity of land, and declining agricultural productivity because of over-grazing, erosion and inefficient techniques of cultivation. They also include taxation, discriminatory grain tariffs imposed to stop the Basotho competing with white farmers, lack of access to markets and lack of capital for investment. The very low wages paid to mine labourers, and the loss of manpower through the out-migration of large numbers of able-bodied men, further depressed indigenous agriculture. Meanwhile, British colonial officials rationalised a policy of administrative and economic neglect by

contradictory principles. On the one hand, they endorsed the philanthropic view that 'native cultures' should not be interfered with. On the other hand, they shared Cecil Rhodes's view that Africans should learn the dignity of labour. In 1903 the Resident Commissioner commended the Basotho who went to work in South Africa for their industrious character in this respect. The principle that expenditure should not exceed revenue became the touchstone of administrative competence. Jack Spence has described this as a 'neat coincidence of interest between private altruism and government parsimony'.

Thus the failure of peasant self-sufficiency must be examined against the background of a larger system of production. This demanded, not that Africans grow sufficient food to preserve their economic independence, but that they contribute their labour to the 'white' economy—to white farmers and mining companies in particular. As the economist Francis Wilson has observed, 'peasant production was "idleness" to the white man in need of labour'. The evidence of decline shows that underdevelopment is not an original state, attributable to a lack of African entrepreneurial ability, or to the deficiencies of African social structure, or to the inhibitions of African culture. Rather, underdevelopment is an historical process. Its explanation must be sought in the specific conditions under which Basotho were in-

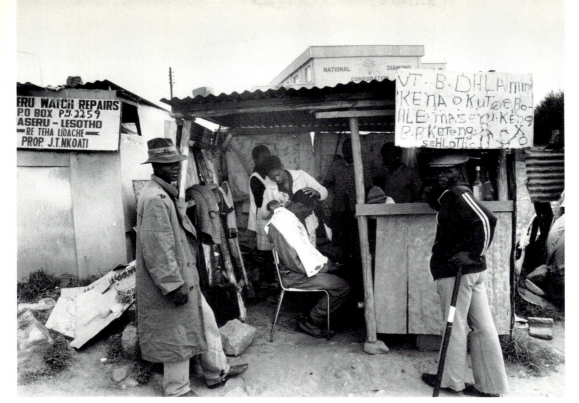

The informal sector in Maseru: a barber and watch repairer.

A Maseru hairdresser, part of the formal sector of the economy.

corporated into a larger political and economic system.

In recent years the Lesotho government has been able to diversify its sources of international aid, to expand tourism greatly, and to initiate an integrated plan for rural development. In view of the long history of agricultural decline, the prospects of the latter are as yet uncertain. The possibility of exploiting Lesotho's water resources has never been realised, owing to the breakdown of negotiations with South Africa. A significant recent development has been the capitalisation of diamond-mining by De Beers at Letseng-la-Terai, a remote site in the northern mountains. Work on the development of the mine began in 1975; and in 1978 diamonds were exported to the value of R16,7 million. They have already overtaken Lesotho's traditional exports in value—R4,8 million of mohair and R2,9 million of wool were exported in 1978.

Technical training: young men and women at the Lerotholi Polytechnic in Maseru.

Botswana: A Story of Burgeoning Inequality

Botswana is a vast and arid table-land, sloping gently from east to west. It is about twenty times larger than Lesotho but has barely more than half of Lesotho's population. More than 50 000 Batswana are employed in the formal sector of the economy. About the same number were estimated to be in South Africa in 1971, reflecting an historical dependence on the export of labour similar to that of Lesotho. Over 40 000 Batswana were recruited for South African mines in 1976. However, the country's economic prospects are significantly different from those of Lesotho in two respects.

Firstly, there is a large commercial livestock industry, which has preferential access to the market of the European Economic Community. Meat and meat products have been the most important exports and the national herd increased enormously in response to the rising price of beef in the 1970s. Secondly, some of the country's extensive mineral

resources are now being exploited on a considerable scale. Diamond production began at the rich Orapa mine in 1971, and other mines have also been developed. The most substantial investment, undertaken by multi-national interests in association with the Botswana government, has been in the copper-nickel deposits at Selebi-Pikwe. There have been many technical difficulties, and a major strike in 1975, but the future potential is considerable. Mineral exports have already overtaken livestock products in value, and provide the government with a vital source of revenue. They do not, however, go very far towards solving the problem of unemployment.

Tribal land—the former Tribal Reserves plus recent additional areas—comprises 71 per cent of the land area of Botswana; while 6 per cent is held under freehold or leasehold, and 23 per cent is State land—mainly sparsely populated sandveld in the northern, central and western parts of the country (see fig. 33). Only about 6 per cent of the total land area is suitable for cultivation. This is concentrated, as is 80 per cent of the population, in the eastern strip of the country which has higher rainfall than elsewhere and lies along the line of rail. The main crops are sorghum, maize, beans and cowpeas. Production is very variable from year to year, depending largely on the distribution of rainfall; and income from crops is far less than income from livestock.

In 1975 the government introduced a Tribal Grazing Land Policy (T G L P). The policy has three avowed aims: to arrest the long-term degradation of the veld arising out of a large increase in the national herd and consequent over-grazing and erosion; to reverse the trend of increasing inequalities of wealth and income in the rural areas; and to facilitate the sustained growth of the commercial livestock industry. Under the old system of communal grazing, it proved impossible either to limit absolute numbers of livestock or to conserve the grazing that was available. The T G L P proposed to give stock-owners control over specific grazing areas and thereby to improve herd management.

The policy is to divide the tribal grazing areas into three zones: Commercial Farming Areas, for ranching by large individual cattle owners and by syndicates of smaller owners, under lease from Land Boards; Communal Grazing Areas, in which the traditional system would continue to apply; and Reserved Areas, which would conserve grazing for future use and also accommodate groups which still live mainly by hunting. There are major anxieties relating to all three aims of the policy. Firstly, it is doubtful whether the T G L P can achieve its ecolo-

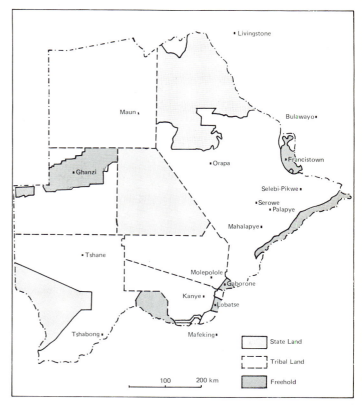

fig. 33 Botswana, showing the recent conversion of some State Land into Tribal Land (compare with the distribution shown in fig. 14).

gical or commercial objectives, because of the lack of credit available for fencing and for bore-holes, and because proficient managers cannot be found. Secondly, the problem remains unresolved of how to protect the interests of those with existing land rights in the commercial areas who do not have livestock. These are mainly Sarwa (Bushmen), but there are also significant numbers of poor Tswana and Kgalagadi. They have not been adequately compensated for the loss of their rights. In practice, the policy is likely to exacerbate existing wealth differentials, which are already wide. A recent proposal that a cattle head-tax should be introduced, as the only effective way of conserving grazing, was rejected by the cabinet.

We have already noted three patterns of population movement in Botswana. One is the traditional seasonal movement between villages and lands. Another is the more recent drift towards permanent settlement in the outlying areas. A third is repetitive migration to work in South Africa, which has been such an important feature of the lives of Batswana

A mine official pays remittances from an absent Tswana migrant labourer to his wife.

for decades. A fourth significant pattern of movement is the rural-urban drift to the 'new' towns (and to a lesser extent to the large tribal capitals) which has taken place mainly as a result of the development of government infrastructure and an accelerated rate of job creation since independence in 1966. These 'new' towns are: Gaborone, the capital of Botswana, which was little more than a police post in 1964; Lobatse, the centre of the beef-export industry; Francistown, the old commercial centre of the Tati company in the north-east; and the mining towns of Orapa and Selebi-Pikwe. The population of these five towns has grown from about 21 000 in 1964 to over 120 000 in 1978. This is a spectacular rate of urbanisation.

Many urban workers have not, however, cut off their links with the rural areas. A study of Selebi-Pikwe by David Cooper has shown that wage employment, the urban informal sector and rural sources of income are complementary. Workers' families retain a base in arable land and livestock; and their wages allow them to invest more effectively in farming than many rural households without direct access to wage employment. Skilled workers with higher wages are much better able to do this than unskilled workers who can barely scrape a livelihood for their families. The drift to the towns does not therefore imply a neat division of the population into rural peasants and urban workers. As with the traditional pattern of dispersal between villages and lands, we are dealing not with discrete populations but with *relationships* encapsulated within the household as the basic unit of production and consumption. Its members continue to distribute their energies and resources between employment in the formal sector—inside or outside the country; participation in the domestic economy based on agriculture and livestock; and opportunities that arise in the informal sector in both rural and urban areas.

Some Evidence of Differentiation

Surveys of income distribution between rural households have revealed considerable inequality in both Lesotho and Botswana. What is this evidence and how can it be interpreted? Before exploring these differences specifically it will be helpful to make two general points.

The first point is that farm incomes in the periphery are to a large extent derived from the investment of migrant earnings. Observers often assume that migrants undertake employment in South Africa in order to *supplement* their income from livestock and domestic agriculture. The myth of 'subsistence' farming dies hard. It is true that the failure of agricultural production to meet subsistence needs is an index of aggregate dependence on the export of labour. On the other hand, under prevailing conditions of population pressure and farming technology, effective cultivation depends on the availability of male and female labour and on the use of intensive methods: the hire of oxen or a tractor, the purchase of seed and fertilizer. The most common difficulty rural households face is a scarcity of capital inputs in the form of cash, equipment or traction animals. Migrants also invest their savings in livestock. Thus farming is not conducted independently of a regular cash income. The implication of

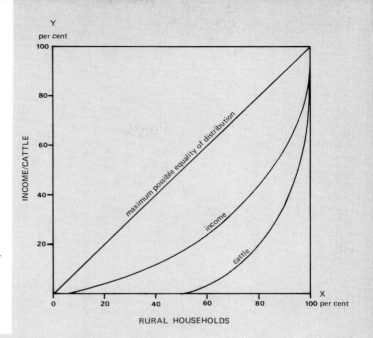

RURAL HOUSEHOLDS

Two different ways of representing inequality amongst rural households in Botswana:
fig. 34a Distribution of income and cattle-ownership. A point on the curve shows that X per cent of households have Y per cent of cumulative income or cattle.
fig. 34b Size of settlement.

LOCATION OF HOUSEHOLD	MEAN INCOME (RANDS) FROM				MEDIAN INCOME (RANDS)
	Crops	Livestock	Employment	Trading	
small villages, lands areas, cattle posts	76	411	258	196	610
*large villages	140	616	739	806	887

* Maun, Serowe, Palapye, Mahalapye, Mochudi, Molepolole, Ramotswa, Kanye.

this is that migrant earning-capacity, rather than farm income, must be viewed as the independent variable in assessing the manner in which individual households dispose their resources. This generalisation applies throughout the periphery, except to the small number of commercial farmers in Botswana who have achieved a self-sustaining level of turnover in livestock.

The second point follows from this. Rural households vary in size and demographic composition (the age and sex of their members). The identi-

fication and comparison of 'richer' and 'poorer' households must allow for the fact that these variables affect both household consumption requirements and migrant earning-capacity. This means that what anthropologists call the *developmental cycle* of the household—the way in which its size and composition change through time—must be built into any explanation of observed differences in in-

fig. 35 The distribution of rural household income in Lesotho.

INCOME STRATUM (RANDS)	HOUSEHOLDS		MEAN HOUSEHOLD INCOME (RANDS)	MEAN HOUSEHOLD SIZE
	Number	Percentage		
less than 100	347	27%	66	3,1
200–599	257	20	408	4,9
600–999	347	27	859	5,1
1000 and more	335	26	1 739	7,7
TOTAL	1 286	100	783	5,2

come and wealth between rural households. Life histories help to reveal the way in which strategies of household viability vary with the phase in the developmental cycle; above all, with the presence and relative size, or absence, of an income from migrant labour.

These two points together explain why the class position of inhabitants of the labour reserves is a controversial issue. Rural households engage in a diversity of activities in order to make ends meet. They are certainly not peasants, conventionally defined as small producers for the market who neither employ nor sell labour. Neither are they a proletariat, in the classical sense of having been 'freed' from the land and depending solely on the sale of their labour-power. We use the term rural

proletariat here, to indicate both that the inhabitants of the periphery are heavily dependent on wage labour and that many of them continue to extract a part, albeit a decreasing part, of their livelihood from the land. Many households, also, are 'marginalised' in the sense that they neither have access to wage employment nor have been able to establish an effective resource-base in farming. Poverty is rampant in both relative and absolute terms.

Land and livestock are the two most important assets in the rural economy. In Lesotho scarcity of land relative to the needs of the population is acute. But most surveys show a relatively equitable distribution of the arable land that is available. This is plausibly attributed to a system of land tenure that recognises the right of every married man to usufructuary title to some arable land, and theoretically allows reallocation of land in accordance with the demography of household needs. The mean household holding is, however, only about half the traditional entitlement of three fields per landholder. Perhaps 15 or 20 per cent of households have no land. In view of Botswana's vast size and relatively small population, it has generally been assumed that there is no absolute scarcity of land. The evidence is equivocal, however, since so much of the country is semi-desert scrub or otherwise marginal in respect of arable potential. Particularly in the relatively densely populated areas of the south-east, many Batswana are now experiencing land shortage. The drift outwards to permanent settlement at the lands is one symptom of this.

Livestock are much more unevenly distributed. A survey in 1975 in Lesotho revealed that 48 per cent of households own no livestock, whereas 10 per cent of households own nearly 60 per cent of all livestock. The Rural Income Distribution Survey in Botswana, conducted in 1974–5, showed a similarly skew pattern of livestock distribution: 45 per cent of rural households have no cattle; while 10 per cent of rural households control about 65 per cent of the cattle. The difference is, however, that cattle are far more important in the national economy of Botswana than in that of Lesotho—in absolute numbers, export earnings and proportional contribution to rural household incomes. Botswana's national herd was about three million cattle in 1976; that of Lesotho nearly half a million.

Accordingly livestock are the most important source of income for the richest rural households in

Peaches are the only fruit growing in abundance in some parts of Lesotho.

A General Dealer, 'where right-up-to-date things can be found'.

Botswana; whereas income from employment predominates in the middle-income strata. The mean rural household in Lesotho derives about 70 per cent of its income from migrant earnings, and only 17 per cent from farming (crops and livestock) (see fig. 35). Migrant labour predominates as the major source of income for households in all income strata other than the quarter of rural households identified as 'very poor'. These latter have meagre domestic resources and very little access to migrant earnings. In general, there appears to be an approximate correlation between household size, domestic productive capacity (crops and livestock) and migrant earning capacity. This is contrary to the assumption commonly made that income from migrant earnings varies inversely with farm income.

Many development programmes are now designed with an explicit 'poverty focus'. But knowledge of who the poor are is a prerequisite of effective intervention to help them. One way of identifying the poor is to investigate the characteristics of the poorest 20 or 30 per cent of a given population. The households that predominate in the 'very poor' income stratum in Lesotho—one-quarter of all rural households—appear to have two distinctive characteristics: they are small and they are female-headed. Various evidence from Botswana appears to corroborate this picture. One experienced fieldworker concluded that 'female-headed households make up a disproportionate share of the nation's poorest and economically most vulnerable households'.

BophuthaTswana: An Artificial Economy

BophuthaTswana is also heavily dependent on employment in South Africa. But it is sensible to discuss the nature of this dependence separately from that of Lesotho and Botswana, because of the different political circumstances in which it emerged as an 'independent' national entity. Very little research of a comparable kind has been carried out in BophuthaTswana; and the official figures that are available disguise the similar process of underdevelopment that has been taking place there.

It is helpful to distinguish three aspects of the homeland's 'economy'. One aspect is the inability of rural communities, particularly in the western areas of the homeland, to make a living from the land. BophuthaTswana has the lowest population density of all the 'homelands', at 24 persons per square kilometre in 1970. But its natural vegetation is semi-arid bushveld, much more suitable for pastoral than for arable use. Accordingly, livestock are a much more important source of income than cultivation. There is a nucleus of wealthy farmers, and Chief Mangope's government is committed to encouraging 'progressive' farming by establishing rights of enclosure on tribal grazing land. This inevitably leads to the dispossession of others. Crop yields are low despite the fact that part of the homeland lies within the South African maize triangle. In a review of BophuthaTswana's prospects in December 1977 the *Financial Mail* commented: 'The picture you get is one where females attempt to coax some harvest from small pieces of ground with short-handled broad-bladed hoes, while male children look after miserable livestock and the adult males commute or migrate to industrialised areas to augment family income.' Thus many residents of BophuthaTswana depend on employment outside its constituent territories. In this respect BophuthaTswana conforms with the classic pattern of underdevelopment. The number of male migrant workers temporarily absent was recorded as 37 600 in the 1970 census. That figure represented 27 per cent of the domiciled labour force, defined as males aged 15–64 years. But it very much under-represents the extent of BophuthaTswana's dependence on employment outside its boundaries.

The reason for this is the second aspect of the 'economy' to which it is helpful to draw attention: the large industrial area north and west of Pretoria. Part of this area is situated inside the territory, based on the 'decentralisation' growth point of Babelegi. Employment there amounted to 8 660 jobs for Africans, mainly Tswana, in mid-1977. Much the larger part of it, however, in terms of employment opportunities, consists of the border industries established in 'white' areas in such a way as to use commuter labour drawn from the nearby homeland. In 1975 104 000 people were reported to be travelling daily from the new dormitory towns within BophuthaTswana, such as Ga-Rankuwa, Mabopane and Tlhabane, to the border industries at Brits, Rosslyn, Rustenburg and Pretoria. By 1976 this number had increased to 155 000. Although this is essentially one economic region, legal barriers prevent the free movement of capital, so that the pattern of industrial growth is somewhat different inside and outside the homeland. Wages at Babelegi are very low. They were reported in 1976 to be R9,50 a week for an unskilled labourer, and the rate of job creation is hopelessly inadequate to accommodate a vast influx of people looking for employment. Large numbers of non-Tswana, for example, are unemployed 'squatters' in the sprawling slums of the Winterveld area between Ga-Rankuwa and Mabopane.

In summary of this aspect, north and west of Pretoria there is an ethnically mixed labour force resident in the 'homeland' associated with the Tswana. A few of them have jobs in the Territory. Many have no work at all. Many others commute to work in the 'white' areas but are in a very different legal position from other Africans employed in the same 'white' areas who have rights to reside there. Meanwhile thousands of 'redundant' Africans without such rights are 'endorsed out' of the 'white' areas. Many of them are non-Tswana who filter into the dormitory towns and slums of the homeland region north-west of Pretoria, in the desperate search for work. There they are harassed as foreign squatters by the BophuthaTswana police.

The third aspect is BophuthaTswana's mineral resources, which include platinum, chrome, asbestos, manganese and vanadium. Much the most important of these, in terms of employment and in terms of value in the international market, are three platinum mines: the Impala mine in the Mankwe and Bafokeng districts north of Rustenburg; and the Rustenburg and Western mines, which lie partly on tribal land within BophuthaTswana and partly in 'white' South Africa. The Rustenburg mine is the largest producer of platinum in the world.

The scale of its mining operations, involving 61 000 African employees in 1977, distinguishes BophuthaTswana from all the other 'homelands'. The large majority of these employees, however, come from elsewhere in South Africa and from traditional foreign sources of mine labour such as Malawi, Moçambique, Botswana and Lesotho. Very few are from BophuthaTswana. The reason for this is not that the Tswana are prejudiced against work underground, as in one official view. In 1978, after all, 28 000 men from BophuthaTswana were either recruited or presented themselves for work in mines affiliated to the South African Chamber of Mines. Rather, the reasons appear to be the centralised control of recruitment by the Chamber of Mines; an agreement with the white miners' union to maintain job reservation restrictions on training non-Tswana recruits in BophuthaTswana, making non-Tswana labour cheaper on average than Tswana labour; and the fact that residents of that part of the territory where the mines are concentrated have relatively easy access to the manufacturing industries of the Pretoria-Witwatersrand-Vereeniging complex, where wages and conditions are better than on the mines. In any case, a glance at the map shows that people from other parts of BophuthaTswana are as close to the gold mines near Welkom in the Orange Free State as they are to the platinum mines.

The production of all these mining operations accounts for roughly half of BophuthaTswana's Gross Domestic Product (G D P). But capital investment is drawn from outside the homeland; therefore there is a net outflow of interest payments and dividends to foreign lenders and shareholders. This is generally the case where there is heavy reliance on imported private capital, and particularly so in the mining industry. In the case of BophuthaTswana, however, the earnings of black workers in the homeland's mines, which constitute about half the earnings of all black employees in the homeland, scarcely benefit the resident population. Yet these earnings are also incorporated in the G D P. For these two reasons, the G D P grossly overstates the value to the homeland of the productive activities that take place there. Against this, of course, there are the royalties paid by the Union Corporation, which runs the Impala mine, to the Bafokeng tribe on whose land the mine is situated; and the earnings of commuters and migrants outside Bophutha-Tswana. In 1974–5 it was officially calculated that these earnings represented 67 per cent of the homeland's Gross National Income (G N I = G D P plus earnings of migrants and commuters plus income of non-blacks in the homeland). But these earnings are derived from productive activities that take place in the context of industrial development in Southern Africa as a whole.

The point of all these details is that the 'economy' of BophuthaTswana is integrated so comprehensively with that of South Africa that it is meaningless to construct figures such as the homeland's G D P and G N I per capita. They are wholly artificial. Yet these figures are used to justify and to evaluate the success of the policy of separate development, by comparison with similar figures from other African countries. They overstate the welfare of Bophutha-Tswana's population. Quite apart from this, the use of figures such as G D P per head and G N I per head is discredited because they fail to take account of inequalities of income distribution within the population.

For the same reasons, it is not possible to identify an 'economy' in the Southern Sotho 'homeland' of QwaQwa, which is both the smallest and the most severely over-populated of all the 'homelands'. The land is barren, there is negligible industrial development and very little employment available. During the 1970s the tiny homeland became an urban slum. It absorbed at least an eight-fold increase in its population but was quite unable to provide any means of livelihood for these people. Chief Minister Kenneth Mopeli rejected a suggestion, in 1978, that QwaQwa become a 'city-state' which would act as an administrative centre for all Southern Sotho in South Africa. He has insisted that the option of independence is impossible unless the land area is greatly increased.

Conclusion

In 1976 Roelof ('Pik') Botha, then South Africa's ambassador to the United Nations, addressed the U N Security Council as follows: 'The problem in Southern Africa is basically not one of race, but of nationalism, which is a world-wide problem. There is a white nationalism, and there are several black nationalisms. . . . My Government's principal aim is to make it possible for each nation, black and white, to achieve its fullest potential, including sovereign independence, so that each individual can enjoy all the rights and privileges which his or her community is capable of securing for him or her.'

In the South African government's view, then, the fulfilment of the policy of separate development is a logical expression of ten different 'national' identities.

The evidence presented here leads to a different conclusion. The achievement of 'sovereign independence' is, in fact, compulsory political alienation. More than two million Tswana have already been made 'foreigners' in their own country. The gov-

ernment initially rejected the Wiehahn Commission's recommendation in 1979 that black migrant workers and commuters should be given trade union rights. The Riekert Commission's recommendations in the same year reflect the government's explicit commitment both to ease restrictions on labour mobility for Africans with rights of permanent residence in 'white' South Africa, and at the same time to tighten the mechanisms of influx control applied to workers domiciled in the 'homelands'. On the one hand, these measures will probably improve conditions for urban Africans. On the other hand, they will certainly exacerbate the problems of poverty and unemployment in the barren and isolated areas of the rural periphery.

Migrant workers from the periphery have contributed millions of man-years towards the economic development of 'white' South Africa. Those who come from foreign supplier states such as Lesotho, which remains acutely dependent on South Africa, are most vulnerable to changing labour recruitment policies. But even black South Africans are regarded as 'guest-workers' in 'white' South Africa. They have been deprived of basic political and economic rights in the country of their birth. Thus political boundaries are manipulated in order to export unemployment, to disclaim welfare responsibilities, to suppress class consciousness and to maintain vicarious control of the labour force, through the 'homeland' administrations. In this way the black proletariat is divided and dispossessed.

For these reasons the policy of ethnic nationalism cannot meet the legitimate aspirations of the Tswana and the Southern Sotho peoples.

Phases in the life cycle: herdboys and returning migrants.

Further Reading

A work such as this depends upon the experiences and research of many writers other than its authors. Though the design of the series precludes our use of footnotes, we freely acknowledge our dependence upon those writers and recommend further study of their works. The following list is a sampling of books and articles which will provide greater detail and alternative judgments for the consideration of the reader.

Chapter 1: The Tswana and Southern Sotho People

Doke, C M. 1967. *The Southern Bantu Languages*. 2nd ed. London: Dawsons.

Gluckman, M. 1975. 'Anthropology and Apartheid: The Work of South African Anthropologists.' In *Studies in African Social Anthropology*, ed. M Fortes and S Patterson. London: Academic Press.

Schapera, I. 1976. *The Tswana*. 2nd ed. London: International African Institute.

Setiloane, G. 1976. *The Image of God among the Sotho-Tswana*. Rotterdam: Balkema.

Chapter 2: Early History and Upheaval; Chapter 3: Reconstruction of the Sotho States; Chapter 4: Transitions; Chapter 5: Responses to Colonialism

Agar-Hamilton, J A I. 1928. *The Native Policy of the Voortrekkers*. Cape Town: Maskew Miller.

Butler, Jeffrey; Robert Rotberg and John Adams. 1977. *The Black Homelands of South Africa*. Berkeley: University of California Press.

Chirenje, J Mutero. 1978. *Chief Kgama and His Times*. London: Rex Collings; Cape Town: David Philip.

Du Plessis, J. 1911. *A History of Christian Missions in South Africa*. London: Longmans.

Ellenberger, D Fred, and J C Macgregor. 1912. *History of the Basuto*. London: Caxton Publishing Co.

Gabatshwane, S M. 1961. *Tshekedi Khama of Bechuanaland*. Cape Town: Oxford University Press.

————. 1966. *Seretse Kgama and Botswana*. Cape Town: J Mmusi and S M Gabatshwane.

Germond, Robert C. 1966. *Chronicles of Basutoland*. Morija: Sesuto Book Depot.

Halpern, Jack. 1965. *South Africa's Hostages*. London: Peter Smith.

Horrell, Muriel. 1973. *The African Homelands of South Africa*. Johannesburg: S A Institute of Race Relations.

Lye, William F. 1967. 'The Difaqane.' In *Journal of African History* VIII, pp 107-31.

————. 1969. 'The Ndebele Kingdom South of the Limpopo River.' In *Journal of African History* X, pp 87-104.

————. (ed.) 1975. *Andrew Smith's Journal*. Cape Town: Balkema.

Moffat, Robert. 1842. *Missionary Labours and Scenes in Southern Africa*. London: Snow.

Molema, S M. 1951. *Chief Moroka*. Cape Town: Methodist Publishing House.

Molema, S M. 1966. *Montshiwa*. Cape Town: Struik.

Northcott, Cecil. 1961. *Robert Moffat: Pioneer in Africa*. London: Lutterworth.

Omer-Cooper, J D. 1966. *The Zulu Aftermath*. London: Longmans.

Roux, Edward. 1966. *Time Longer Than Rope*. Madison: Wisconsin University Press.

Sanders, Peter. 1975. *Moshoeshoe, Chief of the Sotho*. London: Heinemann; Cape Town: David Philip.

Schapera, I. 1952. *The Ethnic Composition of Tswana Tribes*. London: London School of Economics and Political Science.

————. 1953. *The Tswana*. London: International African Institute.

————. 1970. *A Handbook of Tswana Law and Custom*. 2nd ed. London: Frank Cass.

————. 1970. *Tribal Innovators: Tswana Chiefs and Social Change*. London: Athlone Press.

Sheddick, V G J. 1953. *The Southern Sotho*. London: International African Institute.

Sillery, A. 1971. *John Mackenzie of Bechuanaland*. Cape Town: Balkema.

————. 1974. *Botswana: A Short Political History*. London: Methuen.

Stevens, Richard P. 1967. *Lesotho, Botswana and Swaziland*. London: Pall Mall Press.

Theal, George McCall. 1964. *Basutoland Records*. Cape Town: Struik.

Thompson, L M. 1965. *Politics in South Africa*. Boston.

————. 1969. *African Societies in Southern Africa*. London: Heinemann.

————. 1975. *Survival in Two Worlds*. Oxford: Clarendon Press.

Walshe, Peter. 1973. *Black Nationalism in South Africa*. Johannesburg: Ravan Press.

Wilson, Francis. 1972. *Migrant Labour in South Africa*. Johannesburg: S A Council of Churches and Spro-Cas.

Chapter 6: The Political Community; Chapter 9: The Contemporary Economic Predicament

(For readers' convenience, references on Lesotho, Botswana, BophuthaTswana and Basotho QwaQwa are listed separately)

Lesotho

Ashton, E H. 1952. *The Basuto*. Oxford University Press for the International African Institute.

Germond, R C. 1967. *Chronicles of Basutoland, 1830-1902*. Morija.

Hamnett, I. 1975. *Chieftainship and Legitimacy*. London: Routledge and Kegan Paul.

Jingoes, S J. 1975. *A Chief is a Chief by the People*. London: Oxford University Press.

Jones, G I. 1951. *Basutoland Medicine Murder*. London: H M S O, Cmnd. 8209.

Murray, C. 1978. 'Migration, Differentiation and the Developmental Cycle in Lesotho.' In *Migration and the Transformation of Modern African Society*, ed. W M J van Binsbergen and H Meilink. Leiden: Afrikastudiecentrum.

Spence, J. 1968. *Lesotho. The Politics of Dependence*. London: Oxford University Press.

Ström, G W. 1978. *Development and Dependence in Lesotho, the En-*

clave of South Africa. Uppsala: Scandinavian Institute of African Studies.

Van der Wiel, A C A. 1977. *Migratory Wage Labour. Its Role in the Economy of Lesotho.* Mazenod.

Botswana

Botswana. 1976a. *National Development Plan 1976-81.* Gaborone: Central Statistics Office.

Botswana. 1976b. *Rural Income Distribution Survey 1974/75.* Gaborone: Government Printer.

Cooper, D. 1978. 'The State, Mineworkers and Multinationals: The Selebi Phikwe Strike, Botswana, 1975.' In *African Labor History,* ed. P C W Gutkind, R Cohen and J Copans. Sage Publications.

Kuper. A. 1970. *Kalahari Village Politics.* Cambridge University Press.

Schapera, I. 1947. *Migrant Labour and Tribal Life.* London: Oxford University Press.

———. 1970. *A Handbook of Tswana Law and Custom.* 2nd. ed. London: Frank Cass.

Sillery, A. 1974. *Botswana. A short Political History.* London: Methuen.

Bophutha Tswana and QwaQwa

1977. *The Republic of Bophutha Tswana.* Johannesburg: Chris van Rensburg Publications.

1977. *Bophutha Tswana.* Fact Paper No. 4. London: International Defence and Aid Fund.

Butler, J, R I Rotberg and J Adams. 1977. *The Black Homelands of South Africa.* Berkeley: University of California Press.

Desmond, C. 1971. *The Discarded People.* Harmondsworth: Penguin Books.

Kane-Berman, J. 1979. *South Africa. The Method in the Madness.* London: Pluto Press. (First published 1978 in South Africa as *Soweto: Black Revolt, White Reaction.* Johannesburg: Ravan Press)

Malan, T, and P S Hattingh. 1976. *Black Homelands in South Africa.* Pretoria: Africa Institute of South Africa.

Rogers, B. 1976. *Divide and Rule. South Africa's Bantustans.* London: International Defence and Aid Fund.

Survey of Race Relations in South Africa. Annually. Johannesburg: South African Institute of Race Relations.

Chapter 7: Kinship

Casalis, E. 1965. *The Basutos.* Cape Town: Struik (facsimile reprint of original 1861 edition).

Comaroff, J. 1978. 'Rules and rulers: political process in a Tswana chiefdom.' *Man* 13, 1, pp 1-20.

Comaroff, J, and A Cohen. 1976. 'The Management of Meaning: On the Phenomenology of Political Transactions.' In *Transaction and Meaning,* ed. B. Kapferer. Philadelphia: ISHI Publications.

Kooijman, K F M. 1978. *Social and Economic Change in a Tswana Village.* Leiden: Afrikastudiecentrum.

Kuper, A. 1975. 'The social structure of the Sotho-speaking peoples of southern Africa.' *Africa* 45, 1, pp 67-81; 2, pp 139-49.

Murray, C. 1977. 'High bridewealth, migrant labour and the position of women in Lesotho.' *Journal of African Law* 21, 1, pp 79-96.

Roberts, S A. 1977. 'The Kgatla marriage: concepts of validity.' In *Law and the Family in Africa,* edited by S A. Roberts. The Hague: Mouton.

Kuper, A. 1970. 'The Kgalagari and the Jural Consequences of Marriage.' *Man* 5, pp. 466-82.

Schapera, I. 1935. 'The social structure of the Tswana ward.' *Bantu Studies* 9, pp 203-24.

———. 1971. *Married Life in an African Tribe.* Pelican Books.

Schapera, I, and S A. Roberts. 1975. 'Rampedi revisited: Another look at a Kgatla ward.' *Africa* 45, 3, pp 259-79.

Wilson, M. 1969. 'The Sotho, Venda and Tsonga.' In *The Oxford History of South Africa,* Vol. I, edited by M Wilson and L Thompson. Oxford: Clarendon Press.

Chapter 8: Ritual Practice and Belief

Ashton, E H. 1943. *Medicine, Magic and Sorcery among the Southern Sotho.* Communications from the School of African Studies (New Series, No. 10). Cape Town: University of Cape Town.

Pauw, B A. 1960. *Religion in a Tswana Chiefdom.* London: Oxford University Press for the International African Institute.

Schapera, I. 1971. *Rainmaking Rites of Tswana Tribes.* Leiden: Afrikastudiecentrum.

Setiloane, G. 1976. *The Image of God among the Sotho –Tswana.* Rotterdam: Balkema.

Index

Kok, Adam, 40; alliance with Moletsane, 50
Kok, Cornelius, 43
Kololo, see Fokeng
Kora (Khoi): interaction with Sotho, 28, 30, 41, 42; raiding by, 33,
39, 48; origins, 39–40; distribution, 40, 42; missionary work
amongst, 54
Kromdraai affair, 104–5
Kruger, Paul: attempt to revise Pretoria Convention, 72
Kuper, Adam, 119
Kuruman, 37, 42, 51; siege of, 72
Kwena, 15; subdivisions, 26; distribution, 27–8; in *Difaqane*, 37;
submission to Boers by, 75; dominance in Lesotho, 90–1, 92*, 93;
and see Moshoeshoe
labour conditions, of Africans, 81
labour control, 136, 149
labour reserves, 21, 135, 135*, 137,
144; and see 'homelands'; rural
periphery
labour unrest, 135
land acts: see land rights
land rights: granted to Voortrekkers, 62, 64; amongst Voortrekkers, 63; amongst Sotho, 63; disputes between Moshoeshoe and
Voortrekkers, 64; 69–71; 71*;
granted to Africans, 76; administered by chiefs, 93; reform of, in
Lesotho, 93, 96; in Botswana, 96,
141; in Lesotho, 144
land shortage: causing expansion,
30; in 'homelands', 99; affecting
residence, 112; in Lesotho, 144
language: use in classification, 9;
clusters, 9–10; spoken by Tswana
and southern Sotho, 9, 12*, 12–15;
relationships between Tswana dialects, 13*; relationships between
southern Sotho dialects, 13*
Lefela, Joseil, 83
Lefela, Maphutseng, 83
Legislative Council (Bechuanaland),
87
Lekganyane, Bishop Edward, 132
Lentswe, Chief, 122
Leselinyana la Lesotho, 12, 68, 132
Lesotho: foundations of, 45, 50;
boundaries, 63, 71*, 91*; environment, 136–7, 137*; migrant labourers from, 137; previous wealth,
137–8; growth of peasantry in,
137–8; imports/exports, 138*; decline of prosperity, 138; economic
developments, 140; education in,
140*
Lesotho Evangelical Church, 132,
132*
Letanka, D S, 81
Letsend-la-Terai mine, 140
levirate, 112
life histories: a migrant worker, 94;

a headman, 95; two rural families,
110–11; and developmental cycle,
144
Life of a South African Tribe, The,
(Junod), 116
Linden, Eugene, 19–20; *The Alms
Race,* 19
lineage, see agnatic lineage
linguistic classification, 9
literature (African), 12–14; missionaries and, 67; role of newspapers
in, 68; Sotho authors and, 68
livestock: reduced by *Difaqane*, 48;
used in bridewealth, 113–15; 116;
125–6; as basis of power, 114; and
sacrifices, 124, 126; in Botswana,
140–1, 144–5; as investment, 143,
143*; in Lesotho, 144–5; in BophuthaTswana, 146; and see raiding; *Difaqane*
Livingstone, David, 61; 65; 65*
London Evangelical Society, 51;
and see missionaries
London Missionary Society, 65–9;
and see missionaries
Ludorf, J D M, *The Tswana People's
Visitor,* 68
Lydenburg heads, 25; and see K L
von Bezing
Lyon, Solomon, 100–1; and see Ma-
boloka affair
Maboloka affair, 100–1, 133
Mackenzie, John, 72
mafisa system, 48–9, 90, 114
Maitland, Sir Peregrine, 64
Maitland Treaty, 69
Makoba II, Chief, 37, 38, 55
Malan, D F, 76
Malawi, 21, 134, 135, 137
malome, see mother's brother
Mangoela, Zakae, 68
Mangope, Chief Minister Lucas, 99,
100, 104, 146
MaNthatisi, Regentess, 31, 32, 33–5;
reputation, 35, 37; extent of con-
quests, 38; alliances with Moshoe-
shoe, 47, 49
Manyeli, G C, 84
Marema-Tlou Freedom Party, 84
Maritz, Gerrit, 59
marriage: definition, 113; and politi-
cal competition, 115–17, 119; rites,
125–6; transactions, 115*; and see
bridewealth
Married Life in an African Tribe
(Schapera), 113
Matiwane, Chief, 31–2; extension
of power of, 48
matrifiliation, 119; and see mother's
brother
matrifocal households, see head of
household
matrilateral kin, 117
Mazenod press, 68
Meeting of the Birds (Sekese), 68
Mekhoa le Maele a Basotho (Sekese),

68
Mhudi (Plaatje), 23, 68
migrant labour, 15; from Lesotho,
15, 73, 76, 137; from Bophutha-
Tswana, 146; from Botswana, 15,
76; causes of, 73; effect on family
life, 108–12; in mines, 135; effect
on farming, 138
Migrant Labour and Tribal Life
(Schapera), 109
migrant wages, 142–3, 145
migration: in the past, 24–6, 30;
affected by land shortage, 30–1,
51; affected by *Difaqane*, 39, 43,
62; and see *Difaqane*; migrant
labour; Great Trek
mineral resources: Lesotho, 140;
Botswana, 141; BophuthaTswana,
146
mines: recruitment of labour by, 73,
76–7, 135; accommodation for
workers offered by, 73, 136*;
areas of recruitment for, 134;
migrants working for, 135; wages
offered at, 138; in 'homelands',
140, 141, 142, 146–7
minority groups: in 'homelands',
14, 100; in South Africa, 20–1; at
Kromdraai, 104
missionaries: report on *Difaqane* by,
36–7; alliances during *Difaqane*, 39;
alliance with Moletsane, 39, 49, 50;
alliances with Griqua, 40, 44; alliances with Sekonyela, 47, 53;
alliances with Moshoeshoe, 50, 53,
66; alliances with Tswana, 51, 65;
as protectors, 51, 52; intervention
in African politics, 52, 63; competition for African influence between, 62; areas of proselytising,
65; welcome by Africans, 66; uti-
lisation of African teachers, 67;
attack on African traditions, 67;
economic changes brought by, 69;
assessment of, 69
Moçambique, 21, 134, 135
Modimo, 123
Moeletsi (Adviser), 132
Moffat, Robert: battle of Dithakong,
37–8; 51; importance of, 65; 67,
67*
Mofolo, Thomas, 68; *Traveller to
the East,* 68; *Pitseng,* 68
Mohale, Chief, 49
Mohlomi, Chief, 30; alliances with
other Sotho, 45
Mojakisane, Chief, 48
Mokgatle, Naboth, 17; *The Auto-
biography of an Unknown South
African,* 17, 80
Mokhehle, Ntsu, 83
Mokuoane, Chief, 49–50
Molefi, Chief, 122
Molema, S M, 69
Moletsane, Chief, 37, 38, 39, 42–3,
50–1, 50*, 52, 54; settlement in

158

Acknowledgement

Grateful acknowledgement is made to the following for photographs or illustrations supplied, or for permission to reproduce previously published illustrations in part or in whole, on the pages indicated:

R Levetan, 19, 22, 96, 97, 113, 121 above, 126, 127, 139, 140, 144, 145, 148–9 and cover, 151; Jean Morris, 10, 11, 13, 18, 21, 78 below, left and right, 79, 95, 110, 111, 118, 120, 121 below, 128, 129, 130 top left and below, 131; A Spiegel, 78 top right, 150; R Webb, 70, 83; M E West, 130 top right, 133, 136; Africana Museum, Johannesburg, 17, 36, 37, 38, 40, 59, 61; McGregor Museum, Kimberley (Duggan-Cronin Collection), 56, 57, 66, 75, 85; McGregor Museum and Kimberley Public Library, 67; S M Gabatshwane for reproduction from *Seretse Kgama and Botswana,* 86; A A Balkema and the South African Museum for reproductions from *Andrew Smith's Journal* edited by William F Lye, 27, 33, 43, 44, 46, 47, 54, 55, 60; La Société des Missions Evangéliques de Paris, 50, 62; Oxford University Press for reproduction from L Thompson: *Survival in Two Worlds,* 68; Macmillan South Africa for reproduction from J L Comaroff: *The Boer War Diary of Sol. T. Plaatje,* 23; Council for World Mission, London, 65; Lesotho Department of Information: *Lesotho, Land of Rolling Mountains and Running Streams,* 84; *Star,* Johannesburg, 80; *Daily News,* Durban, 103 above; *Pretoria News* (Pty) Ltd, 77.

The following diagrams are based on or redrawn with permission from previously published material as follows:

Figs. 1, 2, 3, C M Doke: *The Southern Bantu Languages* (International Africa Institute, London; fig. 11, S M Molema: *Chief Moroka* (Methodist Publishing House, Cape Town); fig. 13, Jean Comaroff: 'Barolong Cosmology: A Study of Religious Pluralism in a Tswana Town' (unpublished Ph.D. thesis, University of London); fig. 14, I Schapera: *A Handbook of Tswana Law & Custom* (Cass, London); figs. 15, 29, W J Breytenbach: *Crocodiles and Commoners in Lesotho* (Africa Institute of South Africa); fig. 17, I Hamnett: *Chieftainship and Legitimacy* (Routledge & Kegan Paul, London); fig. 18, Central Statistics Office, Gaborone; fig. 20, T Malan & P S Hattingh: *Black Homelands of South Africa* (Africa Institute of South Africa); fig. 22, I Schapera: 'The Social Structure of the Tswana Ward', *Bantu Studies* 9, and Schapera & Roberts: 'Rampedi Revisited', *Africa* 45; fig. 31, R G A Feachem et al: *Water, Health & Development* (Tri-Med Books); fig. 33, *National Development Plan* (Government Printer, Gaborone); figs. 34a & 34b, *Rural Income Distribution Survey* (Central Statistics Office, Gaborone; fig. 35, A C A van der Wiel: *Migratory Wage Labour* (Mazenod, Lesotho).

The authors wish to thank Rosemary Hill for compiling the index.